China's foreign trade reforms

Published by the Press Syndicate of the University of Cambridge
The Pitt Building, Trumpington Street, Cambridge CB2 1RP
40 West 20th Street, New York, NY 10011, USA
10 Stamford Road, Oakleigh, Melbourne 3166, Australia

First published 1989

Printed in the United States of America

Library of Congress Cataloging-in-Publication Data
Hsu, John C.
China's foreign trade reforms: impact on growth and stability/
John C. Hsu.
p. cm.
ISBN 0-521-37197-X
1. China – Commercial policy. 2. China – Commerce. 3. China –
Economic policy – 1976– I. Title.
HF 1604.H78 1990   89-32581
382′.3′0951 – dc20   CIP

British Library Cataloguing in Publication Data
Hsu, John C.
China's foreign trade reforms: impact on growth and stability.
1. China. Foreign trade. Policies of government,
history
I. Title
382′.0951

ISBN 0-521-37197-X hard covers

China's foreign trade reforms

Impact on growth and stability

JOHN C. HSU

Department of Economics
University of Hong Kong

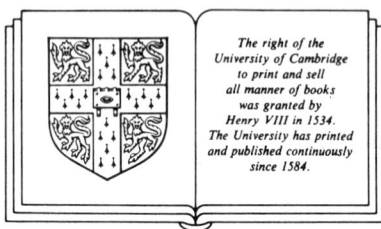

The right of the
University of Cambridge
to print and sell
all manner of books
was granted by
Henry VIII in 1534.
The University has printed
and published continuously
since 1584.

CAMBRIDGE UNIVERSITY PRESS

Cambridge
New York   Port Chester   Melbourne   Sydney

Contents

v

Tables

Preface

During its recent reforms, China's foreign trade has witnessed unusually high growth in comparison with other socialist economies. The pertinent question is this: Has foreign trade served as an engine of growth for China as it has done for other developing countries, including Taiwan and South Korea? This is an important question because both the future relations of China with the rest of the world and the importance of China's foreign trade reforms as an example to other socialist economies depend considerably on the extent to which China has benefited from the reforms.

As an attempt to answer this question, the book provides an overall view of the role of foreign trade in China's economic development before and during the recent reforms, a discussion of the institutional changes involved in the foreign trade reforms, an evaluation of the efficiency of the foreign trade incentive system introduced under foreign trade reforms, a close look into the impact of foreign trade reforms on the growth and commodity composition of foreign trade, a model for the impact of foreign trade growth on shortage and price stability, an empirical analysis of the relation between foreign trade and consumer goods shortage, and some views on the future prospect of the foreign trade reforms, stressing the need for further reforms of the economic system and for a change in the attitude of the political leadership toward the role of foreign trade in China's economic development.

In writing this book, I owe special thanks to Colin Day. The research would not have been undertaken without his encouragement and valuable suggestions. I am also indebted to Gavin Peebles, Yew-Kwang Ng, Henry C.Y. Ho, Chris D. Hall, George A. Selgin, and, in particular, the readers of this manuscript for their valuable comments on earlier drafts of this manuscript, without implying that they necessarily agree with me on the entirety of the analysis. Research assistance from W.K. Hui, Amy Chan, Ivar Tam, Mary Gerson, and Mike Leong was crucial to various stages of the project. Research grants from the University of Hong Kong provided financial resources needed for research assistantships and other expenses. I am also grateful to my economics editor at Cambridge, Ina M. Isobe, and production editor, Louise Calabro Gruendel, for their efficiency and consideration, and to the Center for Chinese Studies, University of California at Berkeley, for its support during my work on the final stages of this book. Finally, I would like to thank the libraries at the Hoover Institute, the Center for Chinese Studies at the University of California at Berkeley, and the Chung-Hua Institution for Economic Research in Taipei for allowing me access to their facilities.

John C. Hsu

Center for Chinese Studies
University of California at Berkeley

CHAPTER 1

Introduction: Foreign trade in China's economic development

Under China's prereform economic system, foreign trade was determined strictly within the national economic plan. Goods would be imported if planned supply fell short of planned demand, as might occur as a result of natural disasters, inadequate technology of production at home, shortage of domestic resources, or increases in domestic investment. Normally, imports would play the simple role of a shortage breaker; they would rise or fall substantially only if there was a rapid increase or decrease in the level of investment, which would call for a large increase or decrease in the supply of foreign technology and capital equipment.[1] Once the level of imports was determined, planned surpluses would be created of those goods which were relatively abundant in supply so that they could be exported. The level of exports was thus determined indirectly by the level of imports. In the actual formulation of the foreign trade plan, the planners would, of course, take into consideration the export capability of the economy before determining the level of imports.

Since foreign trade was conducted strictly within the national economic plan, there was an obvious advantage in keeping the size of foreign trade small. By limiting its size, the planners would have to create only a comparatively small amount of planned surpluses out of a relatively small range of products in order to finance imports. Thus, fluctuations in the international prices of exports and imports could be easily dealt with and, therefore, would not cause serious disruptions to the economic plan. Partly for this reason, foreign trade was relatively small in prereform China.[2] In the years between 1956 and 1977,[3] China's foreign trade amounted to not more than 4 percent of national product.[4] This foreign trade – national-output ratio was well below those of other large developing countries, such as Brazil and India, in which foreign trade amounted to 13.6 percent and 8.7 percent of national output, respectively, in 1970.[5]

In a dramatic turnaround, China's foreign trade started to rise rapidly in 1979. The main reason for this is that in the period between 1979 and 1985, during which time economic reforms were undertaken, the economy was increasingly decentralized and foreign trade ceased to be deter-

1

mined entirely within the central economic plan (see Chapter 2). The policy change greatly facilitated the growth of foreign trade, which, in real terms, rose by an average of more than 20 percent per annum, in comparison with less than 4 percent for the period between 1956 and 1977. Such a growth rate is higher than that of any other centrally planned economy, including Hungary, which witnessed, on the average, only a 6 percent increase in foreign trade per annum in the same period.[6]

To understand the role of foreign trade in China's recent economic reforms and the problems faced by the Chinese economy in the wake of the rapid expansion of foreign trade, this chapter provides an overview of the relationship between foreign trade and economic growth in the pre- and post-1978 periods. Section 1.1 describes briefly the economic planning system of prereform China. I show that in China's planning system the central planning authorities had little control over the production of individual production units because, in the absence of information on the input–output relationships of individual enterprises, they were unable to set meaningful production targets for individual industries except in the case of a few major industries that relied heavily on centrally allocated supplies. In Section 1.2, I discuss the relationship between foreign trade and economic growth in the prereform period. I show that foreign trade fluctuated closely with national income during this period because of the key role the former played in investment. Section 1.3 discusses the problems incurred in China's Four Modernizations program in 1978 and the policy response to the problems in the ensuing years. Section 1.4 discusses the relationship between foreign trade and economic growth in the period between 1979 and 1985. This relationship had important implications for both the efficiency with which domestic resources were allocated and the macroeconomic imbalance of the economy under economic reforms. Finally, Section 1.5 briefly summarizes the findings in this chapter and Section 1.6 provides an outline of the book.

1.1   The prereform Chinese economic planning system

In the early 1950s, Chinese communists undertook the task of transforming the war-torn market-oriented economy into a command economy. The 1946–9 civil war resulted in a substantial fall in agricultural and industrial production. According to official statistics,[7] the production of steel, coal, and electricity in 1949 fell by 83 percent, 48 percent, and 28 percent from their respective pre-1949 peak levels, while the output of grains, cotton, and peanuts fell by 25 percent, 48 percent, and 60 percent, respectively. The war impoverished the already poverty-stricken economy and intensified farmers' and workers' resentment toward relatively rich land owners and industrialists. The communist government, riding the tide, promoted mass movements against land owners and industrialists and ruthlessly executed a countless number of them to make way for the complete transfer of privately owned property to the state. In the meantime, it adopted the "lean to one side" policy and sought financial and technical assistance from the Soviet Union in its effort to rebuild the economy.[8] By 1956, the process of transformation to a command economy was essentially completed, and nearly all enterprises had been nationalized.[9]

China's planning system was modeled on Soviet practices. However, China started central planning with a much narrower industrial base and a much lower degree of economic development than did Russia in 1928. For this reason, in the First Five Year Plan (1952–7), China concentrated only on establishing new enterprises and paid little attention to the linkage between new and old enterprises. Whole plants were imported, mostly from the Soviet Union, for use in heavy industry,[10] which China regarded as a prerequisite for industrial development. The task of economic planning had obviously become extremely burdensome in the course of the rapid investment growth that was taking place. The planners had to base their investment plans on their forecast of the changes in the demand and supply of individual commodities in the future and their forecast had to be made without the base of adequate information. In the First Five Year Plan, serious sectoral imbalances occurred in the economy in spite of the help from the Soviets with the task of planning. The imbalances occurred primarily because of the biased investment policy which focused on the heavy industrial sector, with little attention paid to agriculture and light industry. For this reason, China's central economic plan, being only a partial economic plan from the start, tended to be economically destabilizing.

In China, the central planning authorities (the State Planning Commission, the Economic Commission, the State Council, and central ministries) put under their control only what they considered to be "key industries," including coal, electricity, petroleum, machinery, iron and steel, chemical fertilizer, and so forth. Each enterprise in these industries received centrally allocated supplies and in the meantime sold its output to the state for allocation to end-users. Other nonkey industries were controlled by the local planning authorities (the bureaus of the State Planning Commission, the Economic Commission, and industrial ministries), which were responsible for the allocation of what they considered as key supplies to these industries. Neither central nor local planning authorities undertook the allocation of "nonessential products." For this reason, most enterprises had to rely partly on contractual or noncontractual supplies from other enterprises, and they had to dispatch a large number of purchasing agents to scout the country for needed materials and equipment.[11] Since interenterprise transactions did not have the blessing of the official scheme of commerce, the supplies thus obtained were inherently unstable, regardless of the importance of the supplies to the enterprises' fulfillment of the output targets. In order to ensure a stable supply of material inputs and provide work to employees, enterprises set up and operated as many ancillary plants as they could to produce for themselves machine parts and intermediate products. As a consequence, each enterprise became a highly verticalized, semi-self-contained production unit, over which the planning authorities, by supplying only a fraction of the required inputs, had little control. Most enterprises could easily excuse themselves for not fulfilling the plan target, by, for instance, blaming the shortage of certain inputs not covered by central allocation.

The formulation of the economic plans

In the prereform years, China's economic planning was hampered by the lack of a comprehensive information system on which a central plan had to work. The central planning authorities had under their control less than 200 products, leaving the rest to be allocated under various levels of local plans.[12] The chief items which were placed under central control, according to Donnithorne (1967, p. 462), included (1) the output targets of major industrial and agricultural products, (2) total national investment expenditure, major investment projects, and new productive capacity for important commodities, (3) the balance and transfers of important types of raw materials, equipment, and consumer goods, (4) the volume of exports and imports, and (5) receipts and payments of the national budget, the upward remittances payable and subsidies receivable by local authorities, credit equilibrium, and the transfer of funds for capital purposes. As for local planning authorities, they were accorded with a wide range of decision-making powers, including the determination of the output targets of a large number of commodities, the allocation of investment funds among relatively unimportant projects, and the balancing and transfers of a large number of items of raw materials, intermediate goods, and finished products.

Because of the importance attached to the local economic plans, China's national economic plan degenerated to an aggregate of remotely mutually related local plans, over which the state had control only through centrally allocated raw materials, intermediate goods, and capital equipment and, to a lesser extent, through taxes and subsidies. The lack of coordination among local plans made it difficult for the central planning authorities to formulate a workable long-term plan under which the output growth of individual sectors would be determined. Therefore, annual plans formed the core of the country's economic planning activity, and long-term plans were always vague and unworkable (Hsu 1982, p. 255).

In each annual plan, the central planning authorities would issue a guideline outlining the output targets of those industries which were under the direct control of the central government. The guideline would be received by specialized ministries and provincial and municipal governments for consideration. Provincial and municipal governments would then coordinate with ministries to determine the amount of shortages to be filled by state supplies and the amount of surpluses to be transferred from one province or city to the other. The former would then issue their own guidelines to the lower planning authorities for their consideration. The process would be repeated at each planning level until it reached the enterprise level. Enterprises would then respond to the plan guideline and submit their input demands to their superiors on the basis of the output targets specified in the guidelines. Material balancing would be worked out at each local planning level and finally aggregated for balancing at the national level. The finalized state plan would then be issued to specialized ministries and local governments for implementation.

In sum, the planning process was characterized by a high degree of decentralization of decision-making powers to local authorities and by the extremely weak control the central planning authorities had over the level and structure of output in those industries which relied predominantly on noncentrally allocated supplies. In some years, including the early 1960s, the central government attempted to strengthen its control over individual industries by recentralizing economic planning power. However, as a result of the lack of a comprehensive centralized information system to work on, central control often proved to be excessively rigid and ineffective, eventually forcing the government to revert to a decentralized system.

Foreign trade, investment, and economic planning

Although the central government had little control over those industries that relied predominantly on noncentrally allocated raw materials and intermediate goods, it still possessed full control over heavy industry, which produced mineral raw materials and intermediate goods. All along, the growth of heavy industry was considered as a key to the industrialization of the economy. For instance, the production of iron and steel was considered to be crucial to the economy because they served as inputs to

Table 1.1. Investment in capital construction by sectors

	Agri-culture	Light industry	Heavy industry	Other	Total
1953–7	4.2	3.8	21.3	29.6	58.8
1958–62	13.6	7.7	65.2	34.2	120.6
1963–65	7.5	1.7	19.4	13.7	42.2
1966–70	10.4	4.3	49.9	33.0	97.6
1971–5	17.3	10.3	87.5	61.3	176.4
1976–80	24.6	15.6	107.6	86.4	234.2
1978	5.3	2.9	24.4	17.4	50.1
1979	5.8	3.1	22.6	20.9	52.3
1980	5.2	5.1	22.5	23.1	55.9
1981	2.9	4.3	17.3	19.8	44.3
1982	3.4	4.7	21.4	26.1	55.6
1983	3.6	3.9	24.4	27.6	59.4
1984	3.7	4.2	29.9	36.4	74.3
1985	3.7	6.3	38.3	59.1	107.4

Note: All values are at current prices in renminbi billion yuan.
Source: State Statistical Bureau, *Statistical Yearbook of China* (Hong Kong: Economic Information and Agency, various issues).

capital construction, machinery, transportation, durable consumer goods, and almost all other industries. Heavy industry, including iron and steel, was therefore consistently given growth priority in economic planning in the prereform period. Between 1956 and 1977, the average growth rate of heavy industrial output was 11 percent per annum, compared to 8 percent for light industrial output and 3 percent for agricultural product.[13]

To accelerate the growth of heavy industry, the government invested proportionally more in this sector than in either light industry or agriculture. As shown in Table 1.1, investment in capital construction was concentrated mainly in heavy industry, which normally received more than 40 percent of the total, compared with the normal shares of 10 percent for agriculture and 6 percent for light industry. In investing in heavy industry, the government would normally see to it that all new projects were as technologically advanced as possible. To fulfill this technological requirement, the government would import whole plants or most of the capital equipment needed. Imported machinery and capital equipment would also be used in other large-scale investment projects. Therefore, foreign trade was closely related to, and fluctuated closely with, the level of investment in all of the years between 1956 and 1977 except for the period from 1970 to 1975, during which time significant fluctuations occurred in the international prices of oil and other related products. Figure 1.1 de-

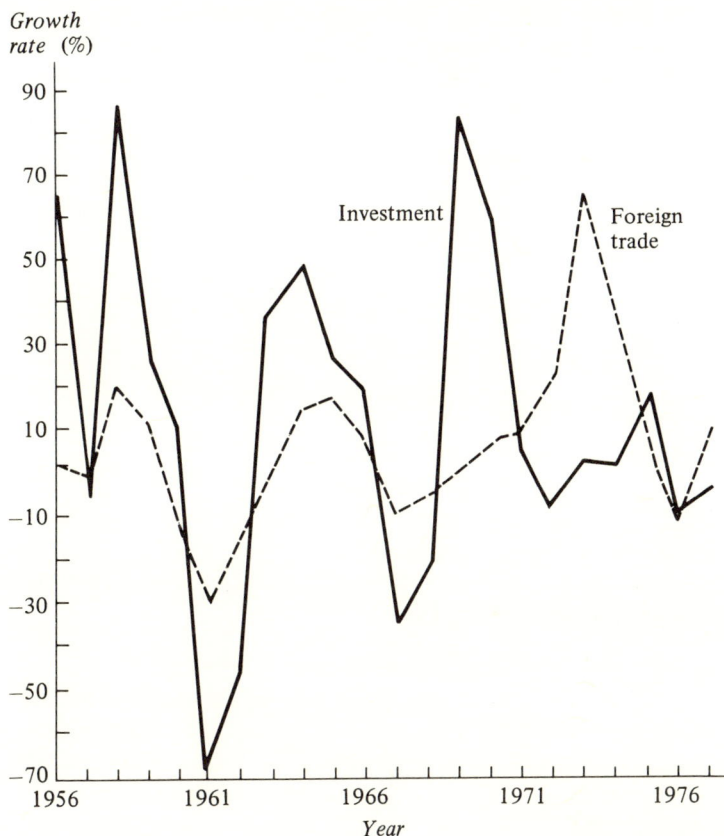

Figure 1.1. Investment and foreign trade growth, 1956–77. *Source:*
Table 1.2.

picts the fluctuations in the growth rates of investment and foreign trade
in the period from 1956 to 1977.[14]

Heavy industry was under the firm control of the central planning
authorities throughout the entire prereform period. It was through heavy
industry that the central planning authorities carried out their role in
economic planning, and it was also through heavy industry that they
gained partial control over the rest of the economy. There had been no
attempt on the part of the central government to improve the effectiveness of its control over the rest of the economy, be it through a reform of
the incentive system or through the establishment of a comprehensive
information system. Therefore, to understand China's economic growth
in the prereform period, it is necessary to look at, among other things, the

Table 1.2. The growth rates of national output, foreign trade, and investment, 1956–77 (in percentages)

	GNP[a,b]	Total[b] trade	Exports	Imports	Investment[b,c]
1956	8.33	2.8	18.9	−10.5	64.80
1957	6.15	−2.1	−2.1	−3.0	−6.09
1958	18.84	23.2	20.1	26.7	88.89
1959	−4.88	13.9	14.9	12.9	29.33
1960	−2.56	−6.9	−12.1	−1.5	11.97
1961	−21.05	−24.4	−22.2	−26.6	−68.77
1962	9.17	−11.4	−0.3	−22.8	−46.17
1963	12.98	3.9	3.6	4.3	38.49
1964	10.81	16.0	11.1	22.5	49.79
1965	12.80	20.5	16.3	25.5	30.79
1966	13.51	9.4	8.6	10.3	21.70
1967	−3.81	−7.8	−11.3	−3.9	−32.21
1968	0.99	−3.3	0.0	−6.6	−17.58
1969	10.78	2.9	5.1	0.5	84.11
1970	16.37	7.8	4.6	11.4	62.82
1971	6.84	11.4	17.6	4.9	8.46
1972	4.63	24.0	27.0	20.5	−3.22
1973	12.93	67.5	58.4	78.9	3.67
1974	3.61	39.3	32.1	47.2	3.57
1975	6.98	3.1	5.9	0.2	18.41
1976	0.00	−8.0	2.0	−18.5	−7.84
1977	8.15	14.4	11.3	18.4	2.47

[a] Figures are at constant prices.
[b] Figures are in U.S. dollars.
[c] Investment refers to "Investment in Capital Construction" in official statistics, deflated by industrial output deflator.
Sources: GNP: Scherer (1980, p. 77). Foreign Trade: Scherer (1984, p. 150). Investment: State Statistical Bureau, Statistical Yearbook of China (Hong Kong: Economic Information and Agency, 1987, p. 404). Industrial output deflator: Calculated from State Statistical Bureau, Statistical Yearbook of China (Hong Kong: Economic Information and Agency, 1987, pp. 31–2).

government's investment policy in relation to the growth of heavy industry, a subject to which we now turn.

1.2   Foreign trade and economic growth in preform China

In a large closed economy such as China's, one might expect the fluctuations in foreign trade to bear little relationship to the level of national income. The reason is that, in such an economy, an increase or decrease in national income will not necessarily lead to an increase or decrease in foreign trade and neither will an increase or decrease in foreign trade, through the multiplier effect, have a significant effect on national income. Surprisingly, however, foreign trade went up and down closely with national output in prereform China. As shown in Table 1.2, high national income growth tended to be associated with high trade growth, and low or negative national income growth tended to be associated with low or negative trade growth. To explain this phenomenon, I first discuss the problems involved in the measurement of national income in China and then examine the relationship between foreign trade and national income.

The measurement of national output

Most economists, including Liu (1968), Eckstein (1966, 1980), and Ashbrook (1982), agree that China witnessed rapid economic growth in the prereform period. Table 1.3 presents various estimates of the growth rates of China's national output, all of which feature high rates of growth. However, they differ rather widely from one another. Take the year of 1963 as an example: The lowest estimate is the -5 percent arrived at by Eckstein, whereas the highest is the 13 percent arrived at by the CIA. In between these two extremes are 7 percent (Liu), 11 percent (State Statistical Bureau), and 12 percent (Ashbrook). The significant differences in these estimates arise as a result of the enormous difficulty involved in the task of estimation.

One of the greatest difficulties involved in the estimation of China's national output in the prereform period is the scarcity of data. In the estimation of national output, one may adopt either of the following approaches: by aggregating all expenditures on currently produced goods and services incurred by the private sector, the public sector, and the foreign sector (the expenditure approach), or by adding up incomes received in the form of wages, profits, interest, and rent (the income approach). However, before China's first publication of the *Statistical Yearbook of China* in 1981, the data needed for the adoption of these two approaches was practically nonexistent, and economists had to base their estimation on the values of output of individual sectors, data which were relatively abundant at the time.[15]

This method is based on the assumption that there is some fixed relationship between the value-added and the level of output in individual sectors. There is, however, a great danger in using this method. First, the values of output appearing in China's official statistics are the aggregates of the values of output at all processing stages. For instance, according to

Table 1.3. The growth rates of national output, 1956–77 (in percentages)

	NDP[c] (Liu)	GNP1 (Ashbrook)	GDP (Eckstein)	GNP2 (CIA)[a]	NI[d] (SSB)[b]
1956	11.91	7.14	12.00	8.33	14.11
1957	3.47	6.00	3.60	6.15	4.51
1958	13.33	13.21	14.98	18.84	22.03
1959	−3.33	−5.56	6.72	−4.88	8.25
1960	−8.14	−8.24	−6.94	−2.56	−1.43
1961	−3.86	−19.87		−21.05	−29.72
1962	2.06	12.00		9.17	−6.50
1963	7.12	12.86	−5.36	12.81	10.70
1964	3.37	15.19		10.81	16.49
1965	3.74	11.54		12.80	17.00
1966		14.29		13.51	16.96
1967		−2.59		−3.81	−7.23
1968		0.88		0.99	−6.49
1969		10.53		10.78	19.31
1970		11.90		16.37	23.25
1971		6.73		6.84	6.99
1972		3.65		4.63	2.92
1973		12.50		12.93	8.29
1974		3.70		3.61	1.08
1975				6.98	8.31
1976				0.00	−2.68
1977				8.15	7.80

Note: All estimates of national output are at constant prices.
[a] CIA = Central Intelligence Agency, United States of America.
[b] SSB = State Statistical Bureau, China.
[c]NDP = Net domestic product.
[d] NI = National income.
Sources: NDP: Liu (1968, p. 165). GNP1: Ashbrook (1982, p. 104). GDP: Eckstein (1966, p. 45; 1980, p. 11). GNP2: Scherer (1980, p. 77).

Qian Jiaqu, a prominent Chinese economist, the value of the output of cloth is arrived at by adding up the values of cotton, cotton yarn, cotton cloth, and even dyed cotton.[16] The values of output thus obtained can be many times the values of the final products, depending on the number of processing stages, and the value-added per unit of output will change with changes in the proportion of output at each processing stage to total output.

Second, the reliability of official output statistics is subject to question. Like other developing countries, China did not and still does not have a sophisticated statistical system to collect and process economic information. In economic planning, annual plans had to be formulated on the basis of the information supplied by local authorities. Similarly, national statistics on production, consumption, employment, prices, and so forth had to rely on information supplied by local planning units. The information thus obtained was likely to have been severely distorted, since local planning units, to gain politically or to guard against unfavorable political consequences, tended to have a strong incentive to disclose as little true information to their superiors as possible. The level of output might be under- or overreported, depending on the benefits associated with the two strategies. For instance, during the Cultural Revolution (1967–76), a factory manager had to be extremely cautious not to appear to be "too enthusiastic" about the factory's production if he was to avoid being criticized as a Capitalist Roader. Under these circumstances, the factory's output was likely to be underreported. The output statistics reported by the local planning authorities could be further distorted by the manipulation of the central government to serve propaganda purposes, particularly in the 1950s when the government was eager to show to the rest of the world the superiority of the new communist regime over the previous Nationalist regime. The problem of statistical manipulation was most serious in the period of the Great Leap Forward (1958–60), when output growth was pushed in great earnest.[17] All production units were assigned high growth targets so that the economy could be modernized and catch up with developed countries within 15 to 20 years (Lin 1981, p. 42). To give support to the Great Leap and to glorify the results, local authorities greatly inflated the level of agricultural output by increasing substantially their delivery to the central government at the expense of local food consumption. The problem was so serious that it resulted in millions of peasants being starved to death during the movement. In industry, enterprises turned out low-quality and unusable products to meet the output targets. Under these circumstances, it was difficult to make a meaningful comparison of the values of output in the Great Leap with those in other years.

Third, the official statistics on sectoral outputs are based on administered prices, which featured the so-called price scissors. As pointed out by Liu and Yeh (1965), Perkins (1966), Donnithorne (1967), Lardy (1983), Xue (1985), and a number of other economists, the Chinese government deliberately depressed the terms of trade of agricultural products for industrial products in order to transfer resources from agriculture to industry. By a deliberate depression of agricultural prices, the government succeeded in lowering peasants' incomes as well as their demand for food and industrial products, making it possible for "surplus resources" to be transferred from agriculture to industry.[18] In addition, the high prices of industrial producer goods imposed a squeeze on the profits of industrial consumer goods, on the one hand, and accelerated the accumulation of investment funds in the industrial producer goods sector, on the other. Thus, the price scissors discriminated in favor of heavy industry and against both light industry and, in particular, agriculture. Such a pricing practice, by assigning an unduly low weight to nonindustrial goods and an unduly high weight to industrial goods, inevitably distorted the actual level of national output.

In view of these factors, there was a tendency for the level of industrial output to expand more quickly than that of the rest of the economy and for the fluctuations in national output to be exaggerated by the fluctuations in industrial output. To explain, let Y be the national output, A the value-added in agriculture, and N the value-added in industry. Then, we have, in a simplified two-sector model,

$$Y = N + A, \tag{1.1}$$

which states that national output is the sum of the value-added in agriculture and industry. Also, let Y', N', and A' stand for the estimates of Y, N, and A on the basis of the official output statistics. Then the following relationship holds:

$$\begin{aligned} Y' &= N' + A' \\ &= \alpha N + \gamma A, \end{aligned} \tag{1.2}$$

where $\alpha = N'/N$ and $\gamma = A'/A$. α and γ reflect the degree of distortion in the estimation of the value-added in industry and agriculture using official output statistics as a basis.

Based on equation (1.2), the estimated growth rate of national output equals

$$\dot{Y'} = \frac{\alpha N}{Y'} \dot{N} + \frac{\gamma A}{Y'} \dot{A} \tag{1.3}$$

as compared with

$$\dot{Y} = \frac{N}{Y} \dot{N} + \frac{A}{Y} \dot{A}. \tag{1.4}$$

The dot denotes the growth rate of the variable. In view of the presence of the bias in the estimation of national output arising from the aforementioned factors, α can be significantly greater than γ. Therefore, $\alpha N/Y' > N/Y$ and $\gamma A/Y' < A/Y$. That is, in the estimation of national output growth, an unduly high weight has been assigned to industry and an unduly low weight has been assigned to agriculture. It follows that if $\dot{A'}$ is relatively stable but $\dot{N'}$ fluctuates significantly, as was the case in prereform China, the fluctuations in $\dot{Y'}$ will be greater than the fluctuations in

Table 1.4. *The growth rates of output by selected sectors, 1956–85 (in percentages)*

	Agriculture	Heavy industry	Light industry	Total
1956	5.06	39.74	19.68	28.06
1957	3.57	18.45	5.77	11.57
1958	2.40	78.79	33.70	54.81
1959	−13.62	48.10	22.00	36.11
1960	−12.68	25.90	−9.80	11.21
1961	−2.39	−46.50	−21.62	−38.19
1962	6.16	−22.59	−8.42	−16.61
1963	11.71	13.80	2.32	8.51
1964	13.53	21.00	17.82	19.59
1965	8.21	10.21	47.69	26.40
1966	8.68	27.50	14.51	20.91
1967	1.48	−20.00	−7.09	−13.81
1968	−2.45	−5.11	−4.91	−5.00
1969	1.15	43.90	25.21	34.30
1970	11.46	42.30	18.09	30.70
1971	3.07	21.40	6.50	14.90
1972	−0.18	7.00	6.19	6.60
1973	8.42	8.70	10.60	9.50
1974	4.15	−1.60	2.70	0.30
1975	4.61	16.80	13.00	15.10
1976	2.47	0.50	2.41	1.30
1977	1.69	14.30	14.30	14.30
1956–77 (Average)	2.69	12.29	8.65	9.62
1978	9.02	15.60	10.73	13.50
1979	8.62	7.70	9.67	8.50
1980	3.89	1.40	18.40	8.70
1981	6.60	−4.70	14.10	4.10
1982	11.08	9.80	5.70	7.70
1983	9.58	12.40	8.70	10.50
1984	17.61	14.20	13.90	14.00
1985	14.19	17.90	18.10	18.00
1979–85 (Average)	10.39	8.21	13.05	10.41

Note: All outputs are at constant prices.
Source: State Statistical Bureau, *Statistical Yearbook of China* (Hong Kong: Economic Information and Agency, 1987, pp. 31–2).

$\dot{Y}$. In other words, the fluctuations in actual national output can be grossly exaggerated by the fluctuations in the values of national output estimated on the basis of official output statistics.

Table 1.4 shows the growth rates of output of individual sectors in the prereform period.[19] Industrial output is shown to fluctuate more significantly than other sectors. The fluctuations originated primarily in heavy industry, which went up by 915 percent from 1956 to 1977, compared with 528 percent for light industry and 85 percent for agriculture. These fluctuations had an increasingly important impact on the stability of Y' as the share of industrial output in total social product rose gradually from 37 percent in 1956 to 60 percent in 1977. For these reasons, the national output estimates in Table 1.2 all exhibit sharp fluctuations. We point out the possible cause for the upward and downward bias in these estimates not to discredit them but to emphasize the great difficulty involved in the estimation. In this study, we do not attempt to undertake the task of eliminating such a bias; it suffices to say that great caution must be taken in using China's national output statistics. In the following discussion, we make use of the CIA's estimates, which cover the entire period of our study. A comparison of the CIA estimates with China's official national income statistics is given in Table A.1 in Appendix A.

Partly because of the statistical bias pointed out above and partly because of the policy bias against consumption, the rapid output growth that China experienced in the prereform period did not translate into a concomitant improvement in the standard of living. Based on the CIA estimates, China's real GNP went up by an average of 6 percent per year during this period. According to Xue (1985), however, the standard of living of peasants in terms of per capita food consumption was lower in 1976 – 7 than in 1956 – 7 (Xue 1985, p. 419). Xue's argument is supported by official statistics, which show that the country's per capita consumption of food grains decreased from 245 kilograms in 1956 to a low of 191 kilograms in 1962 and then rose slowly to 230 kilograms in 1977. That is, Chinese were less well-fed in 1977 than in 1956. Official statistics also show that Chinese were less well-clothed in 1977 than in 1956. The per capita consumption of cloth dropped from 8.6 meters in 1956 to a low of 2.8 meters in 1961 and then rose slowly to 7.7 meters in 1977.[20] In China's recent history, the lack of an improvement in the standard of living has led to struggles between one political faction which seemingly despised material well-being and advocated austere and simple living and another faction which pressed for economic modernization and an improved standard of living.

Foreign trade and economic growth

In general, economists believe that foreign trade has played an important role in China's economic growth (Eckstein 1966; Chen 1975; Hsiao 1977). The main reason for this belief is that through foreign trade China has obtained much needed raw materials and technologically advanced machinery and equipment to expand its productive capacity. Although this view is undoubtedly true in the long run, the short-run relationship between foreign trade and economic growth remains to be examined.

In the short run, foreign trade served as one of the channels through which resources were transferred from agriculture to industry and from consumption to investment. In the process of the transfer, agricultural goods, minerals, and industrial products were exported in exchange for the imports of those industrial machinery, equipment, and raw materials which were unavailable at home. The amount of resources thus transferred was closely related to the amount of investment goods that had to be imported. For this reason, the level of foreign trade was influenced considerably by the governments' investment policy.

Consider first the case where the government raised the level of investment. In the short run, the investment increase would require resources to be transferred from the consumer goods sector, including agriculture, to the producer goods sector. Insofar as the resources thus transferred contributed to an increase in the growth rate of national income, foreign trade would be seen to grow with national output. If the increased output comprised mainly consumer goods, the economy's import capacity would expand, making it possible for foreign trade and investment to expand further. However, if the increased output comprised mainly producer goods, the growth of foreign trade and investment would be limited by the extent to which the standard of living could be lowered. In China, sharp rises in foreign trade often took place with sharp increases in investment in heavy industry and infrastructure, both of which were characterized by long gestation periods before leading to a substantial increase in the production of consumer goods. Therefore, the sharp rises in investment and foreign trade often proved unsustainable as they invariably caused an immediate decrease in the standard of living.

Now consider the case where investment decreased for reasons of political instability, such as during the Red Guard rampages in 1967–8. In this case, national output would decline both because of the (autonomous) decrease in investment and because of the political changes which interfered with economic planning. Suppose that the economy was unwilling to incur foreign trade deficits. The absorption approach to the balance of payments (Alexander 1952) suggests that the decrease in national output would have to be accompanied by a decrease in investment or consumption, or both. If consumption were already at the subsistence level, the burden of adjustment would fall mostly on investment. That is, the decrease in national output would accentuate the decrease in investment. As investment decreased, the amount of resources transferred through foreign trade and other channels from consumption to production would also decrease. Therefore, foreign trade would be seen to decrease hand in hand with national output.

An overview of the relationship among foreign trade, investment, and national output in China between 1956 and 1977 follows. The period is divided into three subperiods: 1956–61, 1962–8, and 1969–77, each of these subperiods starting with an economic boom and ending with an economic decline. For statistics on national output and foreign trade, I use the CIA's estimates[21]; for statistics on investment, I use the level of "investment in fixed capital formation" deflated by the prices of industrial products.[22]

1956–61: China witnessed rapid economic recovery in the years between 1950 and 1957 and sought to achieve an even more rapid growth of the economy by launching the Great Leap Forward program in 1958. In this program, peasants were mobilized to construct dirt dams, backyard steel furnaces, small-scale factories, and so forth, and at the same time put to work in large communes. The aim was to enable the rural sector to support not only itself with its own production of industrial goods but also the modern industrial sector with surplus food and raw materials. In the industrial sector, the government invested heavily in the production of steel, coal, electricity, and so forth, with a view to expanding the industrial base of the economy. For the economy as a whole, fixed capital formation went up by 89 percent,[23] and imports, consisting mainly of machinery and equipment from the Soviet Union, increased by 27 percent (Table 1.2). In order to finance the increased imports, exports rose by 20 percent, drawing primarily on agricultural products, since the nonagricultural sector was still small and underdeveloped. As a result, national output, based on official prices, rose by 19 percent. Fixed capital formation continued to grow rapidly in the next two years,[24] but the economy, already suffering from widespread supply bottlenecks, began to show signs of weakening. National output decreased by 5 percent and 3 percent in 1959 and 1960, respectively, and foreign trade also contracted because of the widespread collapse in agricultural production. To reverse the economic decline, the Great Leap Forward program was called off and efforts were made to revitalize agriculture and light industry in 1961. However, national output suffered a severe decline by 21 percent in that year in the wake of a poor harvest and the Soviet withdrawal of technicians, blueprints, and financial assistance following the disruption in diplomatic relations between the two countries. The decrease in national output was accompanied by a 69 percent decrease in fixed capital formation and a 24 percent decrease in foreign trade.

1962-8: The economy started to recover in 1962. The recovery took place when large communes were divided into smaller collectives and when industry made efforts to revive the old Soviet projects. In this year, national output rose by 9 percent, due mainly to agricultural recovery, while industrial production was still adversely affected by the Soviet pull-out. Between 1963 and 1966, the economy recovered strongly, with national output rising by more than 10 percent per annum. Owing to the rapid investment growth (30 percent per annum as can be obtained from Table 1.2), industrial output expanded rapidly. According to official statistics, industrial output exceeded the 1958 level for the first time in 1966. Agricultural output also expanded quickly and exceeded the 1958 level by 17 percent in that year (Table 1.4). As expected, the recovery was accompanied by a rapid expansion in foreign trade, which went up by as much as 16 percent in 1964 and 21 percent in 1965. Unfortunately, the old guard became increasingly restless as the economy recovered. In late 1966, Mao Zedong launched the so-called Cultural Revolution, in which Mao was idolized and excerpts of his works and speeches, published in the little red book, were publicized as the guiding principles for all facets of life. To make sure that his ideology took precedence over all other thoughts, he mobilized millions of teenage Red Guards to spread his ideology and weed out all elements he considered to be stumbling blocks to the movement. In the Red Guard rampages, numerous officials, factory managers, scholars, teachers, and persons with the slightest contact with Western culture were subjected to beatings, hard labor, public humiliation, and indefinite imprisonment. As a result, production and economic planning were disrupted, causing a decline in foreign trade, fixed capital formation, and national output in 1967 and 1968.

1969-77: The Red Guard outrages were over by 1969, having caused far fewer losses in the physical capacity of production than in human capital. Therefore, domestic production took little time to recover, whereas the long-term damage to the growth of the economy had yet to be felt. In 1969 and 1970, national output increased by an average of more than 13 percent per annum (Table 1.2), due mostly to the rapid recovery of industry, the major victim of the Red Guard rampages. Therefore, as in the economic recovery in 1962 and 1963, foreign trade grew only slowly, rising by an average of 4 percent per annum. In the years between 1971 and 1975, the average growth rate of national output decreased to 7 percent per annum, with agriculture, light industry, and heavy industry expanding simultaneously, thanks to the balanced growth strategy of Chen Yun, the then vice-premier of the State Council. During these years, foreign trade witnessed spectacular growth as a result of China's open

door policy, which enabled it to establish diplomatic and trade relations
with an increasing number of Western countries. On the average, the U.S.
dollar value of foreign trade went up by 31 percent per annum between
1971 and 1975, due considerably, of course, to the oil crisis which inflated
the prices of Chinese exports and imports in U.S. dollars. As in previous
years, the rise in foreign trade was associated with the economy's investment policy which concentrated on the industrial sector. Fixed capital
formation witnessed an average growth rate of 6 percent per annum. The
growth of national output, foreign trade, and investment suffered a temporary setback in 1976, the year of the deaths of Mao Zedong and Zhou
Enlai and of the downfall of the "Gang of Four," but it was back on a
growing track by 1977.

   In short, the prereform Chinese economy was characterized by erratic
fluctuations in foreign trade, investment, and national income. When
national output rose rapidly, as in 1956-8 and 1969-77, the level of
investment increased, raising the demand for imports. Conversely, when
the economy suffered a recession, as in 1961-5, the level of investment
decreased, lowering the demand for imports. As the import demand increased or decreased, exports also increased or decreased in response to
the increase or decrease in the demand for foreign exchange. On the
whole, foreign trade fluctuated closely with national income.

   It should be noted that the composition of foreign trade also changed
with the fluctuations in national output. The detail is shown in Table 1.5.
In general, during economic upturns the share of producer goods in total
imports rose in response to the rise in the demand for imported machinery, capital equipment, and raw materials. At the same time, the
share of agricultural products in total exports increased because of their
relatively inelastic supply. In contrast, during economic downturns, the
share of producer goods in total imports fell in response to the decrease in
the demand for imported capital goods and raw materials. At the same
time, the share of agricultural products in total exports also fell to release
them for domestic consumption.

   The erratic changes in foreign trade and investment point to the fact
that in China's economic plans the level of investment was determined
without a careful assessment of its impact on the economy in the short run
and the long run. To assess the impact, the planners would have needed
information on the input-output relationships between new and old
industries, as might be obtained through elaborate statistical modeling, a
technique the planning system of China was not equipped with. In the
absence of such an assessment, the planners could only act on rule of
thumb or on the will of political leaders. As a result, the years between
1956 and 1971 were characterized by sharp increases in investment in

Table 1.5. The commodity composition of exports and imports, 1956–84 (in percentages)

	Exports		Imports	
	Agricultural products	Manufactures and minerals	Producer goods	Consumer goods
1956	73.9	26.1	91.5	8.5
1957	71.6	28.4	92.0	8.0
1958	72.5	27.5	93.1	6.9
1959	76.3	23.7	95.7	4.3
1960	73.3	26.7	95.4	4.6
1961	66.6	33.4	61.9	38.1
1962	65.3	34.7	55.2	44.8
1963	67.1	32.9	56.0	44.0
1964	67.1	32.9	55.5	44.5
1965	69.1	30.9	56.5	43.5
1966	73.4	26.6	72.2	27.8
1967	75.6	24.4	76.0	24.0
1968	78.2	21.8	77.2	22.8
1969	76.5	23.5	82.4	17.6
1970	74.4	25.6	82.7	17.3
1971	71.1	28.9	83.9	16.1
1972	72.3	27.7	79.4	20.6
1973	75.3	24.7	76.4	23.6
1974	66.2	33.8	75.7	24.3
1975	60.7	39.3	85.4	14.6
1976	61.1	38.9	86.8	13.2
1977	61.5	38.5	76.1	23.9
1978	62.6	37.4	81.4	18.6
1979	56.0	44.0	81.3	18.7
1980	48.2	51.8	78.9	21.1
1981	43.7	56.3	72.8	27.2
1982	39.5	60.5	70.8	29.2
1983	42.6	57.4	78.7	21.3
1984	44.4	55.6	81.0	19.0

Sources: State Statistical Bureau, *Statistical Yearbook of China* (Hong Kong: Economic Information and Agency, 1984, p. 396). State Statistical Bureau, *Statistical Yearbook of China* (Hong Kong: Economic Information and Agency, 1986, p. 509).

some years and sharp decreases in others. Each adjustment was an attempt to correct the mistakes committed by previous investment policy. As shown in Table 1.2, the sharp rises and falls in investment contributed to sharp rises and falls in the growth rates of GNP in this period. In contrast, in the period between 1972 and 1977, investment rose relatively smoothly, resulting in a relatively stable increase in national income.

It is clear from the above discussion that China's foreign trade policy was firmly embodied in its investment policy. For this reason, the level of foreign trade fluctuated closely with the level of national output. Over the long run, foreign trade, acting as a channel through which the economy obtained needed investment technology and equipment, must have contributed immeasurably to the growth of the economy. In the short run, however, excessive rises and falls in foreign trade frequently occurred, and these must have imposed substantial economic losses on the economy. As a result, the rapid output growth that took place in the prereform period generally failed to be translated into an improvement in the standard of living.

1.3   The opening door, economic reforms, and foreign trade

Soon after the deaths of Mao Zedong and Zhou Enlai and the downfall of the Gang of Four in 1976, China began to reexamine past economic policy and search for a new road to economic modernization. Chinese political leaders believed that the country should upgrade the level of technology by making use of technologically advanced machinery and equipment imported from Western industrialized countries. For this purpose, they launched the Four Modernizations program, which emphasized the use of modern technology in industry, agriculture, defense, and science and technology. In launching the program, Deng Xiaoping remarked in his speech to the Fifth National People's Congress (February 26 to March 5, 1978) that:

By the end of this century, the output of major agricultural products is expected to reach or surpass advanced world levels and the output of major industrial products to approach, equal or surpass that of the most developed capitalist countries. In agricultural production, the highest possible degree of mechanization, electrification and irrigation will be achieved. There will be automation in the main industrial process, a major increase in rapid transport and communication services, and a considerable rise in labor productivity. We must apply the results of modern science and technology on a broad scale, make extensive use of new materials and sources of energy, and modernize our major products and the process of production. Our economic and technical norms must approach, equal or surpass advanced world levels (P. Lin 1981, pp. 39–40).

These remarks were embraced by the same spirit that characterized Mao Zedong's Great Leap Forward, through which he looked forward to bringing about a technological revolution to enable China to surpass Britain within 15 years. However, unlike in the Great Leap Forward, indigenous technology was not to play any significant part in the Four Modernizations. The technological revolution was to take place entirely through the import of advanced technology from developed countries, including Japan, West Germany, and the United States. Improvement in human resources received low priority throughout the entire prereform period. The political leadership in China consistently failed to tackle the problem that the lack of human resources posed to the country's economic modernization.

In the Four Modernizations programs, 120 large-scale projects were proposed, including ten iron and steel mills, ten oil and gas fields, thirty power stations, eight coal mines, five harbors, and nine nonferrous metal complexes (Chen 1983, p. 78). Most of these projects were to use imported machinery and equipment to ensure a thorough technological transformation of domestic industries. All imports were to be financed by oil and other exports, which were expected to grow rapidly with the modernization of the economy. In 1978, China entered contracts with foreign traders for the import of more than $7 billion's worth of machinery and capital equipment, mostly in the form of complete plants, and sought to import $40 billion more for the coming years. According to official statistics, total imports rose from 13.3 billion yuan in 1977 to 18.7 billion yuan in 1978, while total exports rose from 14 billion yuan in 1977 to 16.8 billion yuan in 1978.[25] Foreign exchange spending seemed to be running out of hand, as considerably more equipment had been ordered and was in the process of being delivered.

Associated with the rapid expansion of foreign trade was a rise in fixed capital formation from 52 billion yuan in 1977 to 68 billion yuan in 1978, an increase of 31 percent (Table A.3). New investment projects were concentrated in heavy industry, the sector over which the central government, through the allocation of material inputs, could exercise a relatively high degree of control. As before, the new investment projects were undertaken on the basis of the proposals submitted to the central authorities by local governments and industrial ministries, with the encouragement from the central planning authorities. The projects were carried out without the benefit of any advanced evaluation of their feasibility and their short- and long-term impact on the economy. Serious problems arose as a result. First, there was a sharp rise in the demand for goods and services which were already in short supply, including electricity, coal, skilled personnel, and transportation services. The shortage of these goods and services caused not only delays in the construction and operation of new enterprises but also underutilization of productive capacity among old enterprises. As Xue (1985) points out, many existing factories had to operate on a three-day-week basis because of the shortage of electricity and other inputs and many construction works had to be halted as a result of the shortage of construction materials (Xue 1985, p. 419). Second, because of the lack of coordination among importing authorities, including local governments and industrial ministries, duplication in imports arose. Reports abounded of cases where expensive machinery and equipment had to be left idle simply because similar machinery and equipment had already been imported. Third, economic imbalance arose in external trade. In this year, the economy incurred a trade deficit of 1.1 billion U.S. dollars, which was unprecedented in China's recent history. The deficit could potentially have posed a serious problem for the economy in view of the fact that the economy's foreign exchange earnings had long relied on agricultural and mineral exports, both of which were low in demand and supply elasticities. Fourth, the massive rise in investment caused inflationary pressure to rise as the growth of the supply of consumer goods began to lag behind the growth of money incomes (this problem will be discussed in greater detail in Part II).

In the face of these problems, the Four Modernizations program lost momentum soon after it was launched. In late 1978, the government decided to abolish the program and started to restrict technology imports. The import of technology in 1979 amounted to only $1.8 billion, or less than a quarter of the 1978 level. Meanwhile, the government implemented the program of readjustment and reform, aimed at slowing down the rate of capital formation and improving the productivity of individual production units in agriculture and industry. Under the program of readjustment, many large-scale construction projects, including the Baoshan Steel Mill, were either delayed or halted, mainly to prevent the shortage of electricity, coal, oil, and transportation services from worsening further. In addition, the government increased the allocation of investment resources to agriculture and light industry, with a view to easing consumer goods shortage and to achieving rapid growth without putting undue strain on the supply of energy and other products produced by heavy industry. Furthermore, the target outputs of enterprises in heavy industry were lowered so as to, first, release resources to light industry, second, reduce the accumulation of unusable products turned out by enterprises pursuing quantitative targets, and third, put a halt to the excessive use of machinery and equipment without maintenance, a phenomenon which would have caused long-term damage to the productive capacity of industry.

Under the program of economic reform, the government slowly increased the use of the market mechanism as a supplement to central planning. In the first place, measures were taken to decentralize some economic decision-making power in the sphere of investment, sales, and production to enterprises, production teams, and local governments. The purpose was to increase the sensitivity of commodity supplies to changes in supply and demand conditions, thus raising the productivity of individual production units. In association with this change, material incentives were introduced as a means to motivate workers and management to raise their productivity. In agriculture, the government introduced the household responsibility system, in which farmers were responsible for fulfilling their quotas but were allowed to consume or market above-plan output; in industry, the government introduced the profit sharing scheme, in which enterprises and local governments were allowed to retain certain proportions of the above-plan profits of the enterprises for welfare, investment, and bonus payment purposes.[26] To ensure consistency between private interest and national interest under the incentive scheme, the government permitted a greater price flexibility for products traded outside the central plan and proposed to use tax and credit policy as a means to influence the supply and demand of commodities.

The Chinese government certainly did not consider these measures to be sufficient to bring about economic modernization, a goal it was still anxious to achieve in spite of its decision to abolish the Four Modernizations program in late 1978. It was believed that the economy should continue to pursue technological transformation based on imported technology. Therefore, instead of reverting to a closed-door economy, China continued to promote foreign trade in 1979. Many taboos in foreign trade were broken in light of the setting-up of Special Economic Zones, the promotion of foreign investment, and the decentralization of foreign trade power to local authorities. On breaking these taboos, China intended to strengthen its import capacity, in order to allow the possibility of a rapid technological transformation based on imported technology.

1.4 Economic growth, investment, and foreign trade, 1979–85

In spite of its economic reforms, China was still predominantly a centrally planned economy in the period between 1979 and 1985. A major proportion of goods continued to be placed under a unified distribution system. This was true particularly for heavy industry, which had consistently been kept under the relatively strict control of the central government. Enterprises and individuals still did not have unrestricted power to determine levels of investment, the use of foreign exchange, wage rates and bonuses, and the prices of products. Nevertheless, on account of the readjustment program which shifted investment resources from heavy industry to agriculture and light industry, on the one hand, and the new incentive scheme which to a certain extent rewarded farmers and workers with material benefits for increased work effort, on the other, both agriculture and light industry expanded relatively quickly in comparison with heavy industry.

Table 1.6. The growth rates of national output, foreign trade, investment, and consumption, 1979–85 (in percentages)

	1979	1980	1981	1982	1983	1984	1985
GNP[a]	7.00	5.14	3.05	7.51	9.01		
Total trade[b]	36.98	35.53	4.19	−0.07	5.47	25.85	33.95
Exports	34.49	39.37	15.51	6.16	2.22	19.17	13.32
Imports	39.24	33.04	−6.15	−7.07	9.65	36.95	54.96
Investment[c]	2.85	6.25	−21.10	25.61	6.89	23.26	37.21
Consumption per capita							
All commodities[d]	12.57	15.23	9.69	7.23	8.61	13.79	23.33
Food grains[e]	5.92	3.27	2.51	2.87	3.00	8.23	1.20
Cloth[e]	11.50	11.96	2.83	−2.94	3.30	4.94	7.66

[a] Figures are based on U.S. dollar values and are at constant prices.
[b] Figures are based on U.S. dollar values.
[c] Investment = "Investment in capital construction" in official statistics, deflated by industrial prices.
[d] Figures are based on renminbi values.
[e] Figures are based on the physical units of the products.
Sources: GNP: Scherer (1985, p. 90). Foreign trade: Table A.2 in Appendix A. Investment: Table A.3 in Appendix A. Consumption per capita: State Statistical Bureau, Statistical Yearbook of China (Hong Kong: Economic Information and Agency, 1987, pp. 592 and 632).

As shown in Table 1.4, the levels of output in agriculture, light industry, and heavy industry went up by an average of 10 percent, 13 percent, and 8 percent per annum, respectively, in the period between 1979 and 1985. The relatively rapid growth of agriculture and light industry greatly raised the economy's export capability.

In the face of the enlarged export capability and rising oil prices, coupled with the government's policy of promoting exports, exports rose quickly. As shown in Table 1.6, the U.S. dollar value of exports went up by an average of more than 29 percent per annum in the period between 1979 and 1981. The high growth was interrupted by the world economic recession in 1982 and 1983, during which period exports went up by only 6 percent in the first year and 2 percent in the second. This was the first time in the history of the Chinese Communist regime that fluctuations in the world economy had had a significant depressive effect on the growth of the country's foreign trade. The world economy recovered in the next year, raising China's exports by 19 percent in 1984 and 13 percent in 1985.

The government's promotion of exports was not meant to finance a simultaneous expansion in imports. As indicated earlier, a great effort was made by the state to curtail imports in 1979 in order to restore economic balance. Because of the continued presence of the problem of macroeconomic imbalance, the policy of curtailing imports remained in force in the early 1980s. As a result, imports went up by an average of only 5 percent per annum in the period between 1980 and 1982, compared with 19 percent for exports. In addition, the share of producer goods in total imports decreased steadily from 81 percent in 1979 to 71 percent in 1982 (Table 1.5). These changes suggest that, as foreign exchange reserves accumulated with the rapid expansion of exports, the government became relatively liberal toward the import of consumer goods, including food grains and consumer durables, but was cautious not to increase imports of machinery and equipment by a substantial amount for fear of aggravating the problem of economic imbalance.

In conjunction with the government's curtailment of producer goods imports, the level of investment was also strongly curtailed. As shown in Table 1.6 the growth rates of fixed capital formation were only 3 percent in 1979 and 6 percent in 1980, compared with 31 percent in 1978 (Table A.3). Fixed capital formation even experienced an absolute decline by 21 percent in 1981, the year when the government temporarily recentralized economic decision-making power because of its fear that the investment growth at the local level would again lead to worsening economic imbalance. However, in 1982 economic decision-making powers were again decentralized, and investment rose by 26 percent to compensate for the large decline in the previous year. Note that the low investment growth in the years between 1979 and 1982 was attributable primarily to the decrease in the level of investment in heavy industry. As shown in Table 1.1, the annual growth rates of investment in heavy industry were negative in all of the years from 1979 to 1981, whereas the growth rates of investment in the rest of the economy as a whole were positive in both 1979 and 1980.

Beginning in 1983, imports began to rise quickly. The annual growth rate of imports went up from 10 percent in 1983 to 37 percent in 1984 and increased further to 55 percent in 1985. The average yearly growth rate of imports was 33 percent in the period between 1983 and 1985, compared with 11 percent for exports. Notably, the increase in imports was attributable mainly to the rise in the imports of producer goods, the share of which in total imports rose from 71 percent in 1982 to 81 percent in 1984 (Table 1.5).

The rapid increase in producer goods imports occurred primarily because of the accelerated increase in investment in capital construction at the local and central levels. At the local level, enterprises and local govern-

Table 1.7. Sources of investment funds in state-owned units, 1982–5

	1982	1983	1984	1985
State budget	31.0	38.7	46.2	44.4
Domestic loans	13.7	13.6	18.2	38.7
Foreign investment	1.6	1.6	2.6	4.6
Self-raised fund and				
other sources	38.3	41.4	51.5	80.2
Total	84.6	95.3	118.5	168.1

Note: All figures are in billion yuan.
Source: State Statistical Bureau, *Statistical Yearbook of China* (Hong Kong: Economic Information and Agency, various issues).

ments obtained investment funds not only from state allocation but also from bank loans, retained profits, depreciation funds, and even foreign borrowings. They acquired foreign exchange quotas through the foreign exchange retention scheme as well as through central allocation, and they would use foreign exchange entitlement quotas mainly on the imports of machinery and equipment needed in the investment projects (see Chapter 2 for the discussion of the foreign exchange retention scheme). As soon as the central government loosened its control over imports and investment in 1983, enterprises and local governments rushed to start up new projects, which often involved the use of imported technology in order to win approval from the planning authorities. As shown in Table 1.7, the investment increase in the period between 1983 and 1985 was attributable mainly to the expansion of investment funds outside the state budget.

However, the state investment budget also contributed much to the rise in total investment. To a certain extent, the increase in state finance was a response of the central government to the pressure arising from the rising demand for goods and services produced and allocated by the state, such as steel, coal, electricity, and transportation services. The more rapid the increase in investment at the local level, the greater such pressure became. The investment projects financed by state budgets were predominantly large-scale ones which also involved the importation of machinery and equipment. Therefore, the investment increase at the central level also raised the level of imports.

In summary, China's foreign trade expansion during the period between 1979 and 1985 was growth-led. The expansion of exports was made possible by the smooth growth of GNP (Table 1.6), whereas the expansion of imports was made possible by the expansion of exports and external borrowings. Foreign trade to a certain extent determined the level of investment, rather than responding passively to the government's invest-ment plans. Since the rapid foreign trade and investment growth were preceded by the rapid growth of national output, the former did not cause a drop in the standard of living. Instead, as shown in Table 1.6, the economy witnessed remarkable increases in the per capita consumption of both food grains and cloth in this period. In quantitative terms, each Chinese consumed 30 percent more food grains and 45 percent more cloth in 1985 than in 1978. There was also a significant rise in the con-sumption of other nonbasic necessity items, including pork, eggs, poultry, footwear, watches, and so on. In his private visit to Hong Kong in 1987, Fei Xiaotong, a prominent Chinese sociologist, dubbed this period as the best period in Chinese history. As a result of the continued improvement in the standard of living, the government was able to continue to push the growth of foreign trade and investment without encountering significant resistance from the group which had lost its economic and political power in the process of economic reforms.

1.5   Summary

China's prereform economic planning was hampered by the lack of a comprehensive information system on which a central plan had to work. The central government had under its control only about 200 commodity items, and it was unable to set meaningful long-term output targets for individual sectors. Investment resources were concentrated mainly on the heavy industrial sector, particularly when an ambitious development pro-gram was implemented. Invariably, foreign trade was used as a means for transferring resources from consumption to investment. Thus, foreign trade fluctuated closely with the level of investment in prereform China. The fact that both foreign trade and investment changed erratically in the prereform period suggests that investment was carried out without the benefit of a careful assessment of its short- and long-term economic im-pacts.

In the post-1978 period, foreign trade expanded rapidly, mainly as a result of economic reform which greatly enlarged China's export capabil-ity. The rapid growth of exports in most of the years between 1979 and 1985 made the rapid growth of imports in 1984 and 1985 possible. In this period, foreign trade was not determined by the investment decision at the central government level but by, among other things, the government's policy on imports and exports. Since imports continued to be concen-trated on producer goods, the level of foreign trade to a certain extent determined the level of investment and therefore the level of national output.

1.6   The plan of the book

The purpose of this book is to discuss two of the most important problems incurred in the rapid expansion of foreign trade in China. One is a micro-economic problem, which involves the determination of how much and what to export and how much and what to import within the new economic system. Although the market mechanism had been introduced to help deal with the problem, the operation of market forces was still heavily regulated, and the government still played an important part in export and import decision making. The severity of this problem increased as the volume of foreign trade expanded. The second problem concerns the inflationary effect of foreign trade expansion. Inflationary pressure would change with foreign trade because the latter would affect directly and indirectly the supply of and demand for consumer goods. For instance, an increase in the exports of consumer goods will reduce the supply of consumer goods for domestic consumption, whereas an increase in the imports of consumer goods will have the opposite effect. As the volume of foreign trade expands, the inflationary pressure suffered by the economy will be affected. In the rest of this book, Part I, which includes Chapter 2 and 3, deals with the first problem, whereas Part II, which includes Chapters 4 and 5, deals with the second.

The plan for the following chapters is as follows. In Chapter 2, I discuss the allocative efficiency of exports and imports before and during the economic reforms. The focus will be on whether the allocative efficiency has improved with the decentralization of foreign trade power under the economic reforms. Chapter 3 studies the structural changes in China's exports and imports in the years between 1979 and 1985. Government policies causing these changes will be examined. The analysis shows the presence of strong government intervention in the fundamental problems of what to trade, how much to trade, and with whom to trade. In Chapter 4, a model is set up to analyze the impact of foreign trade growth on inflationary pressure in a centrally planned economy. We show that there is a tendency for foreign trade expansion to raise inflationary pressure in such an economy. Chapter 5 presents the empirical evidence. To determine the changes in the inflationary effect of foreign trade in China, we discuss the use of various imbalance measures and show that our real purchasing power imbalance estimates provide a result strikingly similar to the changes in the degree of imbalance perceived by Chinese economists. In this chapter, we also discuss the policy measures employed by the government to deal with the imbalance problem. Finally, Chapter 6 discusses the prospect of China's foreign trade reform in light of the difficulties it has encountered in its recent push for a reform of the pricing and enterprise management system. The major argument in this chapter is that, in the absence of a fundamental reform of the incentive system, foreign trade cannot possibly be further decentralized and the efficiency with which resources are allocated to the foreign trade sector cannot possibly be significantly improved. In addition, I show that before a further decentralization of foreign trade power or a further reform of the foreign trade system occurs the rapid growth of foreign trade will continue to have a strong tendency to worsen the rate of open inflation in China.

Appendix A

Official statistics on national output, foreign trade, and fixed capital formation

National output

China did not and still does not publish data on GNP or GDP. Nevertheless, in its recently published statistical yearbook, it provides two statistics which closely resemble the Western concept of national output. These are total product of society and national income. Total product of society (TPS) is defined as the sum of (a) the values of intermediate goods and (b) the values of final products in the following five "material production sectors": agriculture, industry, construction, transport, and commerce. Apart from the fact that TPS is arrived at on the basis of administered prices instead of market prices, TPS differs conceptually from GNP in that (a) TPS excludes the value of output created in the "nonmaterial production sectors," including culture, education, health care, research, personal services, public services, police, and the armed forces and (b) TPS is the sum of the values of the products at all stages of production and can be many times the values of final products. As for national income (NI), it is defined as TPS excluding the values of all intermediate products. Therefore, NI is conceptually closer to GNP than TPS is. However, NI understates the level of national output by excluding the incomes generated in the "nonmaterial sectors." Therefore, in the present study we use the CIA's estimates of GNP in place of TPS and NI.

Table A.1 presents the growth rates of TPS, NI, and GNP, all at constant prices. They appear to rise and fall closely with one another. However, the fluctuations in TPS and NI are greater than the fluctuations in GNP, presumably because TPS and NI fail to take account of the relatively stable service sector.

Table A.1. The growth rates of total product of society (TPS), national income (NI), and gross national product (GNP), 1956–85 (in percentages)

	TPS	NI	GNP		TPS	NI	GNP
1956	17.94	14.11	8.33	1971	9.09	6.99	6.84
1957	6.08	4.51	6.15	1972	4.45	2.92	4.63
1958	32.65	22.03	18.84	1973	8.60	8.29	12.93
1959	17.95	8.25	−4.88	1974	1.90	1.08	3.61
1960	4.71	−1.43	−2.56	1975	11.50	8.31	6.98
1961	−33.50	−29.72	−21.05	1976	1.39	−2.68	0.00
1962	−9.99	−6.50	9.17	1977	10.30	7.80	8.15
1963	10.20	10.70	12.98	1978	13.11	12.29	11.56
1964	17.48	16.49	10.81	1979	8.50	6.99	5.18
1965	18.99	17.00	12.80	1980	8.41	6.39	5.14
1966	16.89	16.96	13.51	1981	4.60	4.90	3.05
1967	−9.87	−7.23	−3.81	1982	9.50	8.30	7.51
1968	−4.71	−6.49	0.99	1983	10.30	9.79	9.01
1969	25.31	19.31	10.78	1984	14.70	13.50	
1970	25.65	23.25	16.37	1985	16.50	12.29	

Note: All output measures are at constant prices.
Sources: TPS and NI: State Statistical Bureau, *Statistical Yearbook of China* (Hong Kong: Economic Information and Agency, 1987, pp. 24–5 and 38–9). GNP: Scherer (1980, p. 77; 1985, p. 90).

Foreign trade statistics

Chao (1964) points out two major causes of distortions involved in China's foreign trade statistics in the 1950s: first, the unrealistic and inconsistent exchange rates, and second, the different pricing practices applied to its trade with communist and noncommunist countries. The exchange rates were unrealistic because they were mostly overvalued; the exchange rates were inconsistent because, in the absence of currency arbitrage between convertible and nonconvertible currencies, the official cross rates were not necessarily consistent with the prevailing rates quoted in the foreign exchange markets in Western countries; and the pricing practices were such that China recorded the values of imports from the West on the basis of their international market prices but the values of imports from the East on the basis of the relatively inflexible, negotiated prices. As a result, the trade statistics could not reflect without distortion both the actual level of foreign trade and the shares of the country's trade with communist and noncommunist countries. The problem was particularly severe for the renminbi statistics of foreign trade since they in-

Table A.2. Exports and imports, 1956–85

	Value (in billion U.S. $)				Growth rate (%)			
	Exports		Imports		Exports		Imports	
	CIA[a]	SSB[b]	CIA	SSB	CIA	SSB	CIA	SSB
1956	1.63	1.65	1.66	1.49	18.91	17.02	−10.54	−10.34
1957	1.62	1.60	1.44	1.50	−1.22	−3.03	−3.03	−3.85
1958	1.94	1.98	1.83	1.89	20.12	23.75	26.74	26.00
1959	2.23	2.26	2.06	2.12	14.95	14.14	12.88	12.17
1960	1.96	1.86	2.03	1.95	−12.11	−17.70	−1.46	−8.02
1961	1.53	1.49	1.49	1.45	−22.19	−19.89	−26.60	−25.64
1962	1.52	1.49	1.15	1.17	−0.33	0.00	−22.82	−19.31
1963	1.58	1.65	1.20	1.26	3.62	10.74	4.35	7.69
1964	1.75	1.91	1.47	1.55	11.11	15.76	22.50	23.02
1965	2.03	2.23	1.85	2.02	16.00	16.75	25.51	30.32
1966	2.21	2.37	2.04	2.24	8.87	6.28	10.30	10.30
1967	1.96	2.14	1.96	2.02	−11.31	−9.70	−3.93	−9.82
1968	1.96	2.10	1.83	1.94	0.00	−1.87	−6.65	−3.96
1969	2.06	2.20	1.84	1.83	5.10	4.76	0.55	−5.67
1970	2.16	2.26	2.21	2.33	4.66	2.73	20.54	27.32
1971	2.54	2.64	2.15	2.20	17.63	16.81	4.61	−5.58
1972	3.24	3.44	2.59	2.80	27.56	30.30	22.17	30.00
1973	5.10	5.82	4.63	5.16	57.84	69.19	76.87	80.42
1974	6.76	6.95	7.29	7.62	32.37	19.42	47.05	47.67
1975	7.12	7.26	6.83	7.39	5.36	4.46	1.39	−1.71
1976	7.27	6.86	6.03	6.58	2.04	−5.51	−18.43	−12.15
1977	8.18	7.59	7.12	7.21	12.54	10.64	18.14	9.57
1978	10.17	9.75	11.18	10.89	24.32	28.46	57.12	51.04
1979	13.72	13.67	14.29	15.57	34.49	40.10	39.24	43.89
1980	18.92	18.27	20.72	19.55	38.37	33.75	33.04	24.76
1981	21.85	22.01	19.44	22.01	15.51	20.47	−6.15	12.58
1982	23.20	22.35	18.07	19.28	6.16	1.54	−7.07	−12.40
1983	23.71	22.23	19.81	21.39	2.22	−0.54	9.65	10.94
1984	27.64	26.14	27.13	27.41	19.17	17.59	36.95	28.14
1985	31.32	27.36	42.05	42.25	13.32	4.67	54.96	54.14

[a] SSB = State Statistical Bureau, China.
[b] CIA = Central Intelligence Agency, United States of America.
Sources: SSB Statistics: State Statistical Bureau, *Statistical Yearbook of China* (Hong Kong: Economic Information and Agency, p. 519). CIA statistics: National Foreign Assessment Center, Central Intelligence Agency, *China: International Trade,* Fourth Quarter, various issues; National Foreign Assessment Center, Central Intelligence Agency, *China: International Trade,* 1977–8.

Table A.3. Investment in capital construction in state-owned units, 1956–85

	Value (million yuan)	Growth rate (%)		Value (million yuan)	Growth rate (%)
1956	17,296	64.80	1971	45,300	9.75
1957	17,242	−6.09	1972	43,842	−3.22
1958	30,680	88.89	1973	45,450	3.67
1959	39,646	29.23	1974	47,071	3.57
1960	44,391	11.97	1975	55,735	18.41
1961	13,864	−68.77	1976	51,363	−7.84
1962	7,463	−46.17	1977	52,632	2.47
1963	10,336	38.49	1978	68,855	30.82
1964	15,482	49.79	1979	70,817	2.85
1965	20,249	30.79	1980	75,241	6.25
1966	24,643	21.70	1981	59,363	−21.10
1967	16,707	−32.21	1982	74,568	−25.61
1968	13,769	−17.58	1983	79,706	6.89
1969	25,351	84.11	1984	98,248	23.26
1970	41,277	62.82	1985	134,802	37.21

[a] Investment in capital construction is in real terms, using industrial prices as a deflator. *Sources:* Industrial output deflator: State Statistical Bureau, *Statistical Yearbook of China* (Hong Kong: Economic Information and Agency, 1987, pp. 31–2). Investment in capital construction: State Statistical Bureau, *Statistical Yearbook of China* (Hong Kong: Economic Information and Agency, 1987, p. 404).

volved the conversion of the actual foreign exchange values of exports and imports with unrealistic and inconsistent official exchange rates. Under present economic reforms, the conversion problem has been alleviated by the fact that China has been trading mostly with Western countries since the early 1970s, on the one hand, but accentuated by the presence of a wide range of implicit exchange rates for exported goods, on the other (see Chapter 2 for a more detailed discussion). To avoid the conversion problem, the present study uses the U.S. dollar values of exports and imports published by either the CIA or the State Statistical Bureau (SSB).

Table A.2 presents the official and CIA statistics on foreign trade, both in U.S. dollars. CIA statistics are based on the foreign trade statistics published in countries trading with China. Discrepancies in these two sets of statistics are bound to occur because of the possible difference in the exchange rates used to convert non-U.S. dollar values into U.S. dollar values, the difference in the time exports and imports are recorded in the customs of China and its trading partners, the difference in the values assigned to the barter trade taking place between China and its trading partners, and so forth. The discrepancies, however, are relatively small for most of the years.

Fixed capital formation

The Chinese term for fixed capital formation is "investment in fixed assets," which includes "investment in capital construction" and technical updating and transformation. Investment in capital construction refers to expenditures on the construction of factories, mines, railways, bridges, harbors, stores, houses, schools, hospitals, water irrigation systems, and purchases of machinery and equipment. Technical updating and transformation refers to expenditures on the technical renewal of existing fixed assets. Strictly speaking, the technical renewal of existing fixed assets does not amount to an addition to fixed assets by the full amount, because it usually involves the scrapping of existing fixed assets. Therefore, I use investment in capital construction as an approximation to the level of fixed capital formation.

Table A.3 presents the data on investment in capital construction. Note that the data include only investment by state-owned units and that the investment data of collective-owned units are not available. For interyear comparison, the level of annual investment in capital construction is deflated by the industrial price index.

PART I

Foreign trade reforms, economic efficiency, and trade patterns

CHAPTER 2

Foreign trade reforms and the economic efficiency of foreign trade

The rapid growth of China's foreign trade between 1979 and 1985 was attributable partly to the dramatic reforms of its foreign trade system. Under the reforms, some foreign trade decision-making power was decentralized, but the central government still was responsible for setting overall import and export targets, securing domestic goods for export, and determining the allocation of foreign exchange among different uses. In implementing the foreign trade plan, the central government might resort to discretionary measures, including the adjustment of export procurement targets and the strengthening or loosening of import controls. It might also resort to economic measures, adjusting the export and import incentives provided to enterprises and local governments with a view to influencing their export and import decisions (see Section 2.3).

Undoubtedly, the use of economic measures to regulate foreign trade was a significant departure from the prereform foreign trade system, which was characterized by state monopoly and inflexible import and export plans. Such a change was part of the economywide reform which allowed above-plan production and sales of individual products to be determined by market forces. Because of the introduction of the market mechanism to foreign trade planning, one might expect the economic efficiency of foreign trade, in terms of its effects on the output growth of the economy, to increase, thus inducing China to continue to adopt the open door policy. However, the analysis in this chapter shows that this did not appear to have been the case, considering the heavily regulated framework under which market forces operated.

One important contribution of the foreign trade reforms to China's economic growth is that they have provided the long-closed Chinese economy with a greater exposure to advanced production, marketing, and management techniques. This exposure might not itself bring about immediate and speedy rises in national output, but it could have a long-lasting effect on the future growth of the economy through its influence on the attitude of traders, producers, and administrators toward the role played by market forces, as opposed to ideology and bureaucratic plan-

37

ning, in production, consumption, and exchange. In addition, foreign trade reforms have enlarged the outlet for products with surplus productive capacity and enabled some enterprises to enjoy economies of scale. These dynamic benefits are immeasurable, and they might be so large that the economic efficiency of foreign trade under the foreign trade reforms far exceeds that of prereform foreign trade.

Nevertheless, the present analysis focuses on the less elusive, static benefits of foreign trade reforms. More specifically, I look at the effects of foreign trade reforms on the allocative efficiency of resources in the foreign trade sector. Foreign trade reforms are said to have improved the economic efficiency of foreign trade if they result in an increase in both the efficiency with which domestic resources are allocated in production for export and the efficiency with which foreign exchange is made use of in import. Indeed, static benefits of foreign trade were a major concern in China's launch of the trade reforms, as evidenced by the enthusiastic discussions on the theory of comparative costs by Chinese economists justifying the rapid expansion of foreign trade in recent years (Lin 1985; Huang 1985; Chen and Jiang 1985).[1] In order to determine the effects of foreign trade reforms on the allocative efficiency of foreign trade, I first discuss the differences between the prereform and postreform foreign trade systems and then show how decisions on imports and exports would be made under the two systems.

2.1   The economic efficiency of foreign trade under central economic planning

In prereform China, foreign trade was an integral part of the national economic plan and served to make up for shortages in the plan. As discussed earlier, the level of imports was determined by the shortages to be made up for in the plan, and the level of exports was determined by the amount of foreign exchange required to finance the predetermined level of imports.[2] For analytical purposes, imports may be conceptually classified into two groups: investment-induced imports and noninvestment-induced imports. Noninvestment-induced imports refer to those which are needed to help maintain the planned level of consumption in the current period, whereas investment-induced imports refer to those which are needed to help achieve the planned increase in the level of consumption in the future periods. The planners had relatively little control over the former category of imports, including such goods as rubber and chemical fertilizers, which were required in current production and consumption. Conversely, the planners had full control over the latter category of imports since they had full control over the level of investment expenditure.[3] Such imports included machinery, equipment, raw materials, and intermediate manufactured goods which were required by investment-related projects.

Under strict central planning, the economic efficiency of exports and imports depends on the correspondence between the preference of the planners and that of the consumers. In the case where the two preferences coincide, goods in short supply must be valued more highly than goods in abundant supply, and foreign trade, with the export of goods in abundant supply and the import of goods in short supply, must be economically efficient. In reality, however, the preference of the planners is unlikely to coincide perfectly with that of the consumers. Historically, China's development policy has been biased in favor of the producer goods industry and against the consumer goods industry, as is true in other centrally planned economies. With this bias, planned surpluses were likely to be created out of those consumer goods which were actually in short supply, and planned shortages were likely to occur among those producer goods which were actually in surplus. Therefore, foreign trade could be highly economically inefficient. There were also other policy biases (such as the agriculture-industry price scissors) which could have resulted in an over-expansion in some sectors and underexpansion in some others, thus causing artificial surpluses and shortages in industries. The tendency for the economy to import those goods which were in artificial shortage and export those goods which were in artificial surplus suggests that resources tended to be inefficiently allocated to the foreign trade sector.

In general, the economic efficiency of foreign trade under strict central planning depends on the following two factors: the extent to which domestic production and consumption are distorted by the planners' preference, and the extent to which foreign trade is influenced by the distortion in domestic production and consumption. Nevertheless, since both factors are difficult, if not impossible, to quantify, there is no straightforward way to determine the economic efficiency of individual exports and imports.

However, the difficulty does not prevent us from making a meaningful comparison of the economic efficiency of foreign trade between the periods of low and high investment growth.[4] Given that in prereform China investment decisions were made primarily by the central government, investment growth reflected both the extent to which the preference of the central government had been imposed on the economy and the extent to which the preference of the central government was likely to deviate from that of the consumers. As indicated in Chapter 1, the central government, with relatively little planning skill, had to make its investment decisions without the benefit of a careful assessment of their impacts on domestic production and consumption in advance. Therefore, the policy of high investment growth, such as that which was adopted during the Great Leap Forward and the 1978 Four Modernizations drive, involved the creation of artificial shortages (in producer goods) and surpluses (in consumer goods) in the national economic plan, calling for large increases in imports and exports. The greater the volume of foreign trade, the greater the possibility for foreign trade to depart from what would have been determined by the market. Some of the goods imported to fill a planned shortage might not actually be needed or could not be fully utilized, and some of the goods exported from a planned surplus might actually be in critical shortage at home. In contrast, in the periods of low investment growth, the demand for and supply of commodities in the domestic markets were relatively stable, and so were the demand for imports and the supply of exports. Imports were limited to some essential items which could not be produced at home in sufficient quantities to meet domestic demand or which could be produced at home but only at a cost substantially higher than that of imports; exports were determined by the amount of imports that had to be financed, and items exported were normally limited to those which were relatively abundant in supply. Thus, foreign trade tended to be less economically inefficient in the presence of low investment growth than when investment growth was high.

The impacts of the policy of high investment growth on the economic efficiency of foreign trade can be seen from China's experience with technological reform in 1978. In that year, China launched the Four Modernizations program, which regarded the low level of production technology as a major bottleneck to the modernization of the economy. The planners' solution to the "problem" was to speed up the exports of agricultural, mineral, and light industrial products and raise substantially the imports of technologically advanced machinery and equipment for large-scale investment projects. Thus, planned shortages were made of technologically advanced machinery and equipment, and planned surpluses were created out of agricultural, mineral, and light industrial products. However, as pointed out in Chapter 1, resource allocation became so severely distorted by the high investment and foreign trade growth that the imported machinery and equipment could not be fully utilized, and that those goods which had been exported were faced with the pressure of rising demand at home. It is therefore not surprising that China curtailed imports less than a year after the modernization campaign was launched.

2.2 Economic reforms and foreign trade institution

In order to discuss the economic efficiency of foreign trade before and after economic reforms, I first provide a brief account of the background of the policy changes that occurred in the late 1970s and then discuss in detail the changes in foreign trade institution from the prereform period to the postreform period.

The failure of China's 1978 Four Modernizations drive was attributable to the distortive effects of the high investment and foreign trade growth on the supply of and demand for domestic products. Widespread supply bottlenecks occurred in raw materials, electricity, coal, transportation, and so on as a result of the dramatic rise in the demand for them, since the government had little control over these supplies in the short run under the prereform planning system. Nevertheless, China blamed the rigid and bureaucratized management system for the presence of such bottlenecks. It was argued that, under such a system, the production of domestic products was unresponsive to changes in demand, and that a more flexible, decentralized management system was needed to improve its responsiveness. Indeed, had production responded to the changes in demand, bottlenecks in the supply of many material inputs would not have been as serious as they were, and much imported machinery and equipment would have been more efficiently utilized. However, because of the rigid commodity supplies, the sudden rise in resource demand arising from the new investment projects had to be satisfied largely by the diversion of labor and material inputs from existing uses to new investment projects, thus reducing production in old enterprises and contributing to macroeconomic imbalance. To rectify this problem, China launched economic reforms and started to decentralize economic decision-making power in 1979. As will be shown in latter chapters, the implementation of economic reforms, though having the effect of raising the responsiveness of domestic production to changes in market demand, could not by itself do away with the problem of macroeconomic imbalance in the event of rapid investment and foreign trade growth, the very problem that was faced by the 1978 modernization drive. In the rest of the present chapter, I attempt to show that the implementation of economic reforms has not necessarily improved the economic efficiency of imports and exports.

In the prereform period, foreign trade was an integral part, or, as some economists put it, a residual item of the national economic plan. On the basis of past experience and the sectoral plans submitted by various ministries and local governments, the State Planning Commission issued a preliminary foreign trade plan for execution by the Ministry of Foreign

Trade. In response, the Ministry of Foreign Trade mapped out import and export plans, taking into consideration the following factors: internal and external market conditions, the country's political relations with foreign countries, the existing contractual trade commitments to foreign countries, and the present and future export capability. The foreign trade plan was then passed on to specialized national trade corporations for execution. These foreign trade corporations were empowered to conduct foreign trade negotiations, to manage foreign trade enterprises, and to supervise all the operation procedures of foreign trade.

By putting foreign trade under central control, China envisaged a number of advantages. First, exports and imports could be easily integrated into the national economic plan; second, foreign trade could be conveniently used as a tool to help China achieve its political goals in international politics; and third, the bargaining power of the country in both export and import could be strengthened. However, as the Chinese political leaders began to advocate economic modernization through economic reforms in 1979, these advantages became less important than before. As a consequence of reforms, the economy was no longer strictly centrally planned, and it became unnecessary for the planners to integrate all trade activities into the national plan. Furthermore, because of its emphasis on economic modernization, China saw foreign trade more as a means to foster economic growth than as a means to further its political goals in international relations. For foreign trade to foster economic growth, China believed that it was necessary to speed up exports by making use of the initiatives of individual enterprises and local governments. Therefore, it started to distribute part of foreign trade decision-making power to local governments and enterprises in 1979. The benefits that the economy could obtain from the decentralization of foreign trade power were considered to be far greater than those obtainable from the strengthened foreign trade bargaining power under state monopoly.

Since 1979, the State Planning Commission and Economic Commission have been responsible for the formulation of the foreign trade plan. The plan, as before, is issued to the Ministry of Foreign Economic Relations and Trade (MFERT, which is the amalgamation of the former Ministry of Foreign Trade, the Ministry of Economic Relations with Foreign Countries, the State Administrative Commission on Import and Export Affairs, and the State Foreign Investment Commission) for execution. The MFERT in turn has to formulate its own execution plan and issue the plan to both the subordinate foreign trade corporations and local foreign trade bureaus. The plan covers a major part of China's foreign trade activities, estimated at more than 80 percent of the total trade.[5] The rest is under the control of other ministries and local governments, which are empowered to establish their own foreign trade corporations. These foreign trade corporations are said to have contributed to the overexpansion of imports and the growth of unauthorized exports in recent years (He and Wang 1983, p. 471). However, the problem has been alleviated since the government's strengthening of the export and import licensing system in 1985.

Directive plan and guidance plan

The foreign trade plan formulated by MFERT may be divided into two parts: the directive plan and the guidance plan. In the directive plan, specific quantitative targets of exports and imports are assigned to certain sectors, industries, and enterprises. Such a plan involves mainly (a) the exports of heavy industrial products, for example, petroleum,[6] and (b) the imports of raw materials, machinery, and equipment for those large-scale investment projects which are financed by the state budget.[7] This part of the foreign trade plan is inherited from the prereform foreign trade system, in which foreign trade was entirely under centralized control. As before, because of the relatively large amount of foreign exchange transactions involved, trade negotiations are mostly conducted with the active participation of the MFERT, and the resultant contracts are mostly of long-term nature. In this case, national foreign trade corporations serve merely as the execution arms of the MFERT, and individual enterprises implement passively the foreign trade plans issued to them by MFERT through the foreign trade corporations. Foreign trade reforms have no direct bearing on the trade activities taking place under the directive plan.

In the guidance plan, regional and industry-specific export earning targets and import spending limits, specified in monetary terms, are laid down and issued to the ministries and local governments, empowering them to form their own foreign trade corporations to engage in foreign trade. The fulfillment of the export earning targets depends on various factors, including the availability of material and nonmaterial inputs, the size of foreign markets for the products, and the incentives provided to enterprises and their supervising entities. The planners have relatively little control over the first two factors, but they are able to use the last factor to influence exports. The willingness of individual enterprises to produce for export hinges on the incentives provided for them by the profit-sharing scheme and the foreign exchange retention scheme (these two schemes will be elaborated on in Section 2.3). With regard to imports, they depend on the foreign exchange allocation system as well as the structure of import controls instituted under the foreign trade reforms (these will be elaborated on in Section 2.6). It suffices to say here that a high degree of autonomy has been given to enterprises and local governments with respect to export and import decisions within the guidance plan.

2.3   Economic reforms and foreign trade incentives

The reform of the foreign trade system is an integral part of the general reform. First of all, the autonomy enjoyed by enterprises and local governments in foreign trade derives precisely from the general reform program, which accords them with varying degrees of autonomous decision-making power with respect to production, management, investment, and sales.[8] In the general reform program, the most profound institutional changes took place in agriculture with the implementation of the production responsibility system. In this system, farm households or individuals essentially enter some form of contract with their production teams or brigades that specifies the output quotas to be fulfilled on the basis of the allocated land and farm tools.[9] The quotas include state and brigade levies and household supplies to the state. Above-quota output can be retained for own use or traded in free markets. Moreover, the state has reduced the range of agricultural products which are under the centralized procurement system in order to provide farmers with the freedom to make their own production decisions. A similar but less ambitious enterprise responsibility system has been introduced in the industrial sector. For example, the Petrolchemical Company has signed a contract with the government specifying, among other things, the output targets to be fulfilled in the years between 1985 and 1990 (Deng, Ma, and Wu 1985, p. 189). In return, the central government guarantees its supplies of raw materials, fuel, electricity, transportation services, investment funds, and equipment and manpower needed for future development by the company. However, this scheme has been extended to only a few other industries, including coal and iron and steel, on an experimental basis, obviously because of the limited control that the central government has over input supplies in other industries. So long as the central government cannot guarantee the supply of inputs, especially electricity, there is no way for the enterprise to predict with certainty the amount of output it can produce, and no enterprise would be willing to enter a contract with the state specifying the rate of output growth to be achieved. Major changes in the industrial sector took place not in the form of the responsibility system but in the form of the loosening of bureaucratic centralized control over enterprises. Although enterprises are still required to fulfill the planned target, they can now market above-plan output, design their own management system, invest their own resources, and set the prices for their above-plan production within the limits set by the state. In other words, enterprises can now function as semiindependent economic decision-making units partly in charge of their own production and marketing plans.

The profit-sharing scheme

The new incentive system instituted in foreign trade is based primarily on the profit-sharing scheme instituted in the general economic reform. In this reform, profit is taken as one of the most important indicators of the efficiency with which resources are utilized. Therefore, by allowing enterprises to retain a portion of their profits, the government expects that the enterprises would so operate as to maximize their profits, thereby directing domestic resources to their most efficient uses. The scheme also covers foreign trade activities because it is believed that enterprises engaged in export and import can also improve their economic efficiency if they aim at maximizing their profits. In view of the importance of the scheme to the efficiency of resource allocation in the foreign trade sector, a detailed discussion of its operation is in order.

To understand the profit-sharing scheme, it is helpful first to understand China's pricing system. In spite of the autonomy granted to them under the economic reforms, enterprises have only limited freedom to set their own prices. Commodity prices are partly set by the state and partly determined by market forces. Broadly speaking, there are four sets of prices: planned (list) prices, floating prices, negotiated prices, and free market prices (Zhang and Meng 1985, pp. 602–6). Under the economic reforms, enterprises are required to supply to the government a certain portion of their products at fixed (planned) prices for centralized allocation, the portion depending on the perceived importance of the product to the economy. In the case of "essential" products, such as petroleum, electricity, cement, coal, chemical fertilizers, and some machinery and equipment, the state is wholly responsible for the production and distribution of the products, and planned prices apply to the whole of their output. In the case of "nonessential" products, planned output targets are normally set below the enterprises' capacity output, thus allowing above-plan output to be sold at floating prices, negotiated prices, or free market prices. The floating prices refer to those prices which are permitted to rise or fall by within 20 percent of the planned prices[10]; the negotiated prices refer to those prices which are arrived at between the buyers and sellers of the products, the buyers and sellers being enterprises or the purchasing department of the government[11]; and, finally, the free market prices refer to the prices of those products traded in marketplaces.[12]

In view of the fact that each product can have more than one price, its "profitability" depends considerably on the proportions of it being sold at planned and nonplanned prices. To illustrate the determination of enterprise profits, let P_g and P_f be the government-determined, planned price and the flexible, nonplanned price, respectively, the subscripts g and f referring to the planned and nonplanned sectors. P_g and P_f can be expressed as

$$P_g = lw + m + t_g + s_g, \tag{2.1}$$

$$P_f = lw + m + t_f + s_f, \tag{2.2}$$

where l is physical units of labor input per unit of output, w is the state-determined wage rate, m is the average cost of material inputs, including depreciation, t_g is the average rate of taxes imposed on planned output, t_f is the average rate of taxes imposed on above-plan output, s_g is enterprise retained profits generating from each unit of output sold at planned prices, and s_f is enterprise retained profits generating from each unit of output sold at nonplanned prices.

Equation (2.1) indicates that the state procurement price (or the planned price) is composed of a state-determined wage bill, payments for material inputs, local and state taxes, and an accounting surplus kept by the enterprise. This equation is based on the Marxian labor theory of value, according to which the value of a product is equal to the sum of the value of present labor (lw), the value of past labor (m), which is embodied in the materials and equipment employed in production, and a surplus value created by labor ($t + s$). Equation (2.2) is adapted from equation (2.1) by taking into account the fact that the rate of taxes on above-plan output can be different from the rate of taxes on planned output. Given these two equations, the "profit" of the enterprise, Π, is equal to

$$\Pi = (P_g Q_g + P_f Q_f) - (lw + m)(Q_g + Q_f), \tag{2.3}$$

or

$$\Pi = (t_g Q_g + t_f Q_f) + (s_g Q_g + s_f Q_f), \tag{2.3'}$$

where Q refers to the level of output. In the case where Π is positive, a portion of the profit, $(t_g Q_g + t_f Q_f)$, will be surrendered to the government and the rest, $(s_g Q_g + s_f Q_f)$, will be retained by the enterprise. In the case where Π is negative, the enterprise will be subsidized and equation (2.3') can be written as

$$\Pi = t(Q_g + Q_f), \tag{2.3''}$$

where t is the rate of negative taxes (which implies the presence of a soft budget constraint). Enterprise taxes and subsidies form a major part of fiscal revenues and expenditures in China.

In 1981, enterprises retained about 24 percent of their profits, and the rest went to central and local governments (Ho 1986, p.4). The largest share of enterprise profits went to the central government, and the second largest share went to the local governments to which the enterprises belonged. The profits retained by the enterprise can be used for the following purposes: (a) to improve workers' welfare, including housing, education, recreation, and medical services; (b) to issue bonuses to workers and management; and (c) to provide resources for investments, thus increasing the employment opportunity of the family and relatives of the workers. These incentives are instituted under the economic reforms to motivate enterprises to improve their productive efficiency and invest in the areas where profits can be maximized. Enterprises no longer have to seek approval from the central government for the purchase of spare parts, the building of necessary facilities, and so forth. The profits shared by local governments serve a similar purpose, encouraging them to make use of their knowledge of local conditions and invest in those activities where profits can be maximized.[13]

Taxes play an important role in determining the profitability of individual enterprises. In June 1983, China has implemented the so-called tax-for-profit scheme in place of the previous profit-sharing scheme. Under the new scheme, enterprises pay commodity taxes and resource taxes to the government and keep all after-tax profits. The commodity taxes are a tax on enterprise output, whereas the resource tax is an adjustment tax based on such factors as the geographical location and the technology level of the enterprise. These taxes have to be paid to the government irrespective of the level of before-tax profits. The design of the scheme would have been a dramatic departure from the previous profit-sharing scheme if the tax rates were fixed and uniformly applied to all enterprises in the same product group, since under these circumstances there would be no limit to the share of profits that can be kept by individual enterprises. However, to treat profitable and unprofitable enterprises "equally," tax rates have actually been so designed that they rise with the "profitability" of individual enterprises. Moreover, the tax rates are subject to revision from time to time in accordance with the profitability of the enterprises so that no enterprise would get a disproportionally large share of before-tax profits. For this reason, the new scheme does not differ substantially from the old one, and we shall continue to refer to it as the profit-sharing scheme.

The profit-sharing scheme and foreign trade

The profit-sharing scheme is also used as a base to motivate enterprises to expand their exports so that foreign exchange will be available for the import of foreign technology. In general, there is little difference between export procurement prices and domestic prices so long as the products involved are sold both at home and abroad. The procurement prices of exports are set equal to their planned prices if their procurement falls under the net of the directive plan; otherwise, they are set equal to domestic floating prices or negotiated prices. This pricing policy is done to ensure that any product which is profitable in domestic sales must also be profitable in foreign sales, and vice versa. This does not, however, imply that export procurement prices are passively set equal to the prices in the home market. The importance of the home market varies from one good to another, with correspondingly different effects on the procurement prices. For instance, in the case where products are produced mainly or exclusively for export, their procurement prices will depend mainly on the proportion of their outputs being exported. It is, therefore, quite possible for the procurement prices of "high-quality" consumer goods destined for markets in Western countries to be highly independent of the prices of comparable but lower-quality domestic consumer goods. It is also possible for the domestic price to be determined predominantly by the export procurement price in the case where exports account for a significant proportion of the final demand for the goods. These points are clearly shown in the following principles adopted by the foreign trade authorities in setting export procurement prices. First, export procurement prices should be set on the basis of domestic market prices. Second, agricultural exports, which are supplied by the commerce department, should be priced in terms of their allocation prices at the place of production or in terms of their domestic procurement prices. Third, export procurement prices should take into account the difference in specification, quality, and packaging between products for domestic and foreign sales. Fourth, export procurement prices of those goods which are not sold in the domestic market should be set based on their costs plus taxes and a "reasonable" amount of profit. Fifth, export procurement prices may be set below domestic prices if the latter are substantially higher than the renminbi prices of export sales. Exporting enterprises would be provided with tax reductions or exemptions for the portion of products exported. Sixth, domestic prices may be lowered in the case where domestic sales are substantially more profitable than foreign sales. Seventh, export procurement prices may be set above domestic prices to encourage production if the goods concerned are underpriced at home. Eighth, the prices for the products of export-processing enterprises may be set on the basis of the foreign exchange costs of imported materials. Ninth, the export procurement prices of high-skill handicrafts may be set well above their domestic production costs (Li et al. 1988, pp. 54–5).

In other words, export procurement prices are to a certain extent under the control of the FTCs, which may adjust them upward or downward as may be required by the foreign trade plan. The higher the procurement prices, the more profitable it would be for the enterprises to substitute exports for domestic sales, and the greater their exports would be. It is through the export procurement prices that the MFERT exerts its control over the level and composition of exports under the guidance plan.[14]

The importance of the profit-sharing scheme to the decisions of enterprises on exports has been diminished by the government's introduction of the foreign exchange retention scheme, in which exporting enterprises are provided with foreign exchange entitlement quotas in proportion to the excess of their foreign exchange earnings over last year's earnings or over certain contractual targets. Before 1988, a uniform proportion of 25 percent was applied to all exports. Starting in 1988, the proportions for garments, handicraft, and other light industrial exports have been raised to 70 percent, for electric machinery, to 50 percent, and for electronics, to 100 percent (Li et al. 1988, pp. 62–3). As a result of the differences in foreign exchange earning targets and in the rates of retention, the quotas for individual enterprises vary from a low of 3 percent to a high of 50 percent of their foreign exchange earnings, the exact share depending on the nature and geographical location of the enterprise.[15] Export processing enterprises in special economic zones and coastal provinces would normally be given high retention shares, whereas enterprises located in inner provinces and exporting relatively unsophisticated products would normally be given low retention shares. To use the quotas, enterprises and local governments are required to draw on their own investment funds, which may be accumulated out of the profit sharing scheme, borrowed from banks, or allocated from the central government, but approval has to be sought from various official entities before the quotas can be used. The foreign exchange spendings of enterprises and local governments as a whole are determined within the state export and import plan drawn up by the MFERT. There is no guarantee that enterprises' and local governments' import applications within the retention quotas will be approved; they are subject to the scrutiny of the planning authority, which considers their desirability in the light of the country's balance of payments and general economic conditions. In general, consumer goods imports are severely restricted, and capital goods can only be imported if appropriate domestic substitutes are not available at home. Furthermore, since foreign exchange retention quotas can only be accumulated annually, it is not unusual for enterprises to turn over unused quotas to the state by the end of each year.[16] Nevertheless, any allocation of the undervalued foreign exchange to the enterprises amounts to a subsidy to them. Therefore, enterprises would be tempted to export for the sake of the subsidy so long as the net benefit from exports is positive. They would also be tempted to use up all the foreign exchange retention quotas, if permitted, so as to capture as much rent as possible from the use of foreign exchange.

2.4   The concept of the economic efficiency of foreign trade

Chinese economists advocating economic reforms generally believe that through foreign trade expansion China can economize on "social labor" (or the economic cost of production), thus speeding up the process of economic modernization. The amount of social labor saved is taken as the difference between the amount of labor that would have to be used to produce the substitutes for imports and the amount of labor actually used in the production of the required amount of exports. Here, social labor is in monetary terms and equal to the value of output exclusive of profits. The social labor cost saved in the import of goods j is equal to[17]:

$$\epsilon_j = D_j - hF_j, \tag{2.4}$$

with

$$h = \frac{\sum_i h_i X_i}{\sum_i P_i^* X_i}, \tag{2.5}$$

$$h_i = l_i w_i + m_i, \tag{2.6}$$

where ϵ_j is the social labor cost saved in the import of good j, D_j is the domestic labor cost of import substitute j, F_j is the foreign exchange cost of import j, h_i is the domestic labor cost per unit of the export of good i, X_i is the amount of the export of good i, P_i^* is net foreign exchange earnings per unit of export i, h is the average domestic labor cost of foreign exchange earning.   Here, $\sum_i h_i X_i$ is the total labor cost incurred in the economy's exports and $\sum_i P_i^* X_i$ is the total net foreign exchange earnings of the economy. Equation (2.4) implies that the import of good j is justified only if the domestic labor cost of its substitute (D_j) is greater than the domestic labor cost of foreign exchange spending on imported good j (hF_j).

Dividing each term in equation (2.4) by F_j yields

$$\tau_j = d_j - h, \tag{2.7}$$

where

$$\tau_j = \frac{\epsilon_i}{F_j},$$ (2.8)

$$d_j = \frac{D_i}{F_j}.$$ (2.9)

τ_j is the social labor saved per unit of foreign exchange spent on the import of good j and d_j is the domestic labor cost of a foreign exchange unit of import substitute j. Based on equation (2.7), good j should be imported only if d_j is greater than h.

The concept underlying equation (2.7) is similar to that underlying the domestic resource cost (DRC) measure which has been widely used by economists to evaluate the efficiency of foreign trade-related projects (Bruno 1965; Srinivasan and Bhagwati 1978). The DRC of a project is defined as the direct and indirect resource costs (at shadow prices) of the net foreign exchange earnings or savings attributable to the project. In order to gain from foreign trade, a country should export goods with low DRCs and import goods with high DRCs. Provided that the domestic labor costs in equation (2.7) are arrived at in the same way as domestic resource costs are in DRCs, the two approaches are identical: d_j is nothing but the DRC of import substitute j, and h is nothing but the average DRC of exports (which is the accounting price of foreign exchange). If d_j is greater than h, τ_j will be positive and good j should be imported.

However, the estimation of h_i (or h) and d_j in a centrally planned economy can depart significantly from the estimation of the DRC. The departure arises mainly from the irrationality of prices as well as from the fact that resource allocation in a centrally planned economy is not market determined. In arriving at h_j [equation (2.7)], for example, the labor coefficient (l_i) is determined by the government's (often excessive) allocation of labor to the enterprise, the wage rate (w_i) is fixed by the state, the cost of material inputs (m_i) depends on the state-determined input prices, and the costs of land and capital are excluded from the total cost. Therefore, $l_i w_i + m_i$ does not reflect the domestic resource cost of producing good i. The same problem will occur in the estimation of d_j.

The present study does not attempt to deal with the problem of the estimation of domestic resource costs. Instead, I shall only discuss whether the economic reforms in China have generally improved the sensitivity of enterprises and local governments to the economic costs and benefits (or market conditions) of exports and imports. The greater the sensitivity, the more likely will the actual domestic resource costs be taken into account in export and import, and the more efficient will be foreign trade. This approach is certainly less satisfactory than is the DRC method, but it is much less complicated. I first discuss the sensitivity of exports to market conditions in the following section.

2.5   The economic efficiency of exports under economic reforms

The sensitivity of exports to changes in market conditions, or economic costs and benefits, depends on two factors: the extent to which individual production units are allowed to make their own export decisions and the relevance of the export incentive system to economic efficiency. There is no doubt that the decision-making power of individual production units has increased as a result of the decentralization of the economic system under the economic reforms. Enterprises, unless under strict directive planning, can now negotiate export conditions with foreign trade corporations before engaging in production for export. However, the relevance of the new export incentive system (i.e., the profit-sharing scheme and the foreign exchange retention scheme) to economic efficiency requires a detailed discussion.

Economic efficiency and the profit-sharing scheme

Consider first the profit-sharing scheme which has been used to motivate exports. Based on equations (2.3) and (2.3'), the profit retained by an enterprise, Π^e, is equal to

$$\Pi^e = P_g Q_g + P_f Q_f - [(lw + m)(Q_g + Q_f) + (t_g Q_g + t_f Q_f)] \quad (2.10)$$

and the (after-tax) rate of profit is equal to

$$\pi^e = \frac{\Pi^e}{Q_g + Q_f}. \quad (2.11)$$

Suppose that there are n export enterprises, the profit rates of which are $(\pi_1^e, \pi_2^e, \ldots, \pi_n^e)$. If the π_i^es were positively related to their counterparts in the market economy, the economic efficiency of exports could be improved by increasing the responsiveness of exports to their profit rates.[18] In reality, however, the π_i^es are conceptually different from their counterparts in the market economy, and there is no reason to believe that they should be positively related to each other. This can be seen from equation (2.10), in which $P_g, P_f, l, w, m, t_g, t_f$, and Q_g are all under strict government control and in which the costs of land and capital are excluded from the total cost of production. Any arbitrary adjustment of the aforementioned variables in the equation can have a significant effect on the profit rate of the enterprise. For instance, the government often adjusts t_g and t_f in accordance with the "profitability" of each enterprise in order to control the amount of investment and welfare funds under the control of the enterprise. Higher tax rates are imposed on enterprises with higher before-tax profit rates. Taken to its extreme, the tax adjustment could result in the equalization of all the profit rates, thus obscuring any relationship that might have existed between the profit rates and their counterparts in the market economy. Therefore, even if the enterprise responds to the profit rate given in equation (2.11) in determining the level of exports, the response will not necessarily result in an efficient resource allocation.

It is of interest to note that the common reference to irrational prices as the reason for the profit rate being an inappropriate indicator of economic efficiency is only part of the truth. Adjusting P_g and input prices to a rational level does not guarantee an efficient allocation of resources so long as t_g, t_f, Q_g, l, and m are to a certain extent arbitrarily determined. This implies that any price reform cannot be undertaken independently of a basic reform of the enterprise management system if a substantial improvement in allocative efficiency is to be achieved (see Chapter 6 for a more detailed discussion on price reform).

Over- or underexpansion of exports

In general, Chinese economists argue for some form of responsibility system in which enterprises face fixed rates of taxes and are allowed to keep all after-tax profits. Their reasoning is that the system would reward enterprises for lowering the costs of production and for responding to changes in the prices of their products. Indeed, as shown in equation (2.10), Π^e will increase as a result of an increase in P_f or P_g or a decrease in l or m. An increase in Π^e as a result of cost reduction signals an unambiguous improvement in the economic efficiency of production as far as the enterprise is concerned. Wang (1985, p. 34), however, observes that, in the presence of price inflexibility, a cost-cutting technical change tends to cause a stockpiling of the products which have successfully reduced their production costs. From the view of the economy, the economic efficiency of production may actually have been worsened by the cost-cutting innovation. Allocative efficiency also does not necessarily improve in the case of an increase in Π^e that comes about as a result of the increased responsiveness of production to the price of the product so long as the price does not reflect market demand. An expansion of an overproduced product or a contraction of an underproduced product as a result of the response of the enterprise to the price of the product will actually have a negative effect on the efficiency of resource allocation. This is likely to result in an even greater misallocation of domestic resources. In 1988, for instance, food production was hampered by relatively low procurement prices since peasants were more interested in growing cash crops, which enjoyed flexible and higher prices.

In spite of its implications for resource allocation, the contractual tax system was introduced in some industries in 1985. Under this system, enterprises would be required to pay to the government only the contractual amount of taxes out of their profits. The rest would be retained by them for their own use. In the area of exports, such a system is intended to improve the responsiveness of exporting enterprises to the prices of exports, one of the important objectives of the foreign trade reforms. However, the desirability of the increased responsiveness of exporting enterprises to the prices of exports under the present system is subject to doubt. The reason is that export procurement prices, being administratively set either equal to or in close association with domestic prices, remain largely unresponsive to changes in market conditions abroad. China's use of export procurement prices to insulate exporting enterprises from fluctuations in foreign prices is understandable. As is true in other centrally planned economies, prices in China are irrational, serving both as a fiscal instrument and as a means to influence income distribution. The prices of "essential" goods, including food grains, gas, coal, oil, housing, and transportation services, are generally low and heavily subsidized, whereas the prices of industrial consumer goods, such as watches, radio transistors, bicycles, television sets, and washing machines, are generally high and heavily taxed so as to generate reinvestment funds. In the areas where planned prices still dominate, the foreign exchange-price – domestic-price ratios are highly favorable for those goods which are heavily subsidized and highly unfavorable for those goods which are heavily taxed. Obviously, the country's export structure should not be dictated by such irrational price ratios, which result in a multitude of highly differentiated implicit exchange rates; some measures must be taken to "neutralize" the tax-subsidy effect on exports. The use of export procurement prices and administrative controls over exports serves this purpose. However, so long as administratively determined export procurement prices, rather than market prices, are used, enterprises will not and can not respond to changes in market conditions abroad, even under the contractual tax system. In this regard, it is clear that the level of the official exchange rate is of little significance in the selection of goods to be exported.

In short, government control over the level and composition of exports through export procurement prices is by no means a proper substitute for the market mechanism. Under the present system, there are no objective criteria to determine the acceptable foreign exchange conversion costs

(FECCs, or procurement-price–foreign-exchange price ratios) for individual exports. The foreign trade authorities are obliged to coordinate with the fiscal authorities in determining both the quotas and the acceptable FECCs of individual exports, since exports invariably incur "profits" or "losses," which are the revenues or expenditures of the fiscal branch of the government. Therefore, the export procurement prices are often fixed at the beginning of each fiscal year based on fiscal considerations, and they do not necessarily reflect production costs and market demand. They reflect rather the budgetary position of the foreign trade authority. For this reason, undue incentives or disincentives might be provided to exports, giving rise to an overexpansion in some exports and underexpansion in some others.

The use of retained profits

It should be noted that the material incentives provided by the profit-sharing scheme derive not so much from its effect on the enterprises' capability to increase wages and welfare expenditure as from its effect on the enterprises' accumulation of investment funds. In view of the fact that there is a widespread difference in "profitability" among enterprises, owing to such factors as monopoly, technology, the adequacy of infrastructure, and state-determined input and output prices, the unrestricted use of retained profits for wage increases and bonus payments could cause enormous income inequalities that might or might not be justified on efficiency grounds. In order to preserve income equality and at the same time encourage enterprise investments, progressive taxes have been imposed on "excessive" wage increases.[19] A bonus tax of 30 percent of the total standard wages is levied on an annual bonus payment which amounts to 4 to 5 months of the standard wage. The tax rate increases steeply to 100 percent as bonus payments become equivalent to 5 to 6 months of the standard wage. An even steeper bonus tax of 300 percent applies if bonus payments exceed 6 months of the standard wage. Faced with such progressive taxes, enterprises rarely increase their bonus payments to workers and management by a substantial amount. Instead, they are inclined to invest retained profits in the most profitable projects known to them, or spend them on workers' welfare, including housing, traveling, and education.

Exporting enterprises are motivated to invest in new investment projects because such projects will enhance the power and prestige of management, bring about an increase in the employment opportunity of workers' relatives and families, and provide enterprises with an opportunity to make use of the accumulated foreign exchange quotas under the foreign exchange retention scheme, thus enjoying the benefits associated with imports. These benefits include, first, the competitive edge over domestic and foreign competitors provided to them by the import of advanced technology and capital equipment; second, foreign trips, expensive gifts, and illicit payments provided to persons in charge of imports by foreign exporters; and third, the rent, legal or illegal, obtained from reselling at black market exchange rates the retention quotas or imports to other enterprises or consumers. Since these benefits are a blanket subsidy to enterprises and local governments engaged in exports, they have obviously created a bias in favor of exports and against domestic sales.

In short, the sensitivity of exports to economic costs and benefits does not seem to have improved in spite of the economic reforms which have provided enterprises and local governments with a certain degree of autonomy in making export decisions. The reasons are as follows. First, although enterprises have been made responsive to the profitability of exports by the profit-sharing scheme, that profitability is determined, among other things, within the irrational price structure of the economy and cannot act as a proper indicator of the efficiency with which resources are utilized. Second, the export procurement prices, planned or negotiated, are to a certain extent arbitrarily set by the state on the basis of the irrational domestic price structure and do not reflect the foreign exchange prices of exports. As a result, there exist no channels through which any changes in market conditions can be transmitted to exporting enterprises, and overexpansion and underexpansion of exports become unavoidable. Third, exports as a whole tend to be overexpanded because of the subsidies associated with the foreign exchange retention scheme.

Finally, it must be noted that we have so far assumed the export enterprise to be profitable to begin with. In the case where exports are not profitable, due perhaps to the excessively low procurement prices or to the excessively high production costs, the profit-sharing scheme will have no influence on the enterprise's decision to export, and the foreign exchange retention scheme will provide the major part, if not all, of the export incentives. The enterprise will not be motivated to export if the benefits from export are outweighed by the costs associated with the increase in operation losses. However, in the case where the benefits from exports exceed the costs of the loss increase, the enterprise will still be encouraged to export. To minimize the problem that some goods might be overexported such as to cause severe shortages at home, China has introduced an export-licensing system, under which more than 200 hundred items were included in 1987. This system has further reduced the responsiveness of exports to changes in conditions in international markets. Under these circumstances, there is certainly no guarantee for the export of the enterprise to be economically efficient.

2.6 The economic efficiency of imports under economic reforms

I now turn to the issue of the economic efficiency of imports under economic reforms. In postreform China, imports, or the allocation of foreign exchange, are determined by the economic plans formulated by the local and central governments, and the market mechanism does not play any significant role. In general, the national economic plan deals only with the regional distribution of import quotas at a highly aggregated level, leaving considerable room for enterprises and local governments to determine how much and what to import within their allocated quotas. Therefore, the sensitivity of imports to economic costs and benefits depends to a great extent on the system of import control which the enterprises and local governments are subject to. Thus, a discussion of the system of import control under the current reforms is in order.

The system of import control

During the economic reforms, much of China's efforts to promote exports were for the purpose of financing imports, which serve three main purposes: to improve production technology, to make up for shortages in domestic supply, and to expand the economy's export capability. The first purpose points to the country's continued emphasis on the need to import advanced technology and capital equipment to modernize the economy; the second purpose refers primarily to the import of food grains, raw materials, and intermediate goods arising from inadequate supplies at home; and the third purpose is merely a strategy to boost the country's foreign exchange earning capability. Above all, technology imports are the government's chief concern in its promotion of foreign trade. For this reason, China's import policy is actually an inseparable part of the investment policy laid down in the national economic plan, and the import control system is inseparable from the investment control system. The only exception to this linkage is the use of imports as a means for controlling the money supply, such as in the years of 1984 and 1985 when massive imports of consumer goods were allowed in order to reduce inflationary pressures generated by the expanding budget deficit and bank credits.

To explain the linkage between imports and investment, we look at the process through which import applications of enterprises are approved.[20] Under the economic reforms, enterprises are empowered to propose small-scale investments within the resources at their command, such resources including (a) investment funds accumulated in the form of depreciation funds and retained profits,[21] and (b) borrowings from banks, individuals, and other enterprises. Enterprises may also propose large-scale investments to, and seek centrally allocated investment funds from, the State Planning Commission. In 1984, for instance, the State Planning Commission was responsible for scrutinizing only those investment proposals which exceeded 30 million yuan in investment capital; smaller projects would need only the approval of local governments and ministries (Zheng 1985, p. 4). In the case where imports of machinery and equipment are involved, enterprises are required to have sufficient foreign exchange quotas, which may be accumulated under the foreign exchange retention scheme, allocated from the regional or central government, or, in some cases, borrowed from foreign banks. Then, enterprises may submit their import applications for approvals from the following government organizations: their immediate supervising organizations (the specialized corporations or industrial bureaus), the State Planning Commission or its regional branches, the Economic Commission, the regional branches of MFERT, and the local branches of the State Administration of Exchange Control (SAEC). Only after obtaining these approvals can enterprises join the FTCs to negotiate with foreign exporters over the terms of payments, the delivery of goods, and so forth. In this regard the State Planning Commission and the Economic Planning Commission play an important role in keeping the proposed projects in line with the regional development plan of individual industries; MFERT acts to ensure the consistency of the foreign exchange spending with the foreign trade plan, and SAEC approves the use of foreign exchange within the allocated foreign exchange quotas.

The making of import and investment decisions

Under the import control system and within the constraints of the available market information and the capability of the decision makers, enterprises and local governments, motivated by the profit-sharing scheme, are inclined to invest in projects which they deem profitable. Unfortunately, profitability, which is determined on the basis of irrational prices and subject to various manipulations, is far from an appropriate indicator of economic efficiency. According to the government's pricing policy, products of new projects can be priced on a cost-plus basis, with rent and interest excluded from the cost.[22] Thus, profits are almost guaranteed so long as the goods produced are in demand. Under these circumstances, even if the investment funds have been allocated to the areas where profits are maximized, there is no guarantee that domestic resources would be put to their most efficient uses.

Although enterprises and local governments are inclined to invest in areas where their profits can be maximized, the incentives for them to invest are in fact so strong that they often invest in areas where the realized rates of profits are far lower than what would be considered acceptable by the central government. To the individuals who are responsible for making investment decisions, including enterprise managers, banking staffs, and government officials, investment funds and foreign exchange, all under public ownership, are practically costless. Unused investment funds and foreign exchange cannot be directed to other uses and have to be kept idle or turned over to the government, whereas through imports and investments they can benefit from enlarged political power and material rewards, licit and illicit. Therefore, enterprises and local governments are both compelled to spend all they possess and motivated to seek as much allocation from the provincial or central government as possible, a phenomenon that also characterizes most public enterprises in market economies. In the case where the projects are entirely infeasible, the machinery will be left unused and no operational losses will be made, requiring no subsidies from the government and causing no income losses to the enterprise. In case any losses are made at all, convincing excuses can always be found and the losses will always be paid for directly or indirectly by the state. Under a soft budget constraint, actual investments do not necessarily pursue the goal of profit maximization.

Even if enterprises and local governments were to pursue the goal of profit maximization in making investment and import decisions, there would be insurmountable difficulties to overcome. Within the government and the enterprise, party officials are still very much in command, but their lack of management skill and economic knowledge is a serious obstacle to the improvement in the efficiency with which foreign exchange and investment resources are used. As a result, market research and feasibility studies made before new investment projects are undertaken are often ignored, leading to duplication in imports and overinvestment in certain sectors. New projects often prove unworkable because of the lack of technicians, material inputs, and markets for their output. Even worse, customs warehouses all over the country were recently reported to have been filled with a large amount of unclaimed items, mostly machinery, some of which were probably ordered by enterprises for the sole purpose of using up the allocated foreign exchange quotas.[23]

Economic inefficiency also involves imports at the central level. The investment and import decisions made on the initiatives of enterprises and local governments would necessarily result in a change in the demand for related imports and domestic goods, such as energy, transportation, and iron and steel, all of which require a substantial increase in state-financed investments. A large increase in state-financed investments would in turn require a large increase in state-financed imports. Imports at the central government level are thus to a great extent dictated by the investment decisions made by enterprises and local governments. Such induced imports cannot possibly be economically efficient when imports at the local level are not. As for the case where goods are imported independently of the import decisions made at the local level, the economic efficiency of such imports is also not guaranteed because the channels through which the economic costs and benefits of such imports can be conveyed to the importing authority are lacking. Even if the channels as such did exist, there would still be no guarantee that the import decisions made by the importing authority would take the relevant costs and benefits into account.

In sum, under the economic reforms, MFERT is still fully in charge of bulk imports, including industrial raw materials, food grains, and items which are covered by China's trade agreements with other countries. Once imported, these items will be centrally allocated to their end-users. However, in the case of other imports, MFERT is only responsible for formulating import guidelines and controlling the level of foreign exchange expenditure, whereas enterprises and local governments, allocated with foreign exchange quotas, are accorded the right to propose imports for new investment projects or other purposes. This decentralization of import decision-making power is consistent with the spirit of the general reform under which investment decision-making power has been decentralized. Therefore, the economic efficiency of imports must be understood in the context of the economic efficiency of the investment decisions made by enterprises and various government organizations in relation to imports. In general, the economic efficiency of imports tends to be low because enterprises and governments at the central and local levels are not subject to market discipline when making import and investment decisions; the decision makers are always rewarded with material and nonmaterial benefits for undertaking projects involving imports even if the projects turn out to be unworkable. Under the profit-sharing scheme, imports have at best been made responsive to the profitability of investment projects. But even this does not ensure economic efficiency because profitability is not an appropriate indicator of economic efficiency.

2.7   Summary and conclusion

In prereform China, foreign trade was a state monopoly, and the foreign-trade plan was formulated as part of the national economic plan. During the period, foreign trade played different roles, depending on the rate of investment growth. In the years of low investment growth, foreign trade tended to be relatively inactive, with imports involving those items which were necessary for sustaining steady economic growth. In contrast, in the years of high investment growth, foreign trade was actively promoted, substantially increasing the import of technological items which were considered indispensable to the planners' ambitious development programs. Nevertheless, since high investment and foreign trade growth often could not be fully integrated into the national economic plan, they would often cause supply bottlenecks and result in disruptions to economic growth. Meanwhile, the economy would export much needed domestic goods in exchange for imports which could not be fully utilized and the use of which would cause disruptions to domestic production. Therefore, the economic efficiency of foreign trade tended to be low in the years of high foreign trade growth in comparison with that in the years of low foreign trade growth.

Since the implementation of economic reforms in 1979, China has witnessed high foreign trade growth. In contrast to the prereform years when foreign trade was a state monopoly, the rapid foreign trade growth has taken place to a great extent as a result of the foreign trade decisions made by enterprises and local governments. This change greatly reduces the interference, by the central planning authorities, with resource allocation. The abolition of rigid central planning also makes the integration of foreign trade into the national economic plan less an important problem to the economy than before. However, this is not to say that the economic efficiency of foreign trade has necessarily improved; the improvement now hinges on the sensitivity of foreign trade to economic costs and benefits, which in turn hinge on the incentives provided to enterprises and local governments in importing and exporting.

Under the new foreign trade incentive system, foreign trade enterprises and local governments are encouraged by the profit-sharing scheme to pursue profits and, by the foreign exchange retention scheme, to expand exports. The incentive system discriminates in favor of enterprises which are "profitable" or engaged in export. This discrimination can cause allocative inefficiency because, first, profitability, which is subject to manipulation by the government, is not an appropriate indicator of economic efficiency, and second, exports do not themselves spell economic

```
                    ┌─────────────────┐
                    │   Enterprise    │
                    └─────────────────┘
                             │
                             ▼
              ┌──────────────────────────────┐
              │        Approval by           │
              │  supervising organizations   │
              │     (see Figure B.2)         │
              └──────────────────────────────┘
                             │
                             ▼
              ┌──────────────────────────────┐
              │        Approval by           │
              │   economic and planning      │
              │        commissions           │
              └──────────────────────────────┘
                             │
                             ▼
         ┌──────────────────────────────┐
         │        Approval by           │
         │   local branch of MFERT      │
         └──────────────────────────────┘
                   │                            ┌──────────────────────────────┐
                   │                            │        Approval by           │
                   │                            │   local branch of State      │
                   │                            │     Administration of        │
                   │                            │    Exchange Control          │
                   │                            └──────────────────────────────┘
                   ▼                                           │
         ┌──────────────────────────────┐                     │
         │      Import through          │◄────────────────────┘
         │  foreign trade corporations  │
         └──────────────────────────────┘
```

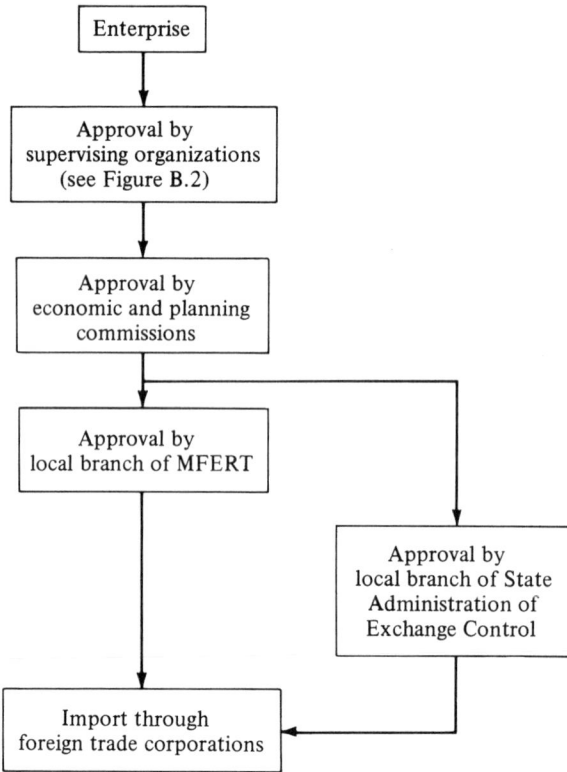

Figure B.1.   The import control system. *Source:* Trade Development Council (1986, Appendix II).

efficiency, particularly when the system for an efficient use of foreign exchange is absent. The foreign exchange earned is partly centrally allocated and partly retained by exporting enterprises and regions. Enterprises, not having to bear the consequences of their investments, are always tempted to use all the foreign exchange allocated to them without regard to the economic benefits of the investment projects. Thus, the incentive system has not in any certain way improved the sensitivity of foreign trade to economic costs and benefits, and the foreign trade reform has not necessarily improved the economic efficiency of foreign trade.

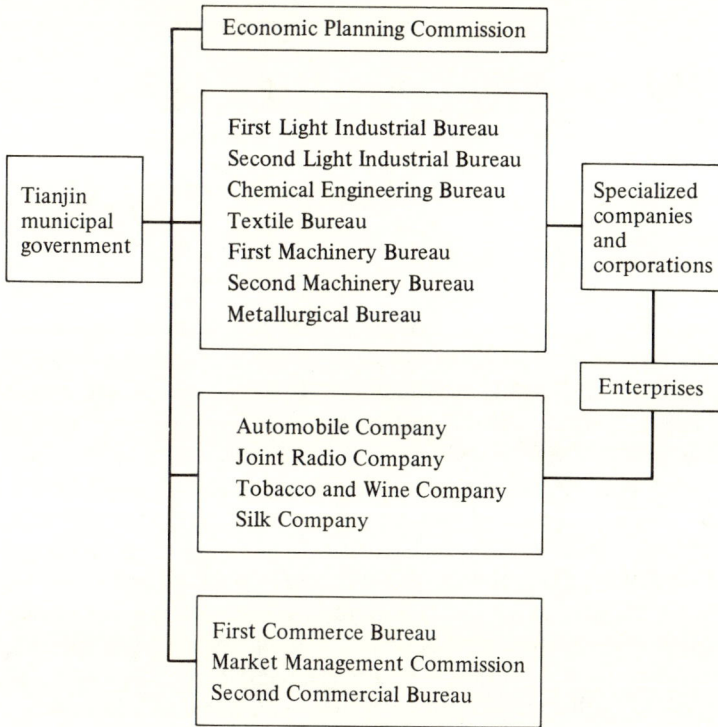

Figure B.2. The management structure of China's industry: the Tianjin case. *Source:* Deng, Ma, and Wu (1985, p. 184).

Appendix B

The import control system

To clarify the import control system, we illustrate the process of importation for an enterprise in Figures B.1 and B.2. Figure B.1 shows the government organizations from which the enterprise has to seek approvals for the import of a certain product, while Figure B.2 shows the management structure of China's industry. It must be noted, however, that the complexity of the importing process varies from one item to the other. In general, the greater the amount of foreign exchange involved, the more government organizations will be responsible for approving the import of the product.

CHAPTER 3

The commodity composition of China's foreign trade, 1978 – 1985

The commodity composition of foreign trade in a centrally planned economy, as in a market economy, depends to a great extent on the structure of national output. In general, an agriculture-based economy will export predominantly primary goods and import predominantly industrial goods whereas an industrialized country will export predominantly technology- and capital-intensive goods and import predominantly labor-intensive goods. Nonetheless, a centrally planned economy has a much greater control over the commodity structure of its foreign trade than does a market economy. This is because in a centrally planned economy foreign trade is embodied in the national economic plan that is subject to the manipulation of the planners, whereas in a market economy foreign trade structure is determined primarily by the relatively stable domestic and foreign market conditions. For this reason, the commodity composition of foreign trade in a centrally planned economy is particularly sensitive to changes in the government's economic policies. In the following analysis I will pay special attention to the effects of government policies on the commodity composition of China's foreign trade for the period between 1978 and 1985. Some new developments in 1986 and 1987 are discussed separately in Appendix C.

Economic reforms represented a major change in China's development strategy and had an important impact on the commodity composition of China's foreign trade. In the period before the economic reforms, China's exports of foodstuffs and crude materials were relatively important and accounted for more than 50 percent of the economy's total exports throughout the period between 1970 and 1977. The economy was able to maintain such a high share for these exports in the wake of the relatively rapid growth of industrial exports mainly because there was among them a rapid growth of oil exports, which went up from 7.4 million U.S. dollars in 1970 to over 1 billion U.S. dollars in 1977. The rapid increase in oil exports came about as a result of a dramatic change from the previous policy that disapproved, in principle, of the depletion and export of the country's "natural wealth" or minerals. The change signaled a gradual opening up of the economy to the West. Under the open door policy, there was also unprecedented growth of industrial exports, which rose from 1,012 million U.S. dollars in 1970 to 3,897 million U.S. dollars in 1977. Nevertheless, the economy's export capacity remained low because, first, exports of foodstuffs and crude materials were limited by low productivity and rising domestic demand,[1] and second, exports of light industrial goods were limited by the government's development policy which focused on heavy industry.[2]

Economic reforms were accompanied by a further strengthening of the government's effort to open and develop the economy. The production and export of industrial goods was promoted with a view to raising technology imports for the economy's modernization need. Manufactured exports increased by 241 percent in this period, compared to the 180 percent increase of foodstuff and crude material exports. As a result, the share of foodstuffs and crude materials in the economy's total exports decreased from 51 percent in 1978 to 44 percent in 1985. In U.S. dollar terms, China's exports went up by more than 200 percent from 10 billion in 1978 to 31 billion in 1985. The rapid growth of exports, accompanied by rising government borrowings from the rest of the world,[3] made it possible for imports to grow at an even higher rate of 283 percent.

The purpose of this chapter is to discuss the changes in the commodity composition of China's foreign trade during the post-1978 period. It can be seen from these changes how foreign trade reforms affected China's foreign trade and whether the reforms were conducive to an improvement in the efficiency of foreign trade. In Section 3.1, I provide an overview of the changes in the structure of national output as a background for the discussion of the changes in the commodity composition of exports. It shows that agricultural and light industrial products witnessed relatively rapid growth in this period. Section 3.2 examines the changes in the commodity composition of China's exports and imports. It is shown that the relative importance of manufactured exports, in terms of their share in China's total exports, rose rapidly under the government's export promotion policy, whereas intermediate goods and machinery and equipment accounted for a major part of the economy's imports. Section 3.3 looks at the changes in China's foreign trade relations with its major trading partners, including Hong Kong, Japan, and the United States. The structural changes in China's exports to and imports from these countries are further examined in Sections 3.4, 3.5, and 3.6. It is shown that the structural changes were influenced by different political and economic factors which characterized the relations between China and these countries. Finally, Section 3.7 provides some concluding remarks.

3.1   Economic reforms and the structure of national output

In the prereform period, China's economic policy focused primarily on the growth of heavy industry, the sector which is considered to be a prerequisite for economic modernization (Chapter 1). Such a policy culminated in the government's launch of the Four Modernizations program in 1978. However, the severe economic imbalance caused by the investment bias led the government to adopt a readjustment program in 1979, aimed at promoting the growth of agriculture and light industry. The readjustment task was completed by 1981. Since 1982, China has stepped up economic reforms, and the reform program has had an important impact on the structure of national output. In the period between 1978 and 1985, in contrast with the prereform period, there was no clearly stated policy on the growth of heavy versus light industry.

To determine the effects of the government's policy on the structure of national output, I have relied on the official statistics on the composition of the gross output of agriculture and industry. It must be borne in mind that the result presented here is inevitably distorted by these statistics, in which the value of a product is defined as the sum of the values of production at all processing stages rather than that of the final product (see the appendix to Chapter 1). Nonetheless, provided that there was a systematic change in the degree of distortion arising from official output statistics, my result will be a good approximation to the actual changes in the structure of national output.

Table 3.1 presents the structure of the output of agriculture and industry, the output of each sector being valued at its 1952 price. By valuing the output of individual sectors at constant prices, the changes in the composition of output shown in the table abstract from the highly unequal changes in agricultural and industrial prices that occurred in the past. In the period between 1978 and 1981, the economy, in contrast with the previous trend, was characterized by a decline in the relative importance of heavy industry in total agricultural and industrial output (TAIO). In this period, the share of heavy industry in TAIO decreased from 51 percent to 44 percent, that of light industry increased from 33 percent to 40 percent, and that of agriculture remained virtually unchanged. This implies that the increase in the share of light industry in TAIO was entirely at the expense of heavy industry.

In the period between 1982 and 1985, the economy experienced few changes in the structure of national output. The share of heavy industry in TAIO rose only slightly to 46 percent, while the share of light industry decreased to 38 percent. It is of interest to note that the rapid rise in the level of investment in fixed capital in 1984 and 1985 resulted in neither a

Table 3.1. Composition of agricultural and industrial output, 1978–85 (in percentages)

	Agriculture	Light industry	Heavy industry
1978	15.82	32.64	51.53
1979	15.84	32.99	51.17
1980	15.33	36.36	48.31
1981	15.73	39.94	44.33
1982	16.12	38.96	44.91
1983	15.99	38.33	45.68
1984	16.40	38.08	45.51
1985	15.95	37.90	46.15

Note: All figures are estimated on the basis of 1952 prices.
Source: Calculated from State Statistical Bureau, *Statistical Yearbook of China* (Hong Kong: Economic Information and Agency, 1987, pp. 31–32).

disproportionately rapid expansion in heavy industry nor a slowdown in the growth of the economy as it did during the Great Leap Forward. The reason is that, under economic reforms, investments, mostly undertaken on the initiative of enterprises and local governments, took place in a wide range of industries and did not incur massive, planned reallocation of domestic resources.

Although the highly aggregated data in Table 3.1 do not provide detailed information about the changes in the structure of outputs within agriculture and industry, they do show that the changes in the structure of national output were conducive to the growth of China's export capability. The rapid growth of agricultural output provided the industrial sector with food and raw materials necessary for the latter's expansion, while the rapid growth of light industry made it possible for the growth of light industrial goods to take place without adversely affecting domestic consumption. Table 3.2 presents the growth rates of the output of selected industries in the periods between 1953 and 1978 and between 1979 and 1985. The growth rates of the outputs of heavy industrial products, including metals, electricity, coal, petroleum, chemicals, and machinery, were all smaller in the second period than in the first. In contrast, food and textiles experienced a much higher rate of growth in the second period than in the first. Most notable is that textiles enjoyed the highest growth rate of 13.6 percent in the second period, followed by machinery (11.9 percent) and building materials (11.3 percent). In the following section, it will be shown that textiles and clothing accounted for an important part of the growth of China's exports during the period of economic reforms.

Table 3.2. Growth rates of output in selected industries (in percentages)

	1953–78	1979–85		1953–78	1979–85
Metallurgy	12.8	7.3	Building materials	11.8	11.3
Electricity	14.7	7.7	Forest	4.4	5.1
Coal	9.2	3.6	Food	6.3	9.4
Petroleum	20.9	4.8	Textiles	6.9	13.6
Chemicals	18.1	10.0	Paper	8.3	9.1
Machinery	16.1	11.9			

Source: State Statistical Bureau, *Statistical Yearbook of China* (Hong Kong: Economic Information and Agency, 1986, p. 226).

3.2   The commodity composition of foreign trade

The discussion in this and the next four sections is based primarily on the foreign trade statistics published by the United States Central Intelligence Agency. These statistics, estimated from trade-partner data and expressed in U.S. dollars, are preferred to official statistics, which are expressed in renminbi, for reasons given in Appendix A. Wherever possible, exports and imports will be classified according to the United Nations Standard International Trade Classification (SITC). All growth rates are based on the U.S. dollar values of exports and imports.

Commodity composition of exports

The changes in the commodity composition of China's exports during the period in question well reflected the changes in the structure of the country's national output. In 1978, about 51 percent of China's total exports were minerals and agricultural products, including chiefly live animals, meat and meat preparations, fish and fish preparations, cereal and cereal preparations, vegetable and fruits, textile fibers and their waste, crude animal and vegetable materials, and petroleum. The share gradually decreased to 44 percent in 1985 in the wake of the decline in the relative importance of all SITC single-digit industries in this category with the exception of mineral fuels (which included mainly petroleum). The rapid growth of petroleum exports occurred both because of the government's continued promotion and because of the rapid increase in international oil prices, which rose by 120 percent in the period from 1978 to 1985.[4] Had it not been for the rising importance of petroleum exports, which accounted for about 23 percent of China's total exports in 1985, the share

Table 3.3. Commodity composition of China's exports, 1978–85 (in million U.S.$)

	1978	1979	1980	1981	1982	1983	1984	1985
Food and live animals	2,331	2,645	3,364	3,409	3,516	3,236	3,543	3,925
Vegetables and fruits	625	762	932	1,045	1,002	1,007	981	984
Beverages and tobacco	99	96	129	127	152	154	136	135
Crude materials	1,198	1,573	1,817	2,058	1,806	2,090	2,570	2,930
Textile fibers	394	506	555	502	561	728	975	1,163
Mineral fuels and products	1,457	2,441	4,362	4,770	5,235	4,790	5,733	7,215
Petroleum and products	1,279	2,232	4,119	4,494	4,908	4,475	5,430	6,631
Animal and vegetable oils	74	89	82	109	76	104	140	128
Chemicals	463	774	1,202	1,363	1,319	1,320	1,407	1,602
Semimanufactured goods	2,664	3,503	4,475	5,296	4,968	4,935	5,882	6,204
Textile yarn and fabrics	1,722	2,265	2,825	3,127	2,898	3,156	4,077	4,380
Machinery and equipment	366	492	675	1,003	863	924	1,143	1,186
Miscellaneous manufactures	1,478	2,004	3,097	3,789	4,171	4,527	5,733	6,675
Clothing	726	1,055	1,691	2,117	2,428	2,738	3,375	3,763
Other transactions	30	36	66	96	1,361	1,632	1,356	1,325
Total	10,170	13,652	19,268	22,020	23,466	23,712	27,645	31,325

Sources: Central Intelligence Agency, China: International Trade Annual Statistical Supplement, 1984–86. Central Intelligence Agency, China: International Trade, Fourth Quarter, 1986.

Table 3.4. China's ten largest exporting industries in 1978 and their
exports in selected years (in million U.S.$)

	1978	1982	1985
Textile yarn and fabrics	1,722	2,898	4,380
Petroleum and petroleum products	1,279	4,908	6,631
Clothing	726	2,429	3,763
Vegetables and fruits	625	1,002	984
Cereals and cereal preparations	454	516	782
Textile fibers	394	561	1,163
Crude animal and vegetable materials	392	463	494
Fish and fish preparations	281	387	407
Meat and meat preparations	278	418	510
Live animals	258	375	329

Note: The industries are on the SITC two-digit division.
Source: Same as Table 3.3.

of minerals and agricultural products in China's total exports would have
been much smaller.

The decrease in the relative importance of minerals and agricultural
products in total exports occurred in the wake of the rapid expansion of
manufactured exports, which rose by 241 percent in the period from 1978
to 1985, compared to the 180 percent increase in mineral and agricultural
exports. As shown in Table 3.3, the shares of all manufactured items in
total exports had risen in this period, with the exception of semimanufactured goods, which included highly resource-based metal products, wood
products, leather products, rubber products, iron and steel, textile yarn,
and so forth. Exports of miscellaneous manufactured goods were the
fastest growing group, with their value rising by 349 percent in the period
between 1978 and 1985 and their share in total exports rising from 14.6
percent in 1978 to 21.3 percent in 1985. The rapid growth of the exports of
miscellaneous manufactures was attributable mainly to the rapid increase
in clothing exports within the group. In 1978, the value of clothing exports
was only 708 million U.S. dollars, but it shot up to 3,763 million U.S.
dollars in 1985. Recall that textiles and clothing were one of the most
rapidly expanding industries during the period. China found the development of these exports a short cut to a rapid expansion of its import
capacity.

The impact of economic reforms on the commodity composition of
exports can be seen more clearly by looking at the industries on the SITC
two-digit level. Tables 3.4 and 3.5 show the values of the exports of the ten
largest exporting industries in 1978 and 1985, respectively. In 1978, the

Table 3.5. China's ten largest exporting industries in 1985 and their exports in selected years (in million U.S.$)

	1978	1982	1985
Petroleum and petroleum products	1,279	4,908	6,631
Textile yarn and fabrics	1,722	2,898	4,380
Clothing	726	2,429	3,763
Textile fibers	394	561	1,163
Vegetables and fruits	625	1,002	984
Military firearms	7	1,288	797
Chemical elements and compounds	138	580	685
Electrical machinery	138	371	665
Coal, coke, and briquettes	178	328	579
Metal manufactures (excluding iron and steel)	218	596	570

Note: The industries are on the SITC two-digit division.
Source: Same as Table 3.3.

exports of these ten industries accounted for more than 63 percent of the economy's total exports. Among them the most important items were textile yarn and fabrics, which accounted for 17 percent of total exports, and petroleum and petroleum products, which accounted for another 13 percent. These two items remained the two most important exports in the years up to 1985, and their share in total exports rose to 35 percent in 1985, 5 percent higher than in 1978, due mostly to the substantial increase in the price of oil in the world market during the period. Three other items which appear in Table 3.4 reappear in Table 3.5, that is, clothing, textile fibers, and vegetables and fruits. The first two items, known for their competitiveness in the world market, were two of the most rapidly expanding items. The growth of clothing exports was facilitated by a number of measures adopted by the government, including the setting up of the Special Economic Zones, the opening up of coastal cities, the provision of incentives for foreign investment, and the adoption of the foreign exchange retention scheme. Also, as a result of the government's policy to promote manufactured exports, five agricultural items (cereals and cereal preparations, crude animal and vegetable materials, fish and fish preparations, meat and meat preparations, and live animals) in Table 3.4 were replaced by one mineral item (coal, coke, and briquettes) and four manufactured items (military firearms, chemical elements and compounds, electrical machinery, and metal manufactures) in Table 3.5. It is of interest to note that all of the four newly added manufactured items belonged to heavy industry. The promotion of items such as these has been criticized by some Chinese economists as being economically inefficient in view of the fact that their export was often to meet the export target assigned by the government with little regard to the cost of production.[5] Indeed, what and how much to export could only be administratively determined under the existing foreign trade system where the exchange rate did not play any part in export decision making.

Commodity composition of imports

As discussed in Chapter 2, China's imports were determined primarily by the government's investment policy. For this reason, the composition of its imports was dictated to a great extent by the focus of the investment policy which, as will be shown, changed significantly from year to year during the period between 1978 and 1985.

Under the Four Modernizations program of 1978, the government focused on imports of heavy industrial items, including iron and steel, which increased by 95 percent, and machinery and transport equipment, which increased by 75 percent. This led to a decrease in the relative importance of imports of minerals and agricultural products, which accounted for about 30 percent of the total imports, compared with 36 percent in the previous year (Table 3.6). In the next three years, a severe economic imbalance occurred and the government made considerable efforts to readjust the economy, causing several major changes in the structure of imports to take place. First, the share of the imports of machinery and transport equipment in total imports continued to rise in 1979 and 1980, up from less than one-fifth to more than one-fourth of the economy's total imports, but most of such imports resulted from the import contracts signed by China with foreign suppliers in 1978. From 1981, the U.S. dollar value of these imports started to decline, and their share in the economy's total imports was lowered to 19.7 percent in 1982, which was slightly below that of 1978. Second, the readjustment program had an immediate dampening effect on imports of iron and steel, the share of which in total imports witnessed a steady decline from a peak of 29 percent in 1978 to a trough of 7 percent in 1981. Third, owing to the government's effort to revitalize light industry and promote light industrial exports, these years featured a rapid increase in imports of crude materials and semimanufactured goods, including textile fibers and textile yarn and fabrics. Imports of textiles alone accounted for 21 percent of the country's total imports in 1981, compared with 11 percent in 1978. Fourth, there was a steady rise in imports of consumer goods, including food grains and consumer durables. By spending foreign exchange on

Table 3.6. Commodity composition of China's imports, 1977–85 (in million U.S.$)

	1977	1978	1979	1980	1981	1982	1983	1984	1985
Food and live animals	1,061	1,367	1,829	2,750	3,171	3,407	2,607	2,035	1,637
Cereals and cereal preparations	653	935	1,362	2,217	2,341	2,449	2,011	1,519	1,050
Beverages and tobacco	—	6	5	32	92	77	80	153	250
Crude materials	1,032	1,406	1,864	3,258	3,205	2,602	2,422	2,684	3,329
Textile fibers	519	897	1,117	2,069	2,271	1,501	1,124	1,190	1,576
Mineral fuels and products	118	155	153	282	195	188	179	213	498
Animal and vegetable oils and fats	154	134	203	203	106	88	58	73	99
Chemicals	871	1,185	1,455	2,092	2,031	2,152	2,190	3,281	3,657
Elements and compounds	302	376	404	537	473	515	565	661	824
Manufactured fertilizers	342	474	619	891	753	609	584	975	886
Plastic materials and resins	99	136	156	372	482	632	585	1,106	1,340
Semimanufactured goods	2,089	3,839	4,632	4,652	4,056	4,234	5,736	7,482	10,844
Textile yarn and fabrics	168	200	295	860	1,587	1,151	1,015	1,513	2,098
Iron and steel	1,537	2,991	3,346	2,251	1,324	1,877	3,291	4,156	5,865
Nonferrous metals	226	331	298	444	191	471	716	848	1,317
Machinery and transport equipment	1,171	2,048	3,833	5,329	4,605	3,329	4,184	7,623	16,375
Miscellaneous manufactures	81	152	297	482	602	669	891	1,492	2,443
Other transactions	32	40	94	167	193	150	161	221	349
Total	6,611	10,331	14,363	19,248	18,254	16,898	18,508	25,256	39,480

Sources: Central Intelligence Agency, China: International Trade Annual Statistical Supplement, 1983–6. Central Intelligence Agency, China: International Trade, Fourth Quarter, 1986.

these "nonessential" items, the government intended to win support from the public for the program of economic reforms, which encountered resistance from ideologists and people who had lost their economic and political power as a result of the reforms.[6]

The government first started economic reforms in 1979, but their impact on imports was not felt until 1982, the year when the task of economic adjustment was essentially completed. Major changes in the structure of imports under the reforms in the period between 1982 and 1985 were as follows. One of the most important achievements of economic reforms was the improvement in agricultural productivity following the implementation of the agricultural household responsibility system. With a substantial increase in agricultural production, the economy was able to reduce its dependence on agricultural imports. The value of grain imports, including wheat and corn, decreased by nearly 60 percent in the period from 1982 to 1985, lowering the share of food and live animals in total imports from 20 percent in 1982 to a mere 4 percent in 1985. Another noticeable change in imports was that as the central government relaxed its control over small-scale investments and allowed enterprises and local governments to participate in making import decisions, investment booms occurred, significantly pushing up the imports of iron and steel, machinery, and transport equipment. In 1985, machinery and transport equipment alone accounted for more than 40 percent of the economy's total imports, while iron and steel accounted for another 15 percent. Furthermore, the rapid growth of textile exports under the export promotion scheme gave rise to a strong increase in the demand for imports of textile yarn and textile fibers, particularly in 1984 and 1985 when the world economy recovered from the economic recession. Finally, in association with the introduction of the foreign exchange retention scheme there was a considerable relaxation of restrictions on consumer goods imports. The policy change resulted in a substantial growth in imports of miscellaneous manufactures, from 669 million U.S. dollars in 1982 to 2,443 million U.S. dollars in 1985.

The movement of the trade balance

Under strict central planning, such as in prereform China, exports and imports would tend to move closely with each other because exports would serve primarily to finance current imports. Under these circumstances, the trade balance would be relatively small and would not normally improve or deteriorate significantly. In postreform China, however, substantial rises and falls in the balance of trade became possible as export and import growth were no longer linked closely with each other. Exports were now promoted independently of the volume of imports and exhibited a relatively high degree of sensitivity to world economic conditions. Imports continued to be dictated by the government's investment policy and tended to rise and fall significantly. As a result, significant improvement or deterioration in the trade balance became possible during the economic reforms.

In 1978 and 1979, as in other prereform years in the 1970s, China had to finance the increase in its imports of raw materials, iron and steel, machinery, and transport equipment mainly with foreign exchange earned from the exports of petroleum and food products. However, as a result of the precipitous rise in the imports of machinery and iron and steel under the Four Modernizations movement, large trade deficits were incurred in those years: 161 million U.S. dollars in 1978 and 711 million U.S. dollars in 1979. The trade balance did not start to improve until 1980, in which year the economy recorded a surplus of 20 million U.S. dollars. The improvement was so substantial that a surplus of 3.8 billion and 6.6 billion U.S. dollars was incurred in 1981 and 1982, respectively. The improvement in the trade balance was due both to the readjustment policy that curtailed producer goods imports and to the precipitous rise in oil exports in those years.

The trade surplus decreased in the next two years when the government stepped up economic reforms. Under the program of foreign trade reforms, individual enterprises were encouraged "to foster exports with imports" and "to join technology with foreign trade." It was expected that, by making use of foreign technology in the production of exports, (a) the technology of domestic production would improve systematically with the expansion of foreign trade and (b) the economy's import capacity would increase in step with the growth of exports. During those years, the imports of raw materials, semimanufactured goods, and machinery and equipment rose quickly with the growth of manufactured exports, including textiles and clothing. Unfortunately, by encouraging the export sector to use imported machinery and equipment, the policy was import-biased and had a tendency to worsen the trade balance. The reason is that, in the short run, if the marginal capital output ratios of exportables were greater than unity, as is normally the case, an increase in one dollar of the output of exportables (or exports) would require an increase of more than one dollar of imported capital input. The increased foreign exchange earnings generated by the exports of manufactured goods would then fall short of the increased spending of foreign exchange on producer goods imports. Partly as a result of this bias, the economy suffered an unprecedented trade deficit of 8 billion U.S. dollars in 1985.

3.3   Foreign trade reforms and foreign trade relations with the rest of the world

China maintained relatively simple trade relations with countries in the rest of the world during the prereform period, during which time foreign trade was relatively small and under central control. However, since 1978 the foreign trade reforms have resulted in a breakdown of state monopoly on foreign trade and the volume of foreign trade has risen rapidly. These changes have coincided with a dramatic change in China's trade relations with the rest of the world. Among the most notable changes was the increase in the relative importance of the West in China's foreign trade. More than 80 percent of China's foreign trade has been conducted with Western countries since as early as 1966. The percentage rose to 85 percent in 1978 and rose further to 93 percent in 1985. The markets in the West were relatively open and large enough to accommodate the unprecedented growth of imports from China. At the same time, Eastern-bloc countries, featuring relatively rigid foreign trade plans, became increasingly unimportant in the country's foreign trade.[7] This section only looks at China's foreign trade relations with the West in the period from 1978 to 1985.

There was an important difference in China's foreign trade relations with the West between the prereform and postreform periods: foreign trade was less of a political tool in the postreform period than it had been in the prereform period. As indicated in Chapter 2, with price irrationality and currency inconvertibility it is difficult, if not impossible, for a centrally planned economy such as that of China in the prereform period to determine unambiguously what, how much, and with whom it should trade. Under these circumstances, political benefits would be a convenient and appealing criterion that the central government may use in forming its foreign trade relations with other countries. Under economic reforms, self-interest, as opposed to political benefits, played an increasingly important role in the determination of China's trade relations with other countries since enterprises and local governments were now empowered to make foreign trade decisions. In addition, as the volume of foreign trade increased, China was no longer faced with perfectly elastic demand for its exports and could no longer have as much say as before about with whom to trade. For these reasons, China's export and import relations with the rest of the world in the postreform period were, as will be seen, determined to a considerable extent by nonpolitical considerations.

Export relations

From 1978 to 1985, about 40 percent of China's exports were destined for developed countries. Among these countries, Japan was (and still is) the most important market, absorbing on the average more than 20 percent of China's total exports (Table 3.7). Broadly speaking, the open door policy and foreign trade reforms had no significant impacts on the relative importance of the Japanese market, which was highly protective against manufactured goods imports from other countries, whereas labor-intensive manufactured goods were the fastest growing exports of China during the economic reforms. These exports had to find their ways in relatively more open economies, including the United States and Hong Kong. Partly as a result, the relative importance of the U.S. market increased more quickly than that of the Japanese market, with imports from China rising from 324 million U.S. dollars in 1978 to nearly 4 billion U.S. dollars in 1985. This sharp increase raised the share of China's exports to the United States in China's total exports from 3 percent in 1978 to more than 12 percent in 1985. China's exports to other developed countries, including the United Kingdom, West Germany, France, and Italy, were relatively small, each accounting for not more than 4 percent of China's total exports throughout the period, partly because of their small sizes and long distance from China and partly because of protectionist measures adopted by the European Common Market on imports from developing countries. The high degree of their concentration on the Japanese and the United States markets among other developed countries was an important characteristic of China's exports during this period.

In contrast with the trade patterns of other developing countries, China's exports were destined primarily for less developed countries. One reason was the relatively high proportion of minerals and agricultural items in the country's exports, and these items had large markets in the neighboring resource-poor developing countries. Another reason was the importance of Hong Kong as an entrepôt of China's exports to both developed and developing countries. Among less developed countries, Hong Kong, China's long-time gateway and a free port, stood out as the most important market for China's exports. In spite of its small size, it consistently absorbed more than 20 percent of China's exports. It retained part of the imports from China for domestic consumption and reexported a major part of them to other countries. Singapore, another free port, was also seen to have performed an increasingly important role as an entrepôt of China's exports. As shown in Table 3.7, the share of China's exports to Singapore rose from 3 percent in 1978 to nearly 7 percent in 1985. The rising importance of Hong Kong and Singapore to China's exports pro-

Table 3.7. China's exports to major trading partners, 1978–85 (in million U.S.$)

	1978	1979	1980	1981	1982	1983	1984	1985
Developed countries	3,776	5,643	8,268	10,043	10,225	9,941	11,878	13,549
	(37.31)	(41.08)	(43.69)	(46.72)	(44.65)	(41.92)	(42.97)	(43.25)
Japan	1,948	2,793	4,139	5,032	5,083	4,846	5,660	6,222
	(19.24)	(20.34)	(21.87)	(23.41)	(22.20)	(20.44)	(20.46)	(19.86)
United States	324	595	1,059	1,875	2,275	2,252	3,074	3,840
	(3.20)	(4.33)	(5.59)	(8.72)	(9.93)	(9.50)	(11.11)	(12.26)
West Germany	319	464	703	669	610	668	740	758
	(3.15)	(3.38)	(3.71)	(3.11)	(2.66)	(2.82)	(2.68)	(2.42)
France	196	284	406	443	380	377	383	434
	(1.94)	(2.07)	(2.15)	(2.06)	(1.66)	(1.59)	(1.38)	(1.38)
Italy	174	344	380	349	372	360	375	516
	(1.72)	(2.51)	(2.01)	(1.62)	(1.62)	(1.52)	(1.36)	(1.65)
United Kingdom	186	255	317	317	295	306	323	344
	(1.83)	(1.85)	(1.67)	(1.48)	(1.29)	(1.29)	(1.17)	(1.10)
Less developed countries	4,782	6,338	8,770	10,209	11,400	12,404	14,151	15,601
	(47.25)	(46.14)	(46.34)	(47.49)	(49.78)	(52.31)	(51.19)	(49.81)
Hong Kong	2,249	3,021	4,401	5,264	5,431	5,847	7,131	7,568
	(22.23)	(21.99)	(23.25)	(24.49)	(23.71)	(24.66)	(25.78)	(24.16)
Singapore	326	392	599	736	839	788	1,283	2,160
	(3.22)	(2.85)	(3.16)	(3.42)	(3.66)	(3.32)	(4.64)	(6.90)
Communist Countries	1,563	1,755	1,887	1,243	1,275	1,366	1,616	2,174
	(15.44)	(12.78)	(9.97)	(5.78)	(5.57)	(5.76)	(5.85)	(6.94)

Note: Figures in parentheses are percentage shares.
Sources: Central Intelligence Agency, China: International Trade, Fourth Quarter, 1980–6.

vided China with an access to markets which it would otherwise have found inaccessible for political and nonpolitical reasons. These markets included Taiwan and South Korea, with whom it had no direct trade relations, and some distant countries such as those in Latin America.[8] More importantly, China was able to ship increasingly large amounts of manufactured goods to developed countries, including the United States and European countries, through Hong Kong and Singapore without being seriously handicapped by its relatively low marketing skill.

One of the major changes in China's trade relations with the rest of the world in the postreform period was therefore the increase in the competition between China and other less developed countries in the exports of labor-intensive manufactures in the markets in developed countries. Even before China began to increase its exports of labor-intensive goods by a substantial amount, the markets for these goods were already limited, and both the United States and the European Common Market countries had already adopted various protectionist measures to limit their imports from developing countries. China's rise as a major exporter of these goods had to take place at the expense of other developing countries, which had to face greater restrictions on their exports as a result. Although it is difficult to assess the impacts of the growth of China's exports on the exports of other less developed countries, it is conceivable that the balance of payments of some small less developed countries, including Sri Lanka and a number of Latin American countries exporting similar products, were adversely affected.[9] In the face of the rapid growth of China's manufactured exports, relatively industrialized developing countries including Taiwan, Hong Kong, and South Korea all witnessed a rapid decline in the growth rate of the exports of textiles and clothing, which constituted a major part of these countries' exports, and they all were forced to "upgrade" their exports by moving toward electronic goods and other technology-intensive goods. Partly as a result, increasing competition in the markets for capital-intensive and technology-intensive goods from these newly industrialized countries has been felt by developed countries. For instance, as a result of the rapid growth of the electronics industry, in 1986 Taiwan exported nearly 9 billion U.S. dollars' worth of electric machinery and apparatus, compared to 7 billion U.S. dollars for textile products.

Import relations

In comparison with its export relations with foreign countries, China's import relations with foreign countries were much more erratic. Under China's export promotion policy, its export relations with the rest of the world depended predominantly on the demand conditions for the coun-

Table 3.8. China's imports from major trading partners, 1977–85 (in million U.S.$)

	1977	1978	1979	1980	1981	1982	1983	1984	1985
Developed countries	4,166	7,268	10,168	13,514	12,739	10,804	11,826	15,451	26,654
	(62.96)	(70.45)	(70.18)	(70.01)	(71.01)	(64.75)	(63.97)	(60.62)	(62.45)
Japan	1,955	3,074	3,674	5,109	5,076	3,500	4,918	7,199	12,590
	(29.54)	(29.80)	(25.35)	(26.46)	(28.29)	(20.98)	(26.60)	(28.24)	(31.90)
United States	171	865	1,724	3,755	3,603	2,912	2,173	3,004	3,856
	(2.59)	(8.38)	(11.90)	(19.45)	(20.08)	(17.45)	(11.75)	(11.79)	(9.77)
West Germany	501	995	1,493	1,145	1,017	853	1,075	1,038	2,230
	(7.57)	(9.65)	(10.30)	(5.93)	(5.67)	(5.11)	(5.81)	(4.07)	(5.65)
France	95	199	339	303	274	336	450	310	781
	(1.44)	(1.93)	(2.34)	(1.57)	(1.53)	(2.01)	(2.43)	(1.22)	(1.98)
Italy	89	188	278	254	331	210	265	442	797
	(1.34)	(1.83)	(1.92)	(1.32)	(1.84)	(1.26)	(1.43)	(1.73)	(2.02)
United Kingdom	109	176	453	394	252	179	244	424	515
	(1.65)	(1.70)	(3.13)	(2.04)	(1.41)	(1.06)	(1.32)	(1.66)	(1.30)
Less developed countries	1,384	1,511	2,378	3,846	3,930	4,166	5,044	7,959	12,132
	(20.92)	(14.65)	(16.41)	(19.93)	(21.90)	(24.97)	(27.28)	(31.23)	(30.73)
Hong Kong	44	63	382	1,249	1,957	1,954	2,495	5,031	7,858
	(0.67)	(0.61)	(2.64)	(6.47)	(10.91)	(11.71)	(13.50)	(19.74)	(19.90)
Singapore	59	58	170	308	179	240	213	243	333
	(0.90)	(0.56)	(1.17)	(1.59)	(1.00)	(1.44)	(1.15)	(0.95)	(0.84)
Communist countries	1,067	1,537	1,942	1,944	1,272	1,716	1,617	2,078	2,694
	(16.12)	(14.90)	(13.41)	(10.07)	(7.09)	(10.29)	(8.75)	(8.15)	(6.82)

Note: Figures in parentheses are percentage shares.
Sources: Central Intelligence Agency, China: International Trade Quarterly Review, Second Quarter, 1979. Central Intelligence Agency, China: International Trade, Fourth Quarter, 1980–6.

try's exports, which were relatively stable. In contrast, its import relations with other countries depended predominantly on the relatively volatile domestic investment policies. As shown in Table 3.8, China imported mostly from developed countries, the share of which was as high as 70 percent in 1978. The high share was due to the fact that the country had to rely on developed countries for its supplies of iron and steel, industrial raw materials, food grains, and technologically advanced machinery and equipment. The large increase in investment in heavy industry under the Four Modernizations program further pushed up the share of China's imports from those countries, which rose from 63 percent in 1977 to more than 70 percent in 1978. The share remained above 70 percent in the next three years, during which time the economy struggled to readjust. Between 1982 and 1985, under the impact of foreign trade reforms which empowered individual enterprises to arrange their own imports through foreign trade corporations, the proportion of China's imports from developed countries started to decline. Individual enterprises and local governments, encouraged by the export incentive scheme, showed considerable interest in machinery and other related imports from more industrialized developing countries. Such imports were mostly for the production of labor-intensive goods and could be more easily adapted to domestic production conditions when compared with those from technologically advanced developed countries. As shown in Table 3.8, an increasingly large proportion of China's imports came from Hong Kong, which served both as a supplier and as an intermediary between China's foreign trade corporations and foreign exporters. In 1985, the proportion of China's imports from developed countries was reduced to 62 percent.

Geographically, the sources of China's imports were highly concentrated. In the period from 1978 to 1985, Japan, being the only developed country in proximity to China, supplied nearly 28 percent of China's total imports, the United States supplied 13 percent, Hong Kong also supplied about 13 percent, West Germany supplied 6 percent, and other countries each supplied less than 2 percent. Nevertheless, China's import relations with these countries were far from stable. Due to the frequent changes in China's import policy, there were dramatic fluctuations in China's imports from Japan, West Germany, and the United States. For instance, China's imports from Japan rose by 161 percent in the period from 1977 to 1980 as a result of the Four Modernizations drive in 1978, but, due to economic readjustment, the U.S. dollar value of the imports suffered a 4 percent decrease in the period from 1980 to 1983. The decrease proved to be short-lived, however, as the amount of imports shot up by 156 percent in the period from 1983 to 1985. A similar growth pattern also characterized China's imports from West Germany and the United Kingdom.

There were two important exceptions to this growth pattern in China's imports from individual countries. One was China's imports from the United States, which increased from 171 million U.S. dollars in 1977 to nearly 4 billion U.S. dollars in 1985. The other was its imports from Hong Kong, which witnessed an even more dramatic expansion. Hong Kong had long been (and still is) one of China's most important export markets, but it played an insignificant role as a supplier of imports to China until the 1980s. In 1978, it exported only 63 million U.S. dollars' worth of goods to China, which was less than one percent of China's total imports. In 1980, the amount of exports shot up to 1,249 million U.S. dollars, which was nearly 20 times as large as the 1978 level. In the next five years, the volume of exports continued to soar, and it reached nearly 8 billion U.S. dollars, or 20 percent of China's total imports, in 1985. This exceptionally high rate of growth in 1985 turned Hong Kong into the second largest supplier of imports to China after Japan. As will be noted in the next section, the rising importance of Hong Kong as a supplier of imports to China was due considerably to the rapid growth of its reexports to China.

In comparison with developed countries, all less developed countries except Hong Kong benefited little from the expansion of China's import capacity. China's imports from less developed countries outside Hong Kong were 14 percent in 1978. The percentage dropped to a trough of 11 percent in 1980 and remained at that level in 1985. The relatively low level of imports from less developed countries stemmed from the fact that these countries had little to offer to China in terms of technology and capital equipment that China regarded as being crucial to its modernization. Their main exports to China were crude materials, which had little likelihood of growing rapidly given that China was richly endowed in natural resources.

3.4   Commodity composition of China's trade with Hong Kong

One of the most important roles of Hong Kong in China's economic development was, and still is, that it provided China with some indispensable facilities to meet with the West. These facilities included an economically different environment in which China could undertake some economic activities which it would find awkward or inefficient to carry on within its own political and economic framework as well as the contacts and arrangements that allowed China to obtain large amounts of foreign exchange earnings through trade with other Western countries (Hsu 1983, pp. 157–8). This unique role was important to the explanation of the changes in commodity composition of the trade between the two economies.

As discussed earlier, China's exports were destined mainly for less developed countries, and it was with these countries that China incurred substantial trade surpluses. China had to rely on these surpluses to finance the trade deficits it incurred with developed countries, from whom technologically advanced machinery and equipment were imported to meet the country's investment need. The largest bilateral trade surpluses that China incurred were those with Hong Kong, which ranged between 2.1 and 3.5 billion U.S. dollars in the years between 1978 and 1984; 1985 was the only year in which a deficit was incurred. The prominent role Hong Kong played in China's foreign trade can be seen from the commodity structure of the bilateral trade between the two countries.

Exports to Hong Kong

In comparison with other markets for China's exports, Hong Kong was unique to China in many aspects. First, it was populated mainly with Chinese who either had fled their motherland for reasons of political or economic hardship or were the descendants of those refugees. They were not only receptive to Chinese products, such as food and household items, but also equipped with the knowledge necessary for acquiring and marketing Chinese products. Some Chinese exports, including handicrafts, specialty food items, and fresh water, were uniquely from Hong Kong's domestic consumption and were unmarketable in the rest of the world. Hong Kong traders also made use of their knowledge of China to help Chinese producers develop products which were marketable in the rest of the world. The samples, product specifications, and even machinery and equipment brought in by them had undoubtedly improved the marketability of Chinese exports in developed countries. Second, Hong Kong was the only relatively industrialized less developed country bordering China. The geographical proximity between the two countries enabled China to export its products to Hong Kong at relatively low information and transportation costs; and Hong Kong's relatively high rate of economic growth enabled China's exports to enjoy a rapidly growing market. Third, the fact that Hong Kong itself was highly dependent on international trade for economic growth allowed China to make use of Hong Kong as a marketing agent for its exports. During the time when China was politically isolated from the rest of the world, such as in the years before 1970, this facility enabled China to widen its indirect contact with the West through foreign trade. In recent years, China's exports to the rest of the world through Hong Kong, which have included mainly manufactured goods, have risen rapidly, given that the marketing of products by Chinese producers themselves is still handicapped by their low communicative skill and the law restricting foreign traveling.

Table 3.9 shows the commodity composition of China's exports to Hong Kong in the period between 1978 and 1985. During this period, the U.S. dollar value of China's exports went up from 2.2 billion to 7.5 billion, an increase of more than 240 percent. Nearly 70 percent of the increase was attributable to the growth of manufactured exports, which rose from 1.1 billion U.S. dollars in 1978 to 5.5 billion U.S. dollars in 1985. The rapid expansion of manufactured exports raised their share in China's total exports to Hong Kong from 48 percent in 1978 to 72 percent in 1985.

China's trade pattern resembled that of other less developed countries in early stages of industrialization in that its manufactured exports were concentrated on textiles and clothing. These were also the major manufactured items China exported to Hong Kong, which relied heavily on China for the supply of textile yarn and which was one of the major investing countries in China. During this period, Hong Kong set up numerous textile and garment factories across the border for export processing purposes.[10] Finished products were mostly shipped back to Hong Kong for either immediate transshipment to other countries or final processing.[11] Another major item of China's exports to Hong Kong was foodstuffs. Hong Kong has always been the most important market for China's food exports. In 1978, about 34 percent of China's food exports were destined for Hong Kong, primarily for the latter's domestic consumption. As China gradually opened up other markets, the percentage share of foodstuffs destined for Hong Kong in China's food exports declined slowly to 22 percent in 1985. The importance of foodstuffs destined for Hong Kong in terms of their share in China's total exports to Hong Kong also witnessed a decline from 36 percent in 1978 to less than 15 percent in 1985.

The export figures in Table 3.9 do not distinguish between the exports destined for Hong Kong's domestic use and those reexported by Hong Kong to the rest of the world. In order to understand the role of Hong Kong in China's foreign trade, it is necessary to make such a distinction. China's total exports to Hong Kong amounted to 2.2 billion U.S. dollars in 1978. Of these, as much as 35 percent, or 762 million U.S. dollars, were reexported. In 1985, China's exports to Hong Kong increased to more than 7.5 billion U.S. dollars, of which 59 percent, or 4.4 billion U.S. dollars, were reexported. Clearly, the rapid growth of China's exports to Hong Kong was sustained by both Hong Kong's promotion of Chinese exports in the rest of the world and, to a lesser extent, by the increase in their competitiveness in Hong Kong's domestic market. The marketability of China's manufactured exports in Hong Kong and other coun-

Table 3.9. Commodity composition of China's exports to Hong Kong, 1978–85 (in million U.S.$)

	1978	1979	1980	1981	1982	1983	1984	1985
Food and live animals	791 (35.99)	893 (29.20)	1,066 (24.90)	1,222 (23.49)	1,190 (23.47)	1,144 (20.78)	1,200 (16.85)	1,115 (14.77)
Crude materials (excluding fuels)	144 (6.58)	168 (5.51)	213 (4.98)	302 (5.82)	248 (4.89)	322 (5.85)	491 (5.10)	541 (7.02)
Petroleum and petroleum products	157 (7.14)	294 (9.62)	437 (10.22)	405 (7.78)	371 (7.32)	344 (6.26)	300 (4.21)	242 (3.21)
Semimanufactured goods	669 (30.46)	966 (31.59)	1,273 (29.74)	1,579 (30.37)	1,449 (28.57)	1,638 (29.75)	2,189 (30.73)	2,138 (28.33)
Textile yarn and fabrics	445 (20.27)	626 (20.47)	807 (18.86)	1,029 (19.80)	905 (17.84)	1,157 (21.01)	1,677 (23.52)	1,646 (21.80)
Machinery and equipment	47 (2.12)	90 (2.93)	181 (4.23)	258 (4.96)	237 (4.68)	285 (5.18)	471 (6.61)	545 (7.22)
Miscellaneous manufactures	266 (12.11)	445 (14.56)	831 (19.42)	1,132 (21.77)	1,241 (24.47)	1,411 (25.63)	2,050 (28.78)	2,463 (32.76)
Total	2,197	3,058	4,278	5,200	5,055	5,504	7,127	7,549

Notes: Figures in parentheses are percentage shares. Figures are computed by converting Hong Kong dollar values into U.S. dollar values at the following exchange rates:

	1978	1979	1980	1981	1982	1983	1984	1985
H.K.$/U.S.$	4.803	4.948	5.130	5.675	6.495	7.780	7.823	7.811

Source: Census and Statistics Department, Hong Kong Government, *Hong Kong Annual Digest of Statistics*, 1986, p. 112.

Sources: Census and Statistics Department, Hong Kong Government, *Hong Kong External Trade*, 1980–6, Table 13. Census and Statistics Department, Hong Kong Government, *Hong Kong Review of Overseas Trade*, 1980–6.

Table 3.10. Hong Kong's reexports of principal commodities from China, 1978–85 (in million U.S.$)

	1978	1979	1980	1981	1982	1983	1984	1985
Textile yarn and fabrics	260	337	383	481	433	479	739	885
Clothing	68	146	252	324	417	526	727	918
Road vehicles	3	7	14	16	14	11	15	13
Watches and clocks	1	2	3	10	10	14	20	19
Toys and sporting goods	3	4	9	19	29	42	182	320
Vegetables and fruits	51	69	68	139	144	148	134	139
Total	762	1,145	1,636	2,262	2,262	2,530	3,593	4,433

Note: Figures are computed by converting Hong Kong dollar values into U.S. dollar values at the following exchange rates:

	1978	1979	1980	1981	1982	1983	1984	1985
H.K.$/U.S.$	4.803	4.948	5.130	5.675	6.495	7.780	7.823	7.811

Source: Census and Statistics Department, Hong Kong Government, *Hong Kong Annual Digest of Statistics*, 1986, p. 112.

Sources: Census and Statistics Department, Hong Kong Government, *Hong Kong Annual Digest of Statistics*, 1986, p. 81. Census and Statistics Department, Hong Kong Government, *Hong Kong Review of Overseas Trade*, 1978–86, Tables 22 and 23.

tries improved remarkably as a result of reforms and the open door policy. Under the open door policy, foreign investments in China in the form of joint ventures rose rapidly, and a majority of the foreign investors were from Hong Kong, who found it profitable to transfer some of their labor-intensive operations to China in the face of rising labor costs at home.[12] They brought with them machinery and management personnel and were responsible for the export of finished products, while China provided land, labor, and raw materials. The marketability of such products in either Hong Kong or other countries in the West was clearly greater than were China's traditional manufactured exports. Under economic reforms, China's domestic enterprises were motivated to improve the quality of their exports, widen their contacts with foreign traders, and respond to changes in foreign demand. During this period, a large number of China's foreign trade corporations set up their branches in Hong Kong to promote their trade relations with the rest of the world.[13] This phenomenon was in sharp contrast with the manner in which foreign trade was conducted in the prereform period, during which time all exports and imports were under the direct control of the National Foreign Trade Corporations. These corporations aimed mainly at fulfilling their export targets and had neither the incentive nor the power to improve the marketability of exports.

The structure of China's products reexported by Hong Kong is shown in Table 3.10. Textile yarn and fabrics were one of the most important reexport items throughout the period between 1978 and 1985. In 1985, the value of such reexports reached 885 million U.S. dollars, or one-fifth of Hong Kong's reexports originating from China. Clothing was another important item, and it also accounted for about one-fifth of Hong Kong's reexports originating from China in 1985. Note that whereas textile yarn and fabrics were aimed mainly at markets in other relatively resource-poor developing countries, including Taiwan and South Korea, clothing was destined mainly for developed countries, including the United States and Japan.[14] Owing to the relatively limited markets in less developed countries, the reexports of clothing grew much faster than did those of textile yarn and fabrics. For the same reason, Hong Kong's reexports of other manufactured products from China in general went up more quickly than did those of raw materials and semimanufactured goods during this period.

Imports from Hong Kong

China's imports from Hong Kong can be classified into two parts: (1) the imports originating in Hong Kong, and (2) the imports shipped in from

Table 3.11. Hong Kong's domestic exports and reexports to China, 1978–85 (in million U.S.$)

	1978	1979	1980	1981	1982	1983	1984	1985
Domestic exports	17	122	313	515	586	800	1,442	1,945
	(27.46)	(31.44)	(25.69)	(26.66)	(23.95)	(23.81)	(28.68)	(24.03)
Reexports	45	266	905	1,418	1,230	1,566	3,587	6,148
	(72.54)	(68.56)	(74.31)	(73.34)	(66.05)	(66.19)	(71.32)	(75.97)
Total	62	388	1,218	1,933	1,816	2,366	5,030	8,092

Notes: Figures in parentheses are percentage shares. Figures are computed by converting Hong Kong dollar values into U.S. dollar values at the following exchange rates:

	1978	1979	1980	1981	1982	1983	1984	1985
H.K.$/U.S.$	4.083	4.948	5.130	5.675	6.495	7.780	7.823	7.811

Source: Census and Statistics Department, Hong Kong Government, *Hong Kong Annual Digest of Statistics*, 1986, p. 112.
Source: Census and Statistics Department, Hong Kong Government, *Hong Kong Annual Digest of Statistics*, 1986, p. 76.

Hong Kong but originating in countries other than Hong Kong.[15] This distinction is necessary because, in contrast to China's imports from other countries, the second component consistently accounted for more than two-thirds of China's imports from Hong Kong in recent years. The U.S. dollar value of both components enjoyed substantial growth in the period from 1978 to 1985: the component originating in Hong Kong went up by a factor of 114, whereas the component originating in countries other than Hong Kong went up by a factor of 136 (Table 3.11). As a result of the rapid growth of China's imports from Hong Kong, there was a substantial drop in China's net foreign exchange earnings from Hong Kong. In the period between 1978 and 1982, China incurred between 2 to 3.5 billion U.S. dollars of trade surplus with Hong Kong. In each of these years, the surplus amounted to more than 20 percent of the value of China's annual imports. China was able to finance a large portion of its imports of technology from developed countries with its foreign exchange earnings from Hong Kong.[16] However, the surplus as well as its proportion to the country's import payments started to decrease in 1983, in which year the surplus was reduced to 3.4 billion U.S. dollars. In 1985, the bilateral trade balance even turned into a deficit of 281 million U.S. dollars. In the face of the decreasing importance of foreign exchange earnings from Hong Kong, China had to turn to foreign borrowings and the expansion of other export markets for foreign exchange. Developed countries, including Japan, the United States, and the European countries, were among the markets to which China significantly raised its exports in the 1980s. They began to face increasingly strong pressure from China to open up their markets for Chinese exports.[17]

Table 3.12 shows the commodity composition of China's imports from Hong Kong. In 1978, China's imports from Hong Kong comprised predominantly raw materials (31 percent) and manufactured goods exclusive of machinery and equipment (44 percent), and the imports of machinery and equipment were relatively unimportant (6 percent). The import structure, however, changed dramatically during the years between 1979 and 1985. The machinery and equipment imports increased dramatically from 4 million U.S. dollars in 1978 to 2,442 million U.S. dollars in 1985 and their share in China's imports from Hong Kong rose from 4 percent in 1978 to 41 percent in 1985. The increase in the percentage share was mainly at the expense of crude materials, the percentage share of which decreased from 31 in 1978 to a mere 3 percent in 1985. The share of other manufactured goods remained around 44 percent in this period but grew most rapidly in absolute terms from 28 million U.S. dollars in 1978 to nearly 3 billion U.S. dollars in 1985. Hong Kong was now acting as an increasingly important middleman for the supplies of machinery and

Table 3.12. Commodity composition of China's imports from Hong Kong, 1978–85 (in million U.S.$)

	1978	1979	1980	1981	1982	1983	1984	1985
Foodstuffs	3	10	37	81	112	157	399	244
	(4.26)	(2.50)	(2.92)	(4.16)	(5.76)	(6.29)	(3.97)	(4.08)
Crude materials	20	49	133	103	137	147	481	196
	(31.11)	(12.87)	(10.62)	(5.27)	(7.05)	(5.88)	(4.77)	(3.28)
Chemicals	9	22	43	93	105	135	520	316
	(13.49)	(5.60)	(3.47)	(4.74)	(5.43)	(5.41)	(5.17)	(5.28)
Machinery and equipment[a]	4	74	213	532	462	671	3,592	2,442
	(6.35)	(19.28)	(17.04)	(27.23)	(23.85)	(26.91)	(35.67)	(40.78)
Electronic machine parts	na	na	na	9	14	31	283	199
Televisions, radios, etc.	1	33	133	144	28	28	156	171
Telecommunication equipment	na[c]	na	na	82	115	157	845	451
Electric tubes and transistors	na	na	na	40	22	33	236	191
Road vehicles/trucks	1	21	57	44	21	42	337	168
Other manufactures[a,b]	28	232	773	1,105	1,096	1,348	4,959	2,716
	(44.44)	(60.46)	(61.84)	(56.59)	(56.55)	(54.02)	(49.25)	(45.35)
Textile yarn and fabrics	13	84	351	670	589	642	2,159	1,108
Watches and clocks	na	na	na	106	75	76	202	120
Sound recorders, reproducers	na	na	na	6	8	7	215	103
Other commodities	—	3	52	36	17	24	112	69
		(4.12)	(1.82)	(0.89)	(0.99)	(1.11)	(1.16)	(1.54)

Notes: Figures in parentheses are percentage shares.

[a] For 1978 to 1980, "Machinery and equipment" is the sum of the following items: power generating equipment, equipment for industry, metalworking machinery, office machines, electric appliances, and road vehicles. "Other manufactures" is obtained by subtracting the sum from all manufactured imports.

[b] For 1981 to 1985, "Other manufactures" is the sum of semimanufactured goods and miscellaneous manufactures.

[c] na = not available.

Source: Central Intelligence Agency, *China: International Trade*, Fourth Quarter, 1980–6.

manufactured goods from industrialized and newly industrialized countries.

The increase in the importance of Hong Kong as a supplier of manufactured imports to China stemmed from both the rapid increase in Hong Kong's investments in China and the change in China's foreign trade institution during the period of economic reforms. As a result of the increased investment in China, Hong Kong investors shipped an increasingly large amount of machinery, raw materials, and semimanufactured goods to China. The shipments originated partly in Hong Kong and partly in other countries, which included particularly Japan, Taiwan, and South Korea. For example, consider China's imports of textile yarn and fabrics in 1985. In that year, these imports amounted to 2.1 billion U.S. dollars, of which about 50 percent were from Hong Kong, and of those from Hong Kong, 86 percent were transshipped from Taiwan and South Korea.[18]

The rapid increase in China's imports from Hong Kong was also due to China's economic reforms which increased China's dependence on Hong Kong for imports from other countries. Under economic reforms, enterprises and local governments were accorded the right which they never had before of spending foreign exchange on goods for their own use. However, lacking experience in foreign trade and not being allowed to travel freely abroad, they had to rely heavily on foreign traders in finding appropriate suppliers and in negotiating with those suppliers for the prices and terms of delivery. In this respect, Hong Kong traders had the advantage of having had a wide range of contacts with the enterprises and government officials who had long exported their products to or through Hong Kong. Such contacts were essential to foreign traders in securing import orders from the Chinese buyers (Fung 1984, p. 165). Foreign traders often report that establishing personal relations with Chinese traders is one of the most important tasks in trading with China; once the relations are established a long-term business relation naturally follows. In addition, the geographical proximity of Hong Kong to China made it possible for a large number of local governments and foreign trade corporations to station their import agents in Hong Kong. They even illicitly placed part of their foreign exchange earnings from Hong Kong in Hong Kong so that they could engage in importation without having to go through the cumbersome import-approving procedure at home (Chapter 2, Section 2.6). These factors greatly facilitated Hong Kong's exports to China.

3.5 Commodity composition of China's trade with Japan

China and Japan are two distinctive economies. Whereas the former is underdeveloped and resource-rich, the latter is industrialized and re-

Table 3.13. Commodity composition of China's exports to Japan, 1978–85 (in million U.S.$)

	1978	1979	1981	1982	1983	1984	1985
Food and live animals	354 (17.41)	425 (14.38)	524 (10.41)	473 (9.31)	493 (10.18)	594 (10.49)	900 (14.31)
Beverages and tobacco	8 (0.40)	6 (0.21)	5 (0.11)	6 (0.12)	5 (0.10)	5 (0.09)	6 (0.09)
Crude materials	359 (17.68)	537 (18.22)	495 (9.84)	495 (0.74)	603 (12.45)	741 (13.08)	788 (12.52)
Mineral fuels and products	821 (40.45)	1,189 (40.23)	2,792 (55.49)	2,908 (52.21)	2,644 (54.59)	2,939 (51.92)	2,885 (45.86)
Crude oil	726 (35.76)	951 (32.19)	2,219 (44.10)	2,224 (43.76)	1,980 (40.89)	2,225 (39.31)	2,133 (33.92)
Animal and vegetable oils	13 (0.63)	13 (0.44)	12 (0.23)	7 (0.14)	12 (0.25)	23 (0.41)	17 (0.27)
Chemicals	53 (2.63)	127 (4.28)	231 (4.60)	216 (4.25)	205 (4.22)	231 (4.09)	289 (4.60)
Semimanufactured goods	278 (13.67)	378 (12.80)	555 (11.03)	528 (10.38)	430 (8.88)	592 (10.46)	619 (9.84)
Machinery and equipment	1 (0.04)	2 (0.05)	37 (0.74)	6 (0.11)	9 (0.18)	9 (0.16)	11 (0.17)
Miscellaneous manufactures	134 (6.59)	267 (9.03)	358 (7.12)	412 (8.10)	399 (8.24)	502 (8.87)	628 (9.99)
Other transactions	10 (0.50)	13 (0.43)	22 (0.44)	32 (0.64)	44 (0.91)	25 (0.44)	147 (2.33)

Note: Figures in parentheses are percentage shares.
Sources: 1978–9: Yamamoto, H., "China," in Economic Interdependence in the Western Pacific Basin in Perspective, T. Iwasaki, ed. (Institute of Developing Economies, Tokyo, Japan: p. 43). 1981–5: Central Intelligence Agency, China: International Trade, Fourth Quarter, 1983–6.

source-poor. This distinction has created a dramatic difference between the pattern of China's imports from Japan and that of Japan from China. Japan supplies China with mainly technologically advanced machinery and equipment, whereas China supplies Japan with mainly crude materials and labor-intensive manufactured goods. The complementarity and geographical proximity between the two economies has made Japan become China's most important trading partner in recent decades, in spite of the anti-Japanese undercurrent that has prevailed among those Chinese who experienced immense suffering from the Japanese occupation in the period between 1937 to 1945 (Nanto 1982).

Exports to Japan

In recent years, Japan has consistently been China's second largest export market after Hong Kong. On the average, about one-fifth to one-fourth of China's exports were destined for Japan in the period from 1978 to 1985. Major growth took place when the value of the exports went up from 2 billion U.S. dollars in 1978 to 5 billion U.S. dollars in 1981 (Table 3.13). This spectacular growth was due partly to China's promotion of exports and partly to the precipitous rise in the prices of oil and other commodities in the world market. However, from 1981 to 1985, the U.S. dollar value of China's exports to Japan rose by only 25 percent, which was much lower than the 46 percent growth in China's total exports. The slow growth was partly a result of China's concentration on agricultural and mineral exports, which accounted for 73 percent of China's exports to Japan in 1985. Petroleum alone accounted for 40 percent of these exports. Low demand and supply elasticities were a hindrance to the growth of these items. At the same time, the highly protective Japanese market greatly limited the growth of China's manufactured exports to Japan. Between 1981 and 1985, China's manufactured exports to Japan increased by 41 percent, which was much lower than the 55 percent increase in China's manufactured exports to the rest of the world as a whole. In the wake of China's promotion of manufactured exports and the decreasing rate of growth of China's oil exports, the relative importance of the Japanese market to China was on a downward trend in the period between 1981 and 1985.

Imports from Japan

China's imports from Japan were much more volatile than were its exports to Japan (Table 3.14). In the period from 1978 to 1980, as a result of the large increase in the value of import contracts that China signed with

Table 3.14. Commodity composition of China's imports from Japan, 1978–85 (in million U.S.$)

	1978	1979	1981	1982	1983	1984	1985
Foodstuffs	—	1	5	6	16	21	21
		(0.00)	(0.10)	(0.17)	(0.33)	(0.29)	(0.16)
Crude materials	79	71	225	150	106	183	269
	(2.60)	(1.75)	(4.44)	(4.29)	(2.16)	(2.54)	(2.11)
Chemicals	420	460	512	457	488	577	690
	(13.76)	(11.32)	(10.09)	(13.05)	(9.93)	(8.02)	(5.41)
Semimanufactured goods	1,884	1,980	1,795	1,720	2,800	3,266	4,197
	(61.78)	(48.75)	(35.35)	(49.15)	(56.97)	(45.37)	(32.92)
Machinery and equipment	630	1,056	2,297	981	1,268	2,758	6,884
	(19.79)	(26.00)	(45.26)	(28.01)	(25.79)	(38.31)	(53.99)
Miscellaneous manufactures	47	91	169	125	185	329	551
	(1.54)	(2.25)	(3.33)	(3.58)	(3.75)	(4.57)	(4.32)
Other transactions	18	40	72	61	52	65	138
	(0.58)	(1.00)	(1.42)	(1.75)	(1.06)	(0.90)	(1.08)
Total	3,049	4,061	5,076	3,500	4,915	7,199	12,750

Note: Figures in parentheses are percentage shares.
Source: Same as Table 3.13.

Japanese exporters in 1978, substantial increases occurred in China's imports from Japan. In those years, chemicals, machinery, capital equipment, and semimanufactured goods were the most important items that China imported from Japan. In 1979, for instance, the share of these goods in China's total imports from Japan was as high as 86 percent. China canceled some of the import contracts it had previously signed with Japanese exporters and issued a moratorium on the signing of new import contracts in 1979, thus resulting in a significant slowdown in China's imports from Japan in the period between 1981 and 1983. Nevertheless, rapid growth resumed in 1984 and 1985 when China loosened its control over investments at the local government level. In 1985, the value of China's imports from Japan reached 12.7 billion U.S. dollars, which was 159 percent over the 1983 level.

The volatility of China's imports from Japan was due mostly to the dramatic rises and falls in the machinery and equipment component of the imports. The value of this category rose from 630 million U.S. dollars in 1978 to 2.3 billion U.S. dollars in 1981. This increase accounted for more than 84 percent of the increase of China's imports from Japan in the same period. From 1981 to 1982, the imports of this category suffered a 56 percent decline, or a decrease of 1,317 million U.S. dollars. This decrease accounted for 84 percent of the decrease in China's overall imports from Japan between the two years. Between 1982 and 1985, the machinery and equipment imports increased by nearly 6 billion U.S. dollars, and this accounted for about 64 percent of the 9.3 billion U.S. dollar increase in China's imports from Japan in the same period. In general, China's imports of machinery and equipment, adjusted by some time lag, served as a good indicator of China's policy on imports and investment. A rapid increase in such imports would suggest the presence of an investment boom in China, whereas a drastic decline would suggest a tightening of the government's control over investment.

It is of interest to note that China imported a proportionally large amount of iron and steel and other semimanufactured goods from Japan. In 1978, they accounted for 62 percent of China's imports from Japan. This percentage share decreased to 49 percent in 1979 in the wake of the relatively rapid increase in the imports of machinery and equipment. In the following years, the percentage share also changed substantially. In U.S. dollar terms, however, imports of semimanufactured goods were relatively stable. Although they tend to rise and fall with the loosening and tightening of the government's investment policy, the fluctuations were relatively moderate. Between 1978 and 1985, the value of these imports rose by 123 percent, as compared with the 993 percent increase of machinery and equipment imports. In 1985, when the imports of machinery and equipment rose by a precipitous 150 percent, the imports of semi-manufactured goods rose by only 28 percent. The relatively stable growth suggests that China was highly dependent on Japan for the supply of certain intermediate goods. The level of their imports had been maintained even during the time when the country tightened its restrictions on the imports of investment goods. The high degree of dependence was attributable partly to China's imports of machinery and equipment from Japan.

3.6   Commodity composition of China's trade with the United States

In 1978, the Carter administration of the United States, enticed by the prospect of a large increase in U.S. exports to China, officially recognized and established diplomatic relations with the Beijing government. This move paved the way for the removal of a number of trade obstacles between the two countries: the frozen claims and assets in both countries, the lack of MFN-status for China's exports to the United States, and the financing of U.S. exports to China from the U.S. Export-Import Bank (Bayard et al. 1982). China sweetened this move by resuming its imports of wheat and corn from the United States in 1978. It also substantially raised the imports of cotton, machinery, and transport equipment from the country. As a result, China's total imports from the United States went up from 172 million U.S. dollars in 1977 to 832 million U.S. dollars in 1978, an increase of 385 percent in a matter of a year. An increasingly close trade relationship was established between the two countries beginning in that year.

Exports to the United States

China's exports to the United States amounted to only 356 million U.S. dollars in 1978, which was less than 4 percent of China's total exports in that year (Table 3.15). The level of China's exports to the United States was low because (a) to China the United States was an unfamiliar market located thousands of miles away in the other hemisphere of the earth; (b) Chinese producers, still accustomed to suppliers' markets at home, were largely unable to cope with the rapidly changing consumer tastes in the United States; and (c) the United States, as a resource-rich country, had little interest in agricultural and mineral imports from China. In that year, manufactures accounted for about 50 percent of China's exports to the United States, and foodstuffs and crude materials accounted for another 50 percent. Clothing and fabrics were two rapidly growing manufactured

Table 3.15. Commodity composition of China's exports to the United States, 1978–85 (in million U.S.$)

	1978	1979	1980	1981	1982	1983	1984	1985
Foodstuffs[a]	30 (8.39)	58 (8.88)	79.5 (7.55)	133.3 (7.05)	168 (7.36)	155 (6.89)	199 (6.78)	216 (5.61)
Crude materials[b]	65 (18.25)	182 (17.86)	262 (24.84)	627 (33.12)	718 (31.44)	529 (23.56)	724 (24.62)	1,113 (28.89)
Petroleum and products		105	135	293	598	430	609	986
Chemicals	39 (15.03)	66 (10.06)	107 (10.19)	126 (6.63)	136 (5.96)	131 (5.84)	153 (5.19)	163 (4.22)
Semimanufactured goods	102 (28.52)	101 (15.40)	235 (22.28)	374 (19.78)	386 (16.88)	390 (17.38)	555 (18.89)	603 (15.65)
Textile fabrics[c]			94	176	173	177	277	270
Machinery and equipment	1 (0.14)	1 (0.18)	6 (0.54)	40 (2.09)	48 (2.21)	41 (1.82)	64 (2.17)	89 (2.31)
Miscellaneous manufactures	120 (33.75)	240 (36.77)	380 (36.08)	621 (32.84)	863 (37.87)	1,027 (45.73)	1,281 (43.57)	1,679 (43.59)
Clothing[d]			249	422	635	774	863	967
Other transactions	1 (0.28)	5 (0.72)	3 (0.30)	6 (0.32)	7 (0.32)	10 (0.45)	19 (0.64)	44 (1.14)
Total	356	653	1,053	1,892	2,284	2,244	2,940	3,853

Notes: Figures in parentheses are percentage shares; figures for 1978 and 1979 are CIF and others are FOB.

[a] Foodstuffs are the aggregate of SITC 0 and 1.

[b] Crude materials are the aggregate of SITC 2, 3, and 4.

[c] Textile fabrics are the aggregate of (1) cotton fabrics, woven, (2) synthetic fabrics, woven, (3) other woven fabrics, (4) special textile fabrics, and (5) fabricated textile products.

[d] Clothing is the aggregate of (1) women's outer garments, (2) men's outer garments, (3) under garments, woven, (4) knitted outer garments, and (5) knitted under garments.

Sources: 1978–9: Gullo (1982, pp. 104–7). 1980–5: Central Intelligence Agency, China: International Trade, Fourth Quarter, 1983–6.

items, which accounted for more than 55 percent of China's manufactured exports to the United States.

In 1979 and 1980, the U.S. dollar value of China's exports to the United States increased by 84 percent and 61 percent, respectively. The dramatic increase was due mainly to the growth of petroleum and clothing exports. China exported oil to the United States for the first time in 1979, in which year the shipment amounted to 105 million U.S. dollars. In the next year, the value of the shipment increased by 44 percent to 151 million U.S. dollars. China's export of oil was part of its effort to finance the large amount of imports of machinery and equipment that were ordered and in the process of being delivered from Japan, West Germany, and other developed countries in 1978. China's clothing exports to the United States were comparatively low in 1978, amounting to only 69 million U.S. dollars. In 1979, they rose by more than 100 percent to 166 million U.S. dollars as a result of the readjustment policy which reallocated investment resources from heavy industry to light industry. Such a policy also made the expansion of other light manufactures possible in 1980, in which year China's manufactured exports to the United States increased by 78 percent.

From 1981 to 1985, China's exports to the United States continued to rise, except in 1982 when the world economy was in recession. Petroleum exports rose from 293 million U.S. dollars in 1981 to 986 million U.S. dollars in 1985. The pace of the growth of clothing and other light manufactures was equally impressive. For instance, manufactures classified under SITC 6 rose from 621 million U.S. dollars in 1981 to 1679 million U.S. dollars in 1985. The growth of China's exports to the United States was not unhindered, however. China's becoming one of the major exporters of textile products to the United States invited the latter to impose restrictive measures on these exports. To maintain export growth, China was forced to shift periodically from restricted items to unrestricted items. Were it not for the economic reforms which increased the responsiveness of Chinese exporters to market conditions, it would have been unlikely for China's exports to the United States to have enjoyed such a rapid growth.

Imports from the United States

In the period between 1978 and 1982, more than 60 percent of China's imports from the United States were foodstuffs and crude materials, including wheat, corn, wood, cotton, and synthetic textile fibers. These items experienced a rapid expansion in the years from 1978 to 1980 – the first three years following the establishment of diplomatic relations be-

Table 3.16. Commodity composition of China's imports from the United States, 1978–85 (in million U.S.$)

	1978	1979	1980	1981	1982	1983	1984	1985
Foodstuffs[a]	362	488	1,265	1,333	1,239	541	580	104
	(31.52)	(28.45)	(33.70)	(36.96)	(42.53)	(24.90)	(19.32)	(2.71)
Crude materials[b]	261	574	1,261	1,128	599	301	468	570
	(31.39)	(33.45)	(33.59)	(31.30)	(20.57)	(13.85)	(15.39)	(14.86)
Chemicals	61	126	386	410	497	355	645	498
	(7.27)	(7.33)	(10.28)	(11.34)	(17.08)	(16.31)	(21.45)	(12.99)
Semimanufactured goods	25	244	425	449	277	219	189	369
	(3.04)	(14.22)	(11.32)	(12.45)	(9.51)	(10.08)	(6.30)	(9.61)
Machinery and equipment	102	268	358	249	256	674	1,014	2,140
	(12.30)	(15.61)	(9.53)	(6.92)	(8.77)	(31.02)	(33.76)	(55.79)
Miscellaneous manufactures	18	33	57	33	42	78	98	139
	(2.14)	(1.89)	(1.53)	(0.90)	(1.45)	(3.61)	(3.26)	(3.61)
Other transactions	3	1	2	3	3	6	11	16
	(0.32)	(0.00)	(0.00)	(0.01)	(0.10)	(0.28)	(0.35)	(0.42)
Total	832	1,717	3,754	3,603	2,912	2,173	3,004	3,836

Notes: Figures in parentheses are percentage shares.
[a] Foodstuffs are the aggregate of SITC 0 and 1.
[b] Crude materials are the aggregate of SITC 2, 3, and 4.
Source: Same as Table 3.15.

tween the two countries (Table 3.16). Beginning in 1981, the values of the imports of most of these items started to decline as a result of the implementation of the agricultural responsibility system, which reduced the shortage of agricultural production at home.[19] The decline was accompanied by a contraction of most manufactured items in 1982 because of the world economic recession. However, China's manufactured imports from the United States started to grow rapidly in 1982, effectively reducing the relative importance of foodstuffs and crude materials in China's imports from the United States. In 1985, foodstuffs and crude materials accounted for only 18 percent of China's imports from the United States, a far cry from the 63 percent of 1982.

The growth of China's manufactured imports from the United States between 1983 and 1985 was attributable mainly to China's increasing interest in the production technology of the United States. In these years, China's imports of machinery and transport equipment from the United States in U.S. dollar terms recorded an annual growth rate of between 50 percent and 163 percent. In 1985, China's imports of aircraft from the United States alone amounted to 657 million U.S. dollars, which was nearly as large as the sum of its foodstuff and crude material imports from the United States. In contrast, China had little interest in consumer goods imports from the United States, as reflected by the relatively small amounts of miscellaneous manufactures in Table 3.16. This was due partly to the lack of competitiveness of consumer goods from the United States in the Chinese market and partly to China's reluctance to spend its "precious" foreign exchange earnings on consumer items. Hong Kong, Taiwan, and other neighboring countries were able to export most of the consumer items needed by the Chinese at relatively low prices.

3.7   Conclusion

Under the economic reforms in China, foreign trade has ceased to be a residual of the central economic plan, and its growth is no longer limited by the size of shortages and surpluses in the economic plan. Exports and imports expand or contract for their own sake and do not have to undergo the process of elaborate material balancing. The growth and structure of exports are determined by, among other things, the system of export incentives, while the growth and structure of imports are determined chiefly by the government's investment policy.

In response to the export incentive scheme implemented under the economic reforms, manufactured exports, particularly textiles and clothing, expanded rapidly in the period between 1979 and 1985. The expansion was undoubtedly due, to a certain extent, to the growth of foreign investment, which was attracted by the relatively low cost of labor. It was, of course, also due to the growth of the level of manufactured exports originating from domestically owned enterprises, which were motivated by the incentives provided by the profit-sharing and foreign exchange retention schemes. Labor-intensive goods were exported by foreign investors for their competitiveness in the world market, but they were exported by domestic enterprises for the "profits" and foreign exchange quotas that could be retained by them or for the simple reason of fulfilling the export target assigned to them. Heavy industrial exports were also seen to have been boosted under the government's efforts to promote foreign exchange earnings. For instance, the exports of oil and coal witnessed a rapid increase during this period even though the domestic sector continued to be faced with shortages of energy following the 1978 modernization drive.

The increased manufactured exports were destined mainly for relatively more industrialized countries, including Hong Kong, Japan, and the United States. The increase in manufactured exports to Japan was relatively insignificant presumably because of the protective measures adopted by Japan against imports. In contrast, there was rapid growth in China's manufactured exports to the relatively open markets of Hong Kong and the United States. Hong Kong increased not only its domestic absorption but also its reexports of China's manufactured goods. Hong Kong's imports increased so rapidly that it remained one of China's most important export markets throughout the period. The growth in China's direct and indirect exports to the United States was, however, seriously limited by the quotas imposed by the latter on textiles and clothing.

The rapid growth of China's exports was aimed at raising the economy's capacity of importing foreign technology. However, the level of imports, in view of their close association with the level of investment, did not grow hand in hand with exports. During the time of economic readjustment, for instance, imports were curtailed for fear that they would worsen the economic imbalance brought about by the Four Modernizations drive in 1978. The accumulation of foreign exchange reserves and the improvement in macroeconomic imbalance led China to ease its curb on imports in 1984 and 1985. During these two years, the level of imports rose so rapidly that China incurred a trade deficit of more than 10 billion U.S. dollars.

China's imports were concentrated on technological items and intermediate goods, supplied mainly by Japan, the United States, and other developed countries. The changes in China's import policy had the greatest impact on the technology imports from Japan and the United States while causing relatively insignificant fluctuations in the imports of intermediate goods. There was a tendency for Japan to benefit most in terms of its exports to China during China's import booms as well as to suffer the most drastic cut in its exports to China during the contraction of China's imports. Among all the suppliers of imports to China, Hong Kong was the only one to enjoy incessantly rising exports to China. They rose so fast during the period between 1978 and 1985 that, starting in 1983, Hong Kong, China's traditionally most important source of net foreign exchange earnings, was transformed into China's second largest supplier of imports after Japan. China's bilateral trade balance with Hong Kong even turned into a deficit in 1985. The change signified the increasing importance of the imports from Hong Kong and other industrialized developing countries to China.

Appendix C
The commodity composition of China's foreign trade with communist countries, 1984–7

China's foreign trade with communist countries witnessed relatively low rates of growth during economic reforms when compared with the country's trade with the West. CIA trade statistics showed that in the period between 1978 and 1985 China's trade with communist countries went up by only 58 percent, compared to the 285 percent increase in its trade with the West, both in U.S. dollars. Part of the reason for the relatively slow growth was that such trade had been adversely affected by China's reform program that accorded individual enterprises and local governments with foreign trade decision-making power. These enterprises and local governments, lacking information about the market conditions for their exports and imports, found it more convenient to deal with Western traders than with the trading organizations of other communist countries. Though they received from Western traders scouting the country for trade opportunities a wide range of information about goods available from and marketable in the West, they had no knowledge of how to trade with their counterparts in other communist countries. Therefore, the growth of China's trade with the West to a certain extent took place at the expense of its trade with communist countries.

The discussion in this appendix is based on official statistics first made available in 1984. As discussed in Appendix A, these statistics inevitably suffer from valuation problems that arise as a result of the inconvertibility of the currencies involved. Because of currency inconvertibility, barter between China and other communist countries was often practiced, in which case there was no objective valuation of the goods traded. Therefore, official statistics had to be compiled based on either domestic prices,

Table C.1. China's exports to communist countries, 1984–7 (in million yuan)

	1984	1985	1986	1987
Food and live animals chiefly for food	722	2,209	2,738	2,925
	(19.68)	(31.95)	(27.56)	(26.76)
Beverages and tobacco	34	46	51	86
	(0.93)	(0.67)	(0.51)	(0.79)
Crude materials, inedible, except fuels	725	1,250	1,871	2,053
	(19.78)	(18.08)	(18.83)	(18.78)
Mineral fuels, lubricants, and related materials	805	886	881	1,194
	(21.94)	(12.81)	(8.87)	(10.92)
Animal and vegetable oils, fats, and waxes	43	63	69	34
	(1.18)	(0.91)	(0.69)	(0.31)
Chemicals and related products	180	296	460	594
	(4.90)	(4.29)	(4.63)	(5.43)
Manufactured goods classified chiefly by materials	658	1,024	1,921	1,705
	(17.96)	(14.82)	(19.34)	(15.60)
Machinery and transport equipment	113	187	312	515
	(3.09)	(2.70)	(3.14)	(4.71)
Miscellaneous manufactured articles	387	942	1,618	1,802
	(10.55)	(13.62)	(16.29)	(16.49)
Commodities, not classified elsewhere	—	11	13	23
		(0.15)	(0.13)	(0.21)
Total	3,667	6,913	9,934	10,931

Notes: Communist countries here include North Korea, Bulgaria, Czechoslovakia, the German Democratic Republic, Poland, Rumania, the Soviet Union, Yugoslavia, and Cuba. Figures in parentheses are percentage shares.
Source: General Administration of Customs, *China's Customs Statistics* (Hong Kong: Economic Information and Agency, January 1985, pp. 36–101, January 1986, pp. 34–98, January 1987, pp. 35–100, and January 1988, pp. 40–107).

which could differ significantly from international prices because of price irrationality, or prices of "comparable" goods in Western trade. Neither method could adequately reflect the actual values of the goods traded. For this reason, the statistics presented in this appendix must be treated with extreme caution.

Table C.1 shows the composition of China's exports to communist countries, which include North Korea, Bulgaria, Czechoslovakia, the German Democratic Republic, Poland, Rumania, the Soviet Union, Yugoslavia, and Cuba. Other communist countries are not included in the official statistics presumably because of their negligible importance in China's total trade. One important feature of China's exports to communist countries was that they were concentrated mainly on agricultural and mineral items, which as a whole accounted for 64 percent of the country's total exports to communist countries in both 1984 and 1985. The percentage dropped to about 56 percent in 1986 and 1987, due mainly to the relatively rapid growth of industrial exports. Food, crude materials, and mineral fuels were all of prominent importance. This export pattern differs considerably from the pattern of China's exports to the West, of which less than 50 percent were minerals and agricultural products. The main reason was that manufactured goods, particularly light industrial products, were relatively unimportant in China's exports to communist countries, which tended to place low priority on consumption in their economic and foreign trade plans.

It is worth noting that China's imports from communist countries comprised mainly heavy industrial products, which included chemicals, semimanufactured goods, and machinery and transport equipment. As shown in Table C.2, these three items alone accounted for as much as between 79 and 86 percent of China's imports from communist countries between 1984 and 1985. It is also worth noting that there was an 89 percent increase in China's exports to as well as imports from communist countries in 1985, the year of an investment boom in China. A precipitous rise such as this was possible only if there were relatively ample trade opportunities existing between China and other communist countries that had not been fully exploited during the earlier years of the economic reforms. In the mid-1980s, China, in the face of rising protectionism against its exports and increased difficulties in opening up new markets in the West, was forced to turn to the Eastern-bloc countries as an outlet for its exports. Table C.3 shows that major growth in China's exports to communist countries took place mainly in the markets of Poland, Czechoslovakia, and the Soviet Union. These three countries could readily expand their trade with China without upsetting their own economic plans either because they were relatively open (Poland and Czechoslovakia) or because they were relatively large in size (the Soviet Union).

Table C.3 also shows that China's bilateral trade with individual communist countries was largely balanced, as is true for the trade between most centrally planned economies. The only exceptions were Rumania, Yugoslavia, and the German Democratic Republic, with each of whom China incurred a large import surplus. In recent years, many of the East-

Table C.2. China's imports from communist countries, 1984–7 (in million yuan)

	1984	1985	1986	1987
Food and live animals chiefly for food	387	435	420	368
	(8.15)	(4.83)	(3.25)	(2.97)
Beverages and tobacco	—	6	9	19
		(0.07)	(0.07)	(0.15)
Crude materials, inedible, except fuels	435	644	1,084	841
	(9.17)	(7.17)	(8.39)	(6.79)
Mineral fuels, lubricants, and related materials	127	128	203	503
	(2.67)	(1.42)	(1.57)	(4.06)
Animal and vegetable oils, fats, and waxes	—	—	—	—
Chemicals and related products	1,223	1,676	1,411	1,616
	(25.73)	(18.64)	(10.92)	(13.05)
Manufactured goods classified chiefly by materials	1,596	3,102	4,781	4,411
	(33.63)	(34.49)	(36.99)	(35.61)
Machinery and transport equipment	947	2,950	4,936	4,506
	(19.96)	(32.80)	(38.19)	(36.38)
Miscellaneous manufactured articles	34	47	72	79
	(0.69)	(0.53)	(0.56)	(0.64)
Commodities not classified elsewhere	—	6	8	43
		(0.06)	(0.06)	(0.35)
Total	4,750	8,994	12,924	12,386

Note: Figures in parentheses are percentage shares.
Source: Same as Table C.1.

ern European countries have incurred substantial external debts with the West and have had to service their debts by expanding their hard-currency exports. These countries no longer maintain strictly balanced bilateral trade with communist and noncommunist countries. Therefore, it was not unusual for China to incur large import surpluses with some of these countries.

Tables C.4 to C.7 show the commodity composition of China's trade with its major communist trading partners: the Soviet Union, Rumania, North Korea, and Poland. China imported mainly chemicals, semi-

Table C.3. China's trade with major communist countries, 1984–7 (in million yuan)

	1984		1985		1986		1987	
	Exports	Imports	Exports	Imports	Exports	Imports	Exports	Imports
North Korea	533 (14.54)	.642 (13.56)	701 (10.14)	787 (8.75)	876 (8.88)	970 (7.44)	1,042 (9.21)	890 (7.01)
Bulgaria	30 (0.82)	84 (1.77)	61 (0.88)	116 (1.29)	90 (0.91)	276 (2.12)	219 (1.93)	321 (2.53)
Czechoslovakia	271 (7.39)	339 (7.16)	674 (9.75)	745 (8.28)	867 (8.79)	1,053 (8.07)	991 (8.76)	1,197 (9.43)
German Democratic Republic	218 (5.94)	335 (7.07)	360 (5.21)	848 (9.43)	787 (7.98)	1,016 (7.79)	959 (8.47)	1,085 (8.54)
Poland	289 (7.88)	327 (6.90)	812 (11.75)	738 (8.21)	1,573 (15.94)	1,890 (14.78)	1,516 (13.39)	1,732 (13.64)
Rumania	707 (19.28)	1,011 (21.35)	835 (12.08)	1,746 (19.41)	936 (9.49)	1,928 (14.78)	1,438 (12.71)	1,665 (13.11)
Soviet Union	1,379 (37.61)	1,593 (33.34)	3,096 (44.79)	3,042 (33.82)	4,302 (43.60)	5,193 (39.81)	4,688 (41.42)	4,849 (38.18)
Yugoslavia	21 (0.57)	120 (2.53)	23 (0.33)	655 (7.28)	108 (1.09)	422 (3.24)	169 (1.49)	672 (5.29)
Cuba	219 (5.79)	299 (6.31)	349 (5.05)	317 (3.52)	329 (3.33)	296 (2.27)	296 (2.62)	288 (2.27)
Total	3,667	4,750	6,913	8,994	9,868	13,044	11,318	12,699

Note: Figures in parentheses are percentage shares.
Source: Same as Table C.1.

Table C.4. Commodity composition of China's trade with the Soviet Union, 1984–7 (in million yuan)

	1984		1985		1986		1987	
	Exports	Imports	Exports	Imports	Exports	Imports	Exports	Imports
Food and live animals chiefly for food	344	2	1,469	4	1,675	1	1,790	15
Beverages and tobacco	—	—	—	—	1	0	—	—
Crude materials, inedible, except for fuels	467	263	661	396	1,060	963	1,368	692
Mineral fuels, lubricants, and related materials	—	—	—	—	63	—	—	256
Animal and vegetable oils, fats, and waxes	33	—	30	—	44	—	21	—
Chemicals and related products	37	389	73	611	58	421	105	826
Manufactured goods classified chiefly by material	304	626	439	1,173	832	2,035	567	2,108
Machinery and transport equipment	10	307	67	850	100	1,650	166	919
Miscellaneous manufactured articles	184	6	356	6	550	8	670	14
Commodities, not classified elsewhere	—	—	—	1	—	—	—	20
Total	1,379	1,593	3,096	3,042	4,320	5,193	4,688	4,849

Source: Same as Table C.1.

107

Table C.5. Commodity composition of China's trade with Rumania, 1984–7 (in million yuan)

	1984		1985		1986		1987	
	Exports	Imports	Exports	Imports	Exports	Imports	Exports	Imports
Food and live animals chiefly for food	62	—	77	—	68	—	164	—
Beverages and tobacco	4	—	5	—	12	—	8	—
Crude materials, inedible, except for fuels	74	67	137	78	155	9	150	8
Mineral fuels, lubricants, and related materials	347	—	362	—	208	—	523	—
Animal and vegetable oils, fats, and waxes	—	—	—	—	1	—	1	—
Chemicals and related products	56	470	76	597	125	547	103	461
Manufactured goods classified chiefly by material	67	223	63	499	138	618	147	397
Machinery and transport equipment	51	245	56	567	124	746	159	793
Miscellaneous manufactured articles	44	5	47	4	99	10	180	5
Commodities, not classified elsewhere	—	—	10	1	6	—	3	—
Total	707	1,011	835	1,746	936	1,928	1,438	1,665

Source: Same as Table C.1.

Table C.6. Commodity composition of China's trade with North Korea, 1984–7 (in million yuan)

	1984		1985		1986		1987	
	Exports	Imports	Exports	Imports	Exports	Imports	Exports	Imports
Food and live animal chiefly for food	21	77	46	124	65	133	74	77
Beverages and tobacco	—	—	—	6	—	8	—	19
Crude materials, inedible, except fuels	11	68	70	116	97	105	159	102
Mineral fuels, lubricants, and related products	448	125	508	125	599	203	654	220
Animals and vegetable oils, fats, and waxes	6	—	20	—	10	—	4	—
Chemicals and related products	12	29	15	5	24	29	46	35
Manufactured goods classified chiefly by material	4	342	16	411	58	486	52	426
Machinery and transport equipment	30	—	19	—	18	6	36	—
Miscellaneous manufactured articles	1	2	5	—	5	—	8	—
Total	533	642	701	787	876	970	1,042	890

Source: Same as Table C.1.

Table C.7. Commodity composition of China's trade with Poland, 1984–7 (in million yuan)

	1984		1985		1986		1987	
	Exports	Imports	Exports	Imports	Exports	Imports	Exports	Imports
Food and live animals chiefly for food	99	7	261	—	450	—	421	—
Beverages and tobacco	—	—	—	—	6	—	—	—
Crude materials, inedible, except fuels	35	14	119	—	187	1	164	11
Mineral fuels, lubricants, and related materials	5	—	11	—	10	—	13	—
Animal and vegetable oils, fats, and waxes	—	—	2	—	8	—	4	—
Chemicals and related products	20	89	31	95	99	149	122	148
Manufactured goods classified chiefly by material	80	156	171	290	364	744	298	752
Machinery and transport equipment	—	59	2	351	20	974	37	790
Miscellaneous manufactured articles	50	2	216	1	426	16	266	30
Commodities, not classified elsewhere	—	—	—	—	4	5	190	—
Total	289	327	812	738	1,573	1,890	1,516	1,732

Source: Same as Table C.1.

manufactured goods, and machinery and equipment from all of these countries except North Korea, being the only relatively underdeveloped country among the four. The patterns of trade between China and these countries differed from one another mainly because the composition of China's exports to these countries was different: The Soviet Union was an important market for all of the major exports of China except mineral fuels, of which the Soviet Union was itself a major producer and exporter; Rumania was mainly a market for mineral fuels; and Poland, like the Soviet Union, imported a wide range of goods from China, including miscellaneous manufactured goods. In its trade with North Korea, China exported mainly mineral fuels and imported mainly food items, crude materials, and semimanufactured goods. The prospect for a rapid growth of trade between the two countries was limited not only because North Korea was relatively small and underdeveloped but also because it remained a strictly centrally planned economy with little interest in expanding its trade with the rest of the world.

In sum, owing to the economic reforms, China's foreign trade has focused increasingly on the West, leaving other communist countries a largely underexploited market for China's exports. These countries could readily absorb a large increase in imports from China while supplying it with semimanufactured goods and technologically advanced machinery and equipment for its investment needs. This explains why China's trade with other communist countries has been relatively small but volatile in past years.

The commodity composition of China's foreign trade, 1986–7

The commodity composition of China's exports and imports in the period between 1985 and 1987 is presented in Table C.8. Figures in the table are official statistics published in the *Statistical Yearbook of China*. Official statistics, instead of CIA statistics, are used because the latter were still not available at the time when the present chapter was written. All figures in the table are expressed in U.S. dollars, as are figures in Tables 3.3 and 3.6.

It should be noted that these official trade statistics are based on China's customs statistics, whereas CIA trade statistics are based on the customs statistics of China's trading partners (Appendix A). Also, the official classification of commodities appear to be different from the CIA classification, as evident from the significant difference between Tables 3.3 and C.8 in their statistics on the commodity composition of foreign trade in 1985. For instance, according to CIA statistics China exported 6.7 billion U.S. dollars of miscellaneous manufactured articles in 1985, but official statis-

Table C.8. Commodity composition of China's foreign trade, 1985–7 (in million U.S.$)

	Exports			Imports		
	1985	1986	1987	1985	1986	1987
Food and live animal chiefly for food	3,803	4,448	4,781	1,553	1,625	2,443
Beverages and tobacco	105	119	175	206	172	263
Crude materials, inedible, except fuels	2,653	2,908	3,650	3,236	3,143	3,321
Mineral fuels, lubricants, and related materials	7,132	3,683	4,544	172	504	539
Animal and vegetable oils, fats, and waxes	135	114	81	122	205	349
Chemicals and related products	1,358	1,733	2,235	4,469	3,771	5,008
Manufactured goods classified chiefly by material	4,493	5,886	8,570	11,898	11,192	9,730
Machinery and transport equipment	772	1,094	1,741	16,239	16,781	14,607
Miscellaneous manufactured articles	3,486	4,948	6,273	1,902	1,877	1,878
Commodities, not classified elsewhere	3,413	6,009	7,387	2,455	3,634	5,078
Total	27,350	30,942	39,437	42,252	42,904	43,216

Sources: State Statistical Bureaus, *Statistical Yearbook of China* (Hong Kong: Economic Information and Agency, 1987, pp. 520–1, and 1988, pp. 722–3).

tics suggest that only 3.5 billion U.S. dollars of such products were exported in that year. By contrast, for the same year, CIA statistics suggest that China exported 1.3 billion U.S. dollars of "commodities not classified elsewhere" (SITC 9) whereas official statistics record a much larger export of 3.4 billion U.S. dollars. Presumably, some manufactured goods classified under "miscellaneous manufactured articles" in the CIA's statistics have been classified under "commodities not classified elsewhere" in official statistics. For these reasons, figures in Table C.8 are not strictly comparable with those in Tables 3.3 and 3.6. For consistency, the following discussion is based entirely on official statistics.

One of the most important changes in the commodity composition of China's foreign trade in 1986 and 1987 was the significant decline in the share of minerals and agricultural products in total exports. As shown in Table C.8, their share decreased from 51 percent in 1985 to 36 percent in 1986 and decreased further to 34 percent in 1987. The decline occurred in the wake of a drastic decline in China's oil exports and a precipitous increase in its manufactured exports during these two years: Oil exports decreased by 37 percent, or 2.5 billion U.S. dollars, while manufactured exports increased by as much as 94 percent, or 13 billion U.S. dollars. The decrease in oil exports was due primarily to the decrease in the international price of oil [which decreased by 37 percent in terms of Kuwaitian crude oil between 1985 and 1987 (International Monetary Fund 1988, p. 463)], while the increase in manufactured exports was due primarily to the rapid expansion of the textile and garment industries, made possible by a large increase in investment from Hong Kong, which was attracted by the low labor costs and increasingly favorable investment conditions across the border, and from other countries. Given that the expansion of manufactured exports more than compensated for the decline of primary exports, there was a net increase in total exports, by as much as 12 billion U.S. dollars.

As for imports, their composition changed less dramatically than did the composition of exports during 1986 and 1987. The U.S. dollar values of all import items changed only slightly, with the exception of "commodities not classified elsewhere," which went up by 2.6 billion U.S. dollars. The exceptionally rapid increase in this category of imports was related to the rapid growth of investment from Hong Kong that brought its own technology, equipment, and materials. As a result of the general decline in the growth rates of manufactured imports, total imports went up by only 2 percent, compared to the 44 percent growth of total exports. The rapid export growth and slow import growth suggest that efforts were being made by the government to reduce the level of the trade deficit, which decreased from 14 billion U.S. dollars in 1985 to 12 billion U.S.

Table C.9. China's foreign trade with developed, developing, and
communist countries, 1985 – 7 (in million U.S.$)

	Exports			Imports		
	1985	1986	1987	1985	1986	1987
Developed countries	11,382	10,437	13,831	23,527	22,211	20,275
	(43.92)	(38.64)	(39.85)	(68.53)	(67.14)	(60.71)
Developing countries	11,797	12,839	16,556	8,094	6,952	9,780
	(45.52)	(47.53)	(47.70)	(23.78)	(20.01)	(29.28)
Hong Kong	5,746	7,562	10,062	5,148	3,956	6,563
Communist countries	2,327	2,909	3,114	2,647	3,808	3,169
	(8.98)	(10.77)	(9.22)	(7.71)	(11.51)	(9.49)

Note: Figures in parentheses are percentage shares.
Source: The Editorial Board of the Almanac of China's Foreign Economic Relations and
Trade, *Almanac of China's Foreign Economic Relations and Trade* (Beijing: The China
Prospect Publishing House, 1988, p. 363).

dollars in 1986 and decreased further to less than 4 billion U.S. dollars in
1987. The government's trade policy resembled that which was employed
in the early 1980s in reaction to the trade imbalance created by the 1978
Four Modernizations drive.

The foreign trade relations of China with communist- and noncom-
munist-bloc countries in the period between 1985 and 1987 are shown in
Table C.9. Most notable in the table is the decline in the relative importance of developed countries in China's foreign trade with the rest of the
world in 1986 and 1987. The share of developed countries in China's total
trade decreased from 47 percent in 1985 to 41 percent in 1987, whereas
the share of developing countries went up from 29 percent in 1985 to 32
percent in 1987. The reason for these changes is twofold. First, as China
attracted a large increase in foreign investment in labor-intensive, export-
processing industries, it became increasingly dependent on Hong Kong
and other developing countries for supplies of machinery and intermediate inputs as well as for the reexport of finished products. Second, as
China curtailed domestic investment in heavy industry for fear of worsening inflation, it also curtailed its imports of iron and steel and machinery
and equipment from developed countries, especially Japan. In short,
although it is evident that enterprises, local governments, and foreign
investors were playing an increasingly important part in the making of
import decisions, China's import relations with the rest of the world were
still very much under central control.

China's exports are likely to become increasingly concentrated in labor-intensive products, and this will have an important implication for China's foreign trade relations with the rest of the world in the near future. As Hong Kong becomes increasingly integrated into China, the trade pattern of China will become increasingly dominated by the trade pattern of Hong Kong. That is, Hong Kong manufacturers will take advantage of low labor costs in China and expand their operations there; they will continue to export such labor-intensive products as garments and footwear to Hong Kong for reexport to developed countries. Faced with increased competition from low-cost imports from China, developed countries such as the United States and the European countries are likely to reassess their trade relations with China and strengthen their trade barriers against China's exports. Under these circumstances, China can no longer be excluded from bilateral or multilateral trade negotiations between developed and developing countries.

PART II

Foreign trade, shortage, and inflation

CHAPTER 4

Foreign trade and consumer goods imbalance: theory

One of the most important features of China's foreign trade is that it fluctuates closely with the level of investment in fixed capital (Chapter 1). The main reason why they fluctuate closely with each other is that when the country raises its level of investment a large proportion of the required machinery and equipment will invariably be imported from abroad, and when the country lowers the level of investment imports of machinery and equipment will be reduced, with foreign trade serving mainly to balance consumer goods and raw material shortages. Because of its close association with investment, the volume of foreign trade, though small in proportion to national output, can have significant effects on the level of aggregate production and consumption, thus indirectly affecting the degree of consumer goods imbalance, or the inflationary pressure, in the economy.

The volume of foreign trade can have direct effects on the degree of consumer goods imbalance as well. On the one hand, any changes in exports will affect the availability of domestic goods for consumption, since the exports of consumer goods will compete directly with domestic consumption, whereas the exports of raw materials, such as petroleum and coal, will reduce their own supplies to industrial uses at home, thus competing indirectly with domestic consumption. On the other hand, change in exports or imports of capital goods will cause a change in the amount of resources employed in the production of consumer goods, thus affecting their supply.

How significantly the consumer goods imbalance might be affected by changes in foreign trade depends on, first, the growth rate of foreign trade, second, the amount of domestic resources mobilized and invested in conjunction with capital goods imports, and third, the allocation of investment resources between the production of consumer goods and the production of nonconsumer goods. The present study is concerned with the case where there is a significant expansion or contraction in foreign trade and where all capital goods imports require proportionally large amounts of domestic resources to work with. In this case, investment will

119

rise or fall quickly with foreign trade, thus having a significant effect on consumer goods imbalance.

The purpose of this chapter is to analyze theoretically the effects of foreign trade on consumer goods imbalance. Section 4.1 reviews the literature on the relationship between investment and consumer goods imbalance advanced by Chinese economists. Section 4.2 develops a two-sector, open economy model, in which the economy is assumed to be strictly centrally planned, and Section 4.3 uses the model to analyze the effect of foreign trade expansion on the level of consumer goods imbalance. Section 4.4 modifies the model by taking into consideration the effects of economic reforms and analyzes with the modified model how a foreign trade expansion may affect the degree of consumer goods imbalance. Section 4.5 discusses whether foreign trade is less inflationary after the reforms than it was before. Finally, Section 4.6 provides a brief summary of the analysis.

4.1   Foreign trade and consumer goods imbalance: a clarification of the concept developed by Chinese economists

The problem of macroeconomic imbalance in a centrally planned economy first attracted the attention of Chinese economists as far back as the late 1950s, during which years the country invested heavily in the heavy industrial sector while paying relatively little attention to other sectors.[1] Many of these economists advocated giving "priority growth" to producer goods, based mainly on the Marxian formula, $I(V + M) > IIC$, in which I and II refer to the producer goods and consumer goods sectors, respectively, V represents wage bill, M represents surplus, and C represents constant capital.[2] This formula suggests that, in order for the economy to achieve expanded reproduction, the output of producer goods should more than satisfy the combined demand for producer goods of the producer goods and consumer goods sectors in the current period.[3] In recent years, the priority growth argument continues to find support from those Chinese economists who concentrate on the same formula, in spite of many previous studies devoted to showing its irrelevance to the argument.[4] To achieve the priority growth of producer goods, these economists argue, the economy should invest more heavily, or bring about more rapid technological change, in the producer goods sector than it should in the consumer goods sector.

Nevertheless, most of the Chinese economists who argue for the priority growth principle fail to show that the Marxian formula does indeed imply the principle. To explain, I make use of equation (2.1), which is based on the Marxian labor theory of value, and set

$$P_1Q_1 = (l_1w_1 + m_1 + \pi_1)Q_1, \tag{4.1}$$

$$P_2Q_2 = (l_2w_2 + m_2 + \pi_2)Q_2, \tag{4.2}$$

where l is physical units of labor input per unit of output, m is the average cost of material input, w is the wage rate, π is the profit rate, Q is the level of output, P is the price, and subscripts 1 and 2 denote producer goods and consumer goods, respectively. Equations (4.1) and (4.2) state that the value of each product is equal to the sum of labor costs, material costs, and profit. Based on these two equations, the Marxian formula can be rewritten as

$$P_1Q_1 > m_1Q_1 + m_2Q_2, \tag{4.3}$$

or

$$\frac{Q_1}{Q_2} > \frac{m_2}{P_1 - m_1}. \tag{4.4}$$

P_1Q_1 is the value of the output of producer goods and $m_1Q_1 + m_2Q_2$ is the aggregate demand for producer goods. Inequality (4.4) indicates that so long as the output ratio of producer goods to consumer goods is greater than $m_2/(P_1 - m_1)$, the supply of producer goods will more than satisfy the demand.

Note that to give priority growth to producer goods is to raise the ouput ratio in the inequality. The question then arises of whether the ouput ratio should be raised, or whether the producer goods sector should be given priority growth. The inequality, however, provides no answer to this question; it only specifies the range of the output ratio of the two sectors that is consistent with the Marxian growth condition and does not make any reference to how the output ratio should change over time. Therefore, it cannot be established from the Marxian formula whether priority growth should or should not be given to the producer goods sector.

Does the Marxian formula represent a necessary condition for expanded reproduction? It can be easily shown that the Marxian formula is the condition for expanded reproduction only if the surplus generated from the producer goods sector constitutes the only element of domestic saving or if the production of consumer goods is always entirely consumed. It can also be easily shown that, as Liu (1962) argues, excessive growth in the producer goods sector can lead to a consumer goods shortage.

To illustrate, let ES_i be the supply of goods i in excess of current consumption. For the economy as a whole, there will be expanded reproduction if the level of saving S is positive,[5] where

$$S = ES_1 + ES_2, \tag{4.5}$$

given that

$$ES_1 = P_1Q_1 - (m_1Q_1 + m_2Q_2), \tag{4.6}$$

$$ES_2 = P_2Q_2 - (l_1w_1Q_1 + l_2w_2Q_2). \tag{4.7}$$

That is, expanded reproduction will be possible if the total value of the outputs of the two sectors exceeds the value of their consumption. Note that the Marxian growth condition, which implies ES_1 must be positive [inequality (4.3)], is a necessary condition for expanded reproduction only if ES_2 is zero or negative. ES_2 will be equal to zero when the domestic production of consumer goods is exactly equal to their (effective) demand, and ES_2 will be negative when the domestic production of consumer goods falls short of their (effective) demand. In both cases, saving has to be generated entirely from the excess of the output of producer goods over their consumption. Note also that when ES_1 is zero or negative, the case when the Marxian inequality is not satisfied, expanded production, or positive saving, is still possible so long as ES_2 is positive and greater than ES_1 in absolute terms. Incidentally, the sum of ES_1 and ES_2 is equal to the level of aggregate profits, Π:

$$\Pi = ES_1 + ES_2. \tag{4.8}$$

As long as the profit rates, π_1 and π_2, are positive as argued by Marx, Π (or S) must also be positive, and expanded reproduction will be possible.

The amount of saving generated by ES_1 and ES_2 may be allocated between the producer goods and consumer goods sectors to achieve the desired rates of growth in the two sectors. Liu (1962) correctly points out that, under consumer goods shortage, the growth of national output hinges crucially on the growth of producer goods. However, he also points out that if the growth of producer goods exceeds a certain limit, consumer goods imbalance will result. To understand more clearly his argument, write the production functions of the two goods as:

$$Q_1 = \frac{K_1}{k_1}, \tag{4.9}$$

$$Q_2 = \frac{K_2}{k_2}, \tag{4.10}$$

where K_i is the amount of capital allocated to sector i and k_i is the capital coefficient of sector i. The stock of capital is an effective input constraint in the two production functions. From equations (4.9) and (4.10), we get

$$\frac{Q_1}{Q_2} = \frac{K_1k_2}{K_2k_1}, \tag{4.11}$$

which states that the output ratio of producer goods to consumer goods is determined by the allocation of the capital stock between the two sectors, given the technology of production. If priority growth is to be given to producer goods, the newly increased capital will have to be so allocated that the rate of increase in capital stock in the producer goods sector is greater than the rate of increase in capital stock in the consumer goods sector, and vice versa. How will such a policy affect consumer goods imbalance?

Based on equation (4.7), consumer goods balance obtains when $ES_2 = 0$ or when

$$\frac{Q_1}{Q_2} = \frac{P_2 - l_2 w_2}{l_1 w_1}. \tag{4.12}$$

This ratio is a constant given P_2, w_1, w_2, l_1, and l_2. From equations (4.11) and (4.12) is derived the ratio of capital stocks allocated to the two sectors that is consistent with consumer goods balance:

$$\frac{K_1}{K_2} = \frac{\sigma k_1}{k_2}, \tag{4.13}$$

where

$$\sigma = \frac{P_2 - l_2 w_2}{l_1 w_1}.$$

If the capital stock ratio is raised (lowered) to a level greater (smaller) than $\sigma k_1/k_2$, there will be a shortage (surplus) of consumer goods. Accordingly, an investment policy based on the priority growth principle will increase the capital stock ratio, K_1/K_2, thus raising the excess demand for consumer goods and inevitably leading to consumer goods shortages.

The relationship between consumer goods imbalance and the capital stock ratio can be further explained with the aid of Figure 4.1. In this figure, the ratio of capital stocks at which the consumer goods market is in equilibrium is given as OC. Line CC represents the time path of consumer goods balance, assuming σ, k_1, and k_2 to be constant. If the economy is initially at point A, at which consumer goods are in shortage, the amount of capital allocated to the producer goods sector should be reduced in order to achieve consumer goods balance. On the other hand, if the economy is initially at point B, at which consumer goods are in surplus, the amount of capital allocated to the producer goods sector should be increased in order to eliminate the surplus. To restore consumer goods balance, the economy can follow such adjustment path as AA' or BB'. Along AA', the producer goods sector is growing slower than is the con-

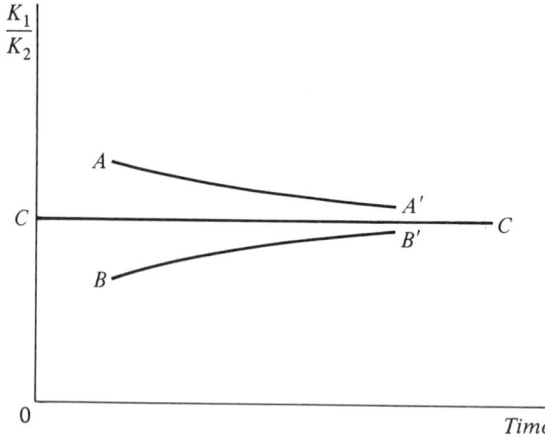

Figure 4.1. Allocation of capital and consumer goods imbalance.

sumer goods sector, and along BB' the producer goods sector is growing more rapidly than is the consumer goods sector. These two adjustment paths suggest that if the economy is to achieve consumer goods balance, it may give priority growth to either consumer goods or producer goods, depending on the initial position of resource allocation in the economy. Clearly, if priority growth is consistently given to producer goods, a shortage of consumer goods will eventually occur irrespective of the initial position of the economy.

Economic institution and consumer goods imbalance

The foregoing discussion is based strictly on the labor theory of value, which assumes that prices reflect the "values" (or labor costs) of the products. In reality, there are no objective rules for setting commodity prices and wage rates, and actual wage rates and commodity prices often function merely as a means of the planners to achieve certain fiscal and distributional goals. For this reason, P_i, w_i, m_i, and, therefore, π_i in equations (4.1) and (4.2) are to a great extent arbitrarily set by the government; once set, they will only be infrequently adjusted. Furthermore, the actual demand for consumer goods is subject to government control, and it can differ significantly from the unconstrained demand for consumer goods, $l_1 w_1 Q_1 + l_2 w_2 Q_2$. These institutional factors have important implications for our analysis of the effects of foreign trade on consumer goods imbalance.

In Figure 4.1, the consumer goods balance schedule CC can now be moved upward or downward depending on the government's policy concerning w_1, w_2, and P_2. Such movement can obviously affect the degree of imbalance in the consumer goods market. Nevertheless, economists observe that consumer goods are normally in short supply in centrally planned economies given the normally inflexible prices and wage rates. The shortage of consumer goods will occur, according to the model, insofar as the economy's production is biased toward producer goods, or, in the terms used by Chinese economists, if producer goods are given priority growth in the sense that they are allocated proportionally more capital than that which corresponds to consumer goods balance. Under these circumstances, producer goods are consistently in excess supply as enterprises stock up unused materials, turn out unusable products, or are allocated machinery and equipment which cannot be fully utilized. At the same time, consumer goods are consistently in short supply, forcing the government to ration their sales and inducing the growth of black markets for greatly sought-after commodities. The economy suffers repressed inflation as a result.

In the presence of repressed inflation, the growth of national output, or expanded reproduction, will now depend on the size of voluntary and involuntary saving. Let RD be the consumer goods demand which is repressed by the government, or the excess of notional demand for consumer goods $(l_1 w_1 Q_1 + l_2 w_2 Q_2)$ over actual demand. Then, the surplus of consumer goods in equation (4.7) should be rewritten as

$$ES_2 = P_2 Q_2 - (l_1 w_1 Q_1 + l_2 w_2 Q_2) + RD \qquad (4.7')$$

and total saving is equal to

$$S = ES_1 + ES_2 = \Pi + RD. \qquad (4.5')$$

The amount of involuntary saving is equal to RD and the amount of voluntary saving is Π. National output will grow with an increase in voluntary or involuntary saving. In the case where national output grows as a result of an increase in involuntary saving, consumer goods imbalance will be worsened with the accumulation of involuntary saving. The consumer goods imbalance so incurred is referred to by Chinese economists (Liao 1985; Xue 1985) as consumption–accumulation imbalance, under which current consumption is crowded out by the increase in investment. This imbalance problem will occur irrespective of whether resources saved are directed primarily toward the consumer goods or producer goods sectors. If they are directed primarily toward the producer goods sector, as is generally the case in China, the imbalance in the consumer goods market will be further worsened, leading to what Chinese economists refer to as an imbalance between heavy industry and light industry, a case where the expansion of heavy industrial output takes place at the expense of light industrial output.

Foreign trade and consumer goods imbalance

Chinese economists have not explicitly related the problem of consumer goods imbalance to foreign trade. However, the fact that foreign trade can be used as a means for making up for domestic shortages and as a channel of access to advanced technology suggests that foreign trade can affect consumer goods imbalance through its influence on both the supply of consumer goods and the allocation of investment resources between producer goods and consumer goods. To explain, let X_i and I_i be the exports and imports of goods i, respectively. Then, the surpluses (or excess supplies) of producer goods and consumer goods are equal to

$$ES_1' = ES_1 + (I_1 - X_1), \tag{4.14}$$

$$ES_2' = ES_2 + (I_2 - X_2). \tag{4.15}$$

From equation (4.15), the repressed demand for consumer goods is equal to

$$RD = (X_2 + l_1 w_1 Q_1 + l_2 w_2 Q_2) - (I_2 + P_2 Q_2). \tag{4.16}$$

The degree of consumer goods imbalance is represented by the level of RD. The higher the value of RD, the greater the degree of consumer goods imbalance. Equation (4.16) shows that the degree of consumer goods imbalance in terms of RD can be worsened (improved) by the export (import) of consumer goods. In China, imports of consumer goods, including food grains, have been relatively insignificant in most years during the past three decades, but they played an important part in making up for the shortage of consumer goods in years such as 1961 and 1962 when the domestic production of food and other consumer goods suffered from the backlash of the Great Leap Forward. Foreign trade under these circumstances will obviously contribute to an improvement in consumer goods imbalance. In contrast, consumer goods have played an important part in China's exports. Foreign trade is a process through which domestically produced consumer goods are converted into investment goods. Therefore, an increase in foreign trade would normally have a negative direct effect on consumer goods imbalance.

It can be argued that the major impact of foreign trade on consumer goods imbalance in China is associated with the role it plays in investment, however. The reason is that any investment decision would not only involve a change in the exports and imports of consumer goods (X_2

and I_2) but also lead to a change in the production of both producer goods and consumer goods (Q_1 and Q_2), which directly or indirectly affects the supply of and demand for consumer goods. This can be seen by combining equations (4.14) and (4.15):

$$S' = (\Pi + RD) + (I - X), \tag{4.17}$$

where $I = I_1 + I_2$, $X = X_1 + X_2$, and S' ($= ES_1' + ES_2'$) is the total amount of resources available for investment. $\Pi + RD$ is the amount of domestic saving and $I - X$ is the net amount of foreign resources available for investment. This equation shows that, under a policy to increase investment, the government can increase domestic saving by increasing RD, given the level of surpluses generated in the two sectors. To increase RD, the government can in turn increase the net exports of consumer goods [equation (4.16)]. The greater is RD, the greater will be S', and the greater will be the level of investment. If investment is concentrated in the producer goods sector, this policy will raise the total wage bill, thus worsening the degree of consumer goods imbalance. Conversely, if investment is concentrated in the consumer goods sector, consumer goods imbalance will improve.

It is of interest to note that, all along, Chinese economists have regarded foreign trade as a sector which has played a key role in China's economic development, even though foreign trade has been relatively small in comparison with national output. This is in sharp contrast with the view of most Western economists who have largely ignored any significant impacts that foreign trade changes might have on real output in centrally planned economies. The reason for the difference is that Chinese economists invariably associate the level of foreign trade with the level of investment, whereas Western economists do not (see Holzman 1974, pp. 113–18; Brada 1982, pp. 231–40). The tendency for Western economists to ignore the relationship between foreign trade and investment is understandable because in a market economy foreign trade cannot be distinguished from other profit-seeking economic activities except for the fact that it involves transactions with foreign residents. Foreign trade does not have any fixed relation to investment in such an economy, and its impact on the economy depends primarily on the relative size of the foreign trade sector.

The foregoing analysis provides a background for understanding the relationship between foreign trade and investment. It shows that foreign trade can influence national output and therefore consumer goods imbalance through its close relationship with the level of investment. The model provides a vigorous treatment of the imbalance concept that has been widely adopted by Chinese economists. However, the model, which is based strictly on the Marxian pricing formula, is not equipped for a vigorous analysis of the relationship between foreign trade and consumer goods imbalance. In the following section, I develop a two-sector model and provide a thorough analysis of the relationship.

4.2   The model

The economy consists of two markets, the goods market and the asset market. The goods market is characterized by a chronic excess demand for consumer goods (Kornai 1980, 1982), and, according to Walras's law, the asset market is characterized by a chronic excess supply of monetary assets. Since only one of these two markets is independently determined, our analysis concentrates on only one of these two markets, the goods market.

The economy produces two goods: consumer goods, C, and producer goods, G. The prices of C and G are fixed by the state, and the level of their outputs is determined by the amount of labor and capital allocated to them. The economy is capital scarce, to the extent that the production of the two goods is explicitly constrained by the limited supply of capital. As will be shown later, a relaxation of this assumption will not alter our analytical result. The producton functions are given as

$$C = a(\overline{C}, R)K''; \ a_c > 0, \ a_R < 0, \tag{4.18}$$

$$G = b(\overline{C}, R)K^*; \ b_c > 0, \ b_R < 0, \tag{4.19}$$

where

$$K = K'' + K^*, \tag{4.20}$$

a is the output–capital ratio of the consumer goods industry, b is the output–capital ratio of the producer goods industry, K'' is the amount of capital allocated to the consumer goods industry, K^* is the amount of capital allocated to the producer goods industry, $\overline{C}$ is the effective demand for consumer goods, and R is the involuntary accumulation of monetary assets.

In equations (4.18) and (4.19), the two output–capital ratios are functions of the physical input of labor (not shown), which is assumed to be fixed, and the purchasing power of wages, realized and unrealized. Since labor cannot be physically withdrawn from productive activities in the model, work effort reponds positively to realized purchasing power, or $\overline{C}$, and negatively to unrealized purchasing power, or R. As for the stock of capital, we assume that it rises or falls with producer goods imports, which are a proxy for the strength of the economy's desire to invest:

$$K = K(M^*). \tag{4.21}$$

This equation signifies that the key role foreign trade plays in China's economic development lies in its linkage with the level of investment. An increase in the level of producer goods imports will be associated with an increase in the level of investment, and vice versa.

Given the two production functions and the exports and imports of consumer goods, the supply of consumer goods, C_s, is equal to

$$C_s = a(\overline{C}, R)K'' + M'' - X'', \tag{4.22}$$

where M'' and X'' are imports and exports of consumer goods, respectively. In a shortage-ridden economy, the effective demand for consumer goods is constrained by its supply:

$$C_d > C_s = \overline{C}, \tag{4.23}$$

where C_d is the desired level of consumption.[6] A similar relationship is given in Barro and Grossman (1971), Muellbauer and Portes (1978), Portes (1979), and Moore (1985). Note that, since $\overline{C} = C_s$, a_c, and b_c reflect the feedback effect suggested by Howard (1976) that an initial decrease in the supply of consumer goods will cause a decrease in the supply of labor (by reducing their work effort in the present model), thus producing a second-round effect reducing the supply of both consumer goods and producer goods.[7]

The shortage of consumer goods is equal to the excess of their notional demand over their supply. Such a shortage will give rise to an involuntary accumulation of monetary assets. Accordingly, we have

$$C_d - C_s = R = W - U(\overline{C}) - \overline{C}, \tag{4.24}$$

where $W \equiv Lw$, with L representing the physical units of labor employed and w the wage rate, and U is the change in the demand for monetary assets, which is a positive function of the volume of transactions in the consumer goods market.[8] Equation (4.24) suggests that in a centrally planned economy a shortage of consumer goods is normally unavoidable because the economy does not allow the price mechanism to operate to equate the change in money supply, $W - \overline{C}$, with the change in money demand, $U(\overline{C})$. Were the price level and the interest rate allowed to adjust freely to equilibrate the money market, the shortage of consumer goods would disappear. However, because of price rigidity and the absence of a bond market, the money market will always be in disequilibrium $[W \neq U(\overline{C}) + \overline{C}]$, and, according to Walras's law, this must also be true for the consumer goods market ($C_d \neq C_s$). The two disequilibria are nothing but the two sides of the same coin.

In the producer goods market, the supply of producer goods, G_s, is the sum of domestic production and net imports:

$$G_s = b(\overline{C}, R)K^* + M^* - X^*, \tag{4.25}$$

where X^* and M^* are exports and imports of producer goods, respectively. The demand for producer goods consists of two components: The portion of demand which is independent of imports, denoted by $\overline{G}$, and the portion of demand which is associated with the demand for producer goods imports, denoted by $\tilde{G}$. Accordingly, we set

$$G_d = \overline{G} + \tilde{G}(M^*), \quad \tilde{G}_m = \frac{\partial \tilde{G}}{\partial M^*} > 0. \tag{4.26}$$

$\tilde{G}_m$ is the increased demand for producer goods resulting from an increase in the imports of producer goods by one unit. It is positive because in a centrally planned economy producer goods imports consist mainly of machinery and equipment, both of which require supplementary investment and additional raw materials.

Since producer goods are centrally allocated, with the state acting as the sole buying and selling agent, supply always equals demand:

$$G_s = G_d. \tag{4.27}$$

Taking into account equations (4.23) and (4.24), we rewrite equations (4.22) and (4.27) as

$$\overline{C} = a(\overline{C}, w)K'' + M'' - X'', \tag{4.28}$$

$$\overline{G} + \tilde{G}(M^*) = b(\overline{C}, w)K^* + M^* - X^*. \tag{4.29}$$

Both output–capital coefficients are now functions of $\overline{C}$ and w. Equation (4.28) determines the supply of consumer goods for domestic consumption and, together with equation (4.24), the shortage of consumer goods. Equation (4.29) is the equilibrium condition in the producer goods market.

The balance-of-payments constraint is

$$B = X'' + X^* - M'' - M^*. \tag{4.30}$$

B is the trade balance exogenously determined by the government. The decision of the government on the level of the trade balance is also a decision on the amount of imports to be financed by foreign borrowings and by the exports of domestic goods.

4.3   Foreign trade growth and internal disequilibrium

In China, foreign trade serves two major purposes: to make up for the shortage of domestic products and to supply the economy with technologically advanced machinery and capital equipment needed in the process of development. Each of these two purposes has an important implication for the degree of consumer goods imbalance. This can be seen clearly by solving the system of equations (4.28) and (4.29). Totally differentiating equations (4.28) and (4.29), we get

$$(1 - a_c K'')d\overline{C} - a \, dK'' = a_w K'' dw + dM'' - dX'', \qquad (4.31)$$

$$b_c K^* d\overline{C} + b \, dK^* = -b_w K^* dw + d\overline{G} + (\tilde{G}_m - 1)dM^* + dX^*. \qquad (4.32)$$

Taking into consideration the balance-of-payments constraint and the effect of producer goods imports on the capital stock, which can be written as

$$dM'' - dX'' = dX^* - dM^* - dB, \qquad (4.33)$$

$$dK^* = K_m dM^* - dK'', \qquad K_m = \frac{\partial K}{\partial M^*} > 0, \qquad (4.34)$$

equations (4.31) and (4.32) can be rewritten as

$$(1 - a_c K'')d\overline{C} - a \, dK'' = a_w K'' dw + dX^* - dM^* - dB, \qquad (4.35)$$

$$b_c K^* d\overline{C} - b \, dK'' = -b_w K^* dw + (\tilde{G}_m - bK_m - 1)dM^* + d\overline{G} + dX^*, \qquad (4.36)$$

or, alternatively,

$$(1 - a_c K'')d\overline{C} - a \, dK'' = a_w K'' dw + dM'' - dX'', \qquad (4.35')$$

$$b_c K^* d\overline{C} - b \, dK'' = -b_w K^* dw \\ + d\overline{G} + (\tilde{G}_m - bK_m)dM^* + dM'' - dX'' + dB. \qquad (4.36')$$

In the system represented by equations (4.35) and (4.36), X'' and M'' are not explicitly shown since they are assumed to change passively with changes in X^*, M^*, B, and $\overline{G}$. Similarly, in the system represented by equations (4.35') and (4.36'), X^* is not explicitly shown since it is assumed to change passively with changes in X'', M'', M^*, B, and $\overline{G}$. To distinguish between the two systems, we use subscripts 1 and 2 to denote the first and second systems, respectively. The model differs from Brada (1982) in that the former explicitly takes into account both the balance-of-payments constraint and the transfer of resources from one sector to the other as a result of changes in exports and imports whereas the latter does not.

Equations (4.35), (4.36), (4.35'), and (4.36') are solved to obtain the effects of changes in exports and imports on $\overline{C}$ and K'' (or K^*). Note that, given the total wage bill, changes in $\overline{C}$ reflect the changes in the degree of consumer goods imbalance or in inflationary pressure.

$$\frac{\partial \overline{\overline{C}}}{\partial \overline{\overline{G}}} = \frac{a}{H} = \frac{\partial \overline{C}}{\partial B}\bigg|_2, \tag{4.37}$$

$$\frac{\partial \overline{C}}{\partial X^*}\bigg|_1 = \frac{1}{H}(a - b), \tag{4.38}$$

$$\frac{\partial \overline{C}}{\partial M^*}\bigg|_1 = \frac{1}{H}[a(\tilde{G}_m - bK_m - 1) + b], \tag{4.39}$$

$$\frac{\partial \overline{C}}{\partial M^*}\bigg|_2 = \frac{1}{H}a(\tilde{G}_m - bK_m), \tag{4.40}$$

$$\frac{\partial \overline{C}}{\partial B}\bigg|_1 = \frac{b}{H}, \tag{4.41}$$

$$\frac{\partial K''}{\partial \overline{G}} = \frac{1}{H}(1 - a_cK'') = \frac{\partial K''}{\partial B}\bigg|_2, \tag{4.42}$$

$$\frac{\partial K''}{\partial X^*}\bigg|_1 = \frac{1}{H}[(1 - a_cK'') - b_cK^*], \tag{4.43}$$

$$\frac{\partial K''}{\partial M^*}\bigg|_1 = \frac{1}{H}[(1 - a_cK'')(\tilde{G}_m - bK_m - 1) + b_cK^*], \tag{4.44}$$

$$\frac{\partial K''}{\partial M^*}\bigg|_2 = \frac{1}{H}(\tilde{G}_m - bK_m)(1 - a_cK''), \tag{4.45}$$

$$\frac{\partial K''}{\partial B}\bigg|_1 = \frac{1}{H}b_cK^*, \tag{4.46}$$

where

$$H = (ab_cK^* + ba_cK'') - b. \tag{4.47}$$

In equation (4.47), a_cK'' and b_cK^* represent the effects of an increase in one unit of consumer goods consumed on the production of consumer goods and producer goods, respectively. Since both effects are positive but considerably smaller than unity, H is negative.

Growth of producer goods exports and consumer goods imports

Equation (4.37) shows the effect on domestic consumption of an increase in the autonomous demand for producer goods by the government, $\overline{G}$. Although the change has no apparent relation to foreign trade, it is shown to be equal to $\partial \overline{C}/\partial B |_2$, which is the effect on domestic consumption of an improvement in the balance of payments brought about by an increase in producer goods exports. The system does not distinguish between the effect of an increase in domestic demand for producer goods and the effect of an increase in producer goods exports. The result suggests that an increase in producer goods exports will worsen consumer goods imbalance. The reason for this result is that, as will be shown, an increase in producer goods exports will require a reallocation of capital from consumer goods production to producer goods production in order to keep the producer goods market in equilibrium.

In equation (4.38), $\partial \overline{C}/\partial X^* |_1$ is the effect on the level of consumer goods for domestic consumption of an increase in the exports of producer goods, together with an increase in the imports of consumer goods by the same amount (since $dX'' = dM^* = dB = 0$). As long as the output–capital ratio of consumer goods is greater than that of producer goods, that is, $a > b$, as is normally the case, $\partial \overline{C}/\partial X^* |_1$ must be negative. That is, an expansion of foreign trade involving an increase in the exports of producer goods and an equal increase in the imports of consumer goods will worsen the shortage of consumer goods. The reason is that, given the domestic demand for producer goods ($d\overline{G} = 0$), an increase in the exports of producer goods will necessitate a reallocation of capital from consumer goods to producer goods, thus reducing the domestic production of consumer goods. The decrease in consumer goods production will be less than fully compensated for by the increase in their imports because of the greater output–capital ratio in the consumer goods sector. More specifically, the decrease in the supply of consumer goods brought about by the reallocation of capital from the consumer goods sector to the producer goods sector will be greater than the increase in imports of consumer goods.

Growth of producer goods imports

In equation (4.39), $\partial \overline{C}/\partial M^* |_1$ is the effect on the supply of consumer goods of an increase in the imports of producer goods, financed entirely by an increase in the exports of consumer goods (since $dX^* = dM^* = dB = 0$). Here, the effect of an increase in the exports of consumer goods is given as $\partial \overline{C}/\partial B\,|_1$, which is negative and equal to b/H [equation (4.41)]; and the effect of an increase in the imports of producer goods is given as $a/H\,(\tilde{G}_m - bK_m - 1)$. The latter effect hinges crucially on the values of $\tilde{G}_m$ and K_m, $\tilde{G}_m$ being the increase in producer goods demand induced by the imports of producer goods and K_m being the rapidity with which producer goods imports are transformed into productive capital stock. In China, $\tilde{G}_m$ tends to be large since imported producer goods, which consist mainly of machinery and equipment, normally require large amounts of domestically produced producer goods to work with. Chao (1982, p. 125) suggests that in China each dollar of goods imported requires an average of two dollars of domestically produced producer goods to work with. That is, $\tilde{G}_m$ is likely to be significantly greater than unity. As for K_m, it depends considerably on the type of producer goods imported. If the imports of producer goods are mainly for investment projects producing heavy industrial products, the gestation periods before any products are turned out by the projects are likely to be long. Then, K_m will be small and close to zero, and $(\tilde{G}_m - bK_m - 1)$ will be positive. That is, imports of producer goods will unambiguously worsen the level of consumer goods imbalance. As a matter of fact, even if K_m is equal to one, bK_m will still be less than one,[9] and $(\tilde{G}_m - bK_m - 1)$ is still likely to be positive. Therefore, imports of producer goods will still contribute to an increase in the shortage of consumer goods in the short run. The only exception is the case where $\tilde{G}_m$ is small or where the imports of producer goods require little domestically produced producer goods to work with.

In equation (4.40), $\partial \overline{C}/\partial M^*\,|_2$ is the effect on the supply of consumer goods of an increase in the imports of producer goods, financed by the exports of domestically produced producer goods (since $dX'' = dM'' = dB = 0$). In view of the arguments in the preceding paragraph, the effect possesses a negative sign.[10] The difference between $\partial \overline{C}/\partial M^*\,|_1$ and $\partial \overline{C}/\partial M^*\,|_2$ can be explained by the fact that they involve different financing methods. That $\partial \overline{C}/\partial M^*\,|_2$ is greater than $\partial \overline{C}/\partial M^*\,|_1$, in absolute terms, suggests that an increase in the imports of producer goods would contribute to a greater shortage of consumer goods if it is financed by the exports of domestically produced producer goods than if it is financed by the exports of consumer goods. The reason is that the exports of producer goods will involve a greater reduction in capital employed in the consumer goods sector than will the exports of consumer goods, given $\overline{G}$. This can be seen more clearly in our discussion of equations (4.42) to (4.46) that follows.

Note that the above analytical results as implied by equations (4.39) and (4.40) hinge crucially on the assumption that increased producer goods imports consist primarily of investment goods which require a large amount of domestically produced producer goods to work with. However, it is not inconceivable for the economy to import some material inputs for use in the consumer goods sector. Such imports would require far less domestically produced producer goods to work with than do investment goods imports. What are the implications of an increase in such imports for consumer goods imbalance in a centrally planned economy?

If the increased imports take entirely the form of material inputs used in the consumer goods sector, then the imports will not add to capital stock ($K_m = 0$) and $\tilde{G}_m$ will possess a value significantly smaller than unity. In this case, the negative effect of the import increase on consumer goods imbalance will be lower than it would be when investment goods are imported instead. Equation (4.39) also shows that when consumer goods are exported to finance the increased imports of material inputs the consumer imbalance will even improve if $\tilde{G}_m$ is so small that it is less than $1 - b/a$. To see this, consider the case where the increased imports of producer goods require no domestically produced producer goods to work with, that is, $\tilde{G}_m = 0$. According to equations (4.25) and (4.26), the import increase will cause no change in the amount of producer goods demanded but will increase the producer goods supply by the amount of the import increase, thus creating an excess supply of producer goods that has to be eliminated by a decrease in their domestic production. As the domestic production of producer goods is reduced, capital will be released from the producer goods sector to the consumer goods sector, raising the production of consumer goods. Note that the resultant increase in the production of consumer goods will be greater than the initial increase in consumer goods exports because the capital requirement in the consumer goods sector is lower than in the producer goods sector. In the end, there will be an improvement in the consumer goods imbalance.

A similar result can be obtained for the case where excess productive capacity is present in the consumer goods sector. If for some reason, such as a drought (which causes a reduction in cotton harvest, for instance), the economy suffers from underutilized productive capacity in the consumer goods sector, the production of consumer goods can be increased by increasing the use of imported inputs (cotton, in the present example), without requiring capital to be released from the producer goods sector to the consumer goods sector and causing a decrease in the production of producer goods. A significant improvement in consumer goods imbalance will be possible. The improvement would be even greater if the import increase is financed by foreign borrowings. This result shows that although the model is so set up that it does not permit underutilized productive capacity in either the consumer goods or producer goods sector it is sufficiently flexible to permit an analysis of how under similar circumstances a foreign trade increase would affect the consumer goods imbalance.

In the real world, all producer goods imports have to work with at least some domestically produced producer goods, such as electricity and transportation, and the level of idle capacity in the consumer goods sector, if any, is unlikely to be large under normal circumstances. For these reasons, one must not overemphasize the positive effect of a foreign trade expansion on consumer goods imbalance that was just presented. This is all the more true if the inputs used in the consumer goods sector are all but a small proportion of the increased imports, as is normally the case in China, which consistently emphasizes the importance of technologically advanced imports to the economy. Our previous analytical result that an increase in the imports of producer goods would worsen consumer goods imbalance should normally hold true, irrespective of whether the imports are financed by producer goods or consumer goods exports.

Foreign trade and sectoral allocation of capital

Equations (4.42) to (4.46) show the effects of changes in foreign trade on the allocation of capital between the consumer goods sector and the producer goods sector. In equation (4.42), $\partial K''/\partial \overline{G}$ and $\partial K''/\partial B|_2$ are negative and equal to each other. The equation suggests that an increase in the exports of producer goods will reduce the amount of capital allocated to the consumer goods sector, since K^* has to rise at the expense of K'' to maintain the same level of producer goods production, given the producer goods demand (since $d\overline{G} = dM^* = 0$). $\partial K''/\partial B|_1$ in equation (4.46) shows the effect of an increase in the exports of consumer goods on K''. This effect is negative because of the need to reallocate capital from the consumer goods sector to the producer goods sector to compensate for the reduced supply of producer goods caused by the reduced work effort. The combined effect of an increase in the exports of producer goods and an increase in the net imports of consumer goods on K'' is given as $\partial K''/\partial X^*|_1$ in equaton (4.43), which can be positive or negative depending on whether $a_c K''$ and $b_c K^*$ are greater or smaller than unity. Since $a_c K''$ and $b_c K^*$ are both small and much smaller than unity, $\partial K''/\partial X^*|_1$ is normally negative, that is, there will be a net decline in the amount of capital employed in the consumer goods sector. Equation (4.44), $\partial K''/\partial M^*|_1$ shows the effect of an increase in the imports of producer goods together with an increase in the net exports of consumer goods by an equal amount on the amount of capital allocated to the consumer goods sector. As in equation (4.39), the sign of $\partial K''/\partial M^*|_1$ depends crucially on the value of $(\tilde{G}_m - bK_m - 1)$, which, as discussed earlier, is most likely to be positive in the case of prereform China. Therefore, $\partial K''/\partial M^*|_1$ is normally negative, suggesting that there will be a decrease in capital allocated to the consumer goods sector following an increase in the imports of producer goods and an equal increase in the net exports of consumer goods.[11] Under the same condition, $\partial K''/\partial M^*|_2$ must also be negative. The reason for both $\partial K''/\partial M^*|_1$ and $\partial K''/\partial M^*|_2$ being negative is that capital has to be released from the consumer goods sector to the producer goods sector to meet the increased demand for domestically produced producer goods.

All in all, the inflationary effects of an expansion of foreign trade as shown in equations (4.37) to (4.41) can be explained by the adverse effects of the trade expansion on the amount of capital allocated to the consumer goods sector as shown in equations (4.42) to (4.46). This result is consistent with the result obtained in Section 4.1, which shows that in a centrally planned economy foreign trade will affect consumer goods imbalance mainly through its effect on the allocation of capital between the producer goods industry and the consumer goods industry. Nevertheless, there are important differences between the two approaches. In the previous approach, the effect of foreign trade on the allocation of existing capital stock between the two sectors is not determined, and foreign trade affects the degree of consumer goods imbalance through both the allocation of newly created capital between the two industries and the resultant change in the total wage bill. By contrast, in the present approach, the effect of a foreign trade expansion on consumer goods imbalance obtains primarily from the resultant reallocation of the existing capital stock between the two sectors while the total wage bill remains unchanged. In other words, I have shown that even without an increase in the total wage bill and without a bias in output growth against consumer goods caused by the increased capital, foreign trade expansion would still cause an increase in inflationary pressure.

4.4 Foreign trade and inflation under economic reforms

The preceding analysis is based on the assumption that the economy is strictly centrally planned, such that all prices are fixed by the state and foreign trade is under strict central control. However, since China has increasingly decentralized its economic decision-making power, distributing it to individual enterprises following the implementation of economic reforms in 1979, the economy is no longer strictly centrally planned. One important change resulting from the decentralization is an increase in price flexibility. As discussed earlier (Chapter 2), prices can roughly be classified into planned prices and nonplanned prices. Planned prices are fixed by the state and applicable to the portion of output which falls into the state procurement plan, whereas nonplanned prices are determined primarily by market forces and applicable to the portion of output which is above or outside the procurement plan. As a result of this change, surplus purchasing power in the controlled market can now find an outlet in the free and semifree markets as far as consumer goods are concerned, and the degree of consumer goods imbalance will now be reflected, at least in part, by the rate of open inflation.[12]

Another important change in relation to our analysis is the decentralization of foreign trade power, which allows enterprises and local governments to make export and import decisions with relatively little interference from the central government. The amounts of some exports and imports are no longer under the direct control of the foreign trade authorities; they may increase or decrease depending on the decisions of enterprises and local governments. As a result of this change, foreign trade has become increasingly large in proportion to national output, and the investment growth which is associated with the import growth has become increasingly important to the economy.

The model in Section 4.3 can be modified to take increased price flexibility into consideration. The price level P is now a weighted average of planned prices P_g, and nonplanned prices P_f:

$$P = (1-\beta)P_g + \beta Pf; \qquad 0 < \beta < 1, \tag{4.48}$$

where $(1-\beta)$ and β are weights assigned to P_g and P_f, respectively. Since P_f is flexible and changes positively with the excess demand for consumer goods in the controlled market, we set

$$P_f = F + \theta(C_d - C_s), \qquad \theta > 0, \tag{4.49}$$

where F is a constant and θ reflects the responsiveness of nonplanned prices to the excess demand for consumer goods in the controlled market. Substituting equation (4.49) into equation (4.48) yields

$$P = \bar{P} + \beta\theta(C_d - C_s), \tag{4.50}$$

where $\bar{P} = (1-\beta)P_g + \beta F$.

Equation (4.50) suggests that under economic reforms, the price level depends on, first, the relative importance of the free market as reflected by the value of β, and, second, the responsiveness of nonplanned prices to the excess demand for consumer goods in the controlled market, θ. This is in contrast with a strictly centrally planned economy, in which $\beta = 0$ and $P = \bar{P} = P_g$. In the first few years of economic reforms in China, β must have been small because of the small size of the free market, and θ must also have been small because consumers were likely to put off their spendings on goods traded in the free market in the expectation for a greater availability of products in future years. Therefore, the price level P could be approximated by $\bar{P}$ in those years, and the analysis in Sections 4.3 and 4.4 is still applicable. However, as both β and θ increase with time, the price level P is becoming more and more responsive to the level of shortage in the controlled market, $(C_d - C_s)$, and the increase in P, or the rate of open inflation, can increasingly better reflect the degree of consumer goods imbalance. When the rate of open inflation becomes an important indicator of the degree of consumer goods imbalance, it will no longer be appropriate to look at the change in the real supply of consumer goods (or the real effective demand for consumer goods, $\bar{C}$) to determine the change in the degree of consumer goods imbalance as we did in the preceding section. Furthermore, work effort will now be a function of the real wage rate, w/P, instead of the actual consumption of consumer goods.

Based on the above considerations, the model is modified as follows:

$$P = \bar{P} + \beta\theta\left[C_d(Lw) - a\left(\frac{w}{P}\right)K'' - M'' + X'' \right], \qquad (4.51)$$

$$\bar{G} + \tilde{G}(M^*) = b\left(\frac{w}{P}\right)K^* + M^* - X^*. \qquad (4.52)$$

Equations (4.51) and (4.52) are equilibrium conditions in the consumer goods and producer goods markets, respectively. Totally differentiating equations (4.51) and (4.52) yields

$$\left(\frac{1}{\beta\theta} - \frac{a'K''w}{P^2}\right)dP + a\,dK''$$
$$= \left(LC_d' - \frac{aK''}{P}\right)dw + dX'' - dM'', \quad (4.53)$$

$$-\left(\frac{b'wK^*}{P^2}\right)dP + b\,dK^*$$
$$= -\left(\frac{b'K^*}{P}\right)dw + d\bar{G} + dX^* + (\tilde{G}_m - 1)dM^*, \quad (4.54)$$

where

$$a' = \frac{\partial a}{\partial\left(\dfrac{w}{P}\right)}, \quad b' = \frac{\partial b}{\partial\left(\dfrac{w}{P}\right)}, \text{ and } C_d' = \frac{\partial C_d}{\partial(Lw)}.$$

Taking into consideration equations (4.33) and (4.34), we get

$$\left(\frac{1}{\beta\theta} - \frac{a'K''w}{P^2}\right)dP + a\,dK''$$

$$= \left(LC_d' - \frac{a'K''}{P}\right)dw - dX^* + dM^* + dB, \quad (4.55)$$

$$-\left(\frac{b'wK^*}{P^2}\right)dP - b\,dK''$$

$$= -\left(\frac{b'K^*}{P}\right)dw + d\overline{G} + dX^* + (\tilde{G}_m - bK_m - 1)dM^*. \quad (4.56)$$

In this system, X'' and M'' are not explicitly shown since they are assumed to change passively with changes in X^*, M^*, $\overline{G}$, and B. Equations (4.33) and (4.34) can also be written as

$$\left(\frac{1}{\beta\theta} - \frac{a'K''w}{P^2}\right)dP + a\,dK''$$

$$= \left(LC_d' - \frac{a'K''}{P}\right)dw + dX'' - dM'', \quad (4.55')$$

$$-\left(\frac{b'wK^*}{P^2}\right)dP - b\,dK'' = \left(\frac{b'K^*}{P}\right)dw$$

$$+ d\overline{G} + dM'' - dX'' + (\tilde{G}_m - bK_m)dM^* + dB. \quad (4.56')$$

In this system, X^* is not explicitly shown since it is assumed to change passively with changes in M^*, X'', M'', $\overline{G}$, and B. The first and second systems are denoted by subscripts 1 and 2, respectively.

Solving the two systems, we get

$$\frac{\partial P}{\partial \overline{G}} = \frac{a}{I} = \frac{\partial P}{\partial B}\bigg|_2, \quad (4.57)$$

$$\frac{\partial P}{\partial X^*}\bigg|_1 = \frac{1}{I}(a - b), \quad (4.58)$$

$$\frac{\partial P}{\partial M^*}\bigg|_1 = \frac{1}{I}[b + a(\tilde{G}_m - bK_m - 1)], \quad (4.59)$$

$$\frac{\partial P}{\partial M^*}\bigg|_2 = \frac{a}{I}(\tilde{G}_m - bK_m), \quad (4.60)$$

$$\frac{\partial P}{\partial B}\bigg|_1 = \frac{b}{I}, \quad (4.61)$$

$$\frac{\partial K''}{\partial \overline{G}} = \frac{1}{I}\left(\frac{a'K''w}{P^2} - \frac{1}{\beta\theta}\right) = \frac{\partial K''}{\partial B}\bigg|_2, \tag{4.62}$$

$$\frac{\partial K''}{\partial X^*}\bigg|_1 = \frac{1}{I}\left[\frac{w(b'K^* + a'K'')}{P^2} - \frac{1}{\beta\theta}\right], \tag{4.63}$$

$$\frac{\partial K''}{\partial M^*}\bigg|_1 = \frac{1}{I}\left[(\tilde{G}_m - bK_m - 1)\left(\frac{a'K''w}{P^2} - \frac{1}{\beta\theta}\right) - \frac{b'wK^*}{P^2}\right], \tag{4.64}$$

$$\frac{\partial K''}{\partial M^*}\bigg|_2 = \frac{1}{I}(\tilde{G}_m - bK_m)\left(\frac{a'K_c w}{P^2} - \frac{1}{\beta\theta}\right), \tag{4.65}$$

$$\frac{\partial K''}{\partial B_1}\bigg|_1 = \frac{-1}{I}\frac{b'wK^*}{P^2}, \tag{4.66}$$

where

$$I = \frac{b}{\beta\theta} - \frac{w}{P^2}(ba'K'' + ab'K^*). \tag{4.67}$$

In equation (4.67), $b/\beta\theta$ is greater than unity, w is in theory less than P, and $(ba'K'' + ab'K^*)$ is normally less than unity. Therefore, I is positive. Given positive I and the conditions that $a > b$ and $\tilde{G}_m - bK_m > 0$, the results in equations (4.57) to (4.66) are all consistent with the analytical results given in equations (4.37) to (4.46). That is, in the presence of price flexibility in the consumer goods sector an increase in foreign trade will tend to raise the rate of open inflation. The reason is that foreign trade growth will result in a decrease of the supply of consumer goods as capital is reallocated from the consumer goods sector to the producer goods sector. The analytical results show that the inflation rate depends crucially on the value of $\beta\theta$, which determines the responsiveness of the price level to the excess demand for consumer goods in the controlled market. The greater $\beta\theta$ is, the greater will be the inflation rate, ceteris paribus. Conceivably, the present model is relevant when $\beta\theta$ exceeds a certain threshold, below which work effort is still determined to some extent by the availability of consumer goods in the controlled market and above which work effort is determined entirely by the real wage rate.[13] In the case of China before 1987, $\beta\theta$ was presumably below such a threshold in view of the relatively large portion of consumer goods which were still under central control. In this case, the rate of open inflation would not reflect fully the change in the degree of consumer goods shortage in the controlled market and consumers would continue to accumulate monetary assets, in the form of savings deposits and unused money balances, out of the expectation that there would be a greater availability of consumer goods at lower prices in the future. This "involuntary" accumulation of monetary assets would be greater the greater the price differentials between the controlled market and the free market. Since 1987, controls on prices have been lifted off of most consumer goods in China. In this case, the rate of open inflation is clearly a good indicator of the degree of consumer goods imbalance.

4.5   Foreign trade effects on consumer goods imbalance under strict central planning and under economic reforms: a comparative analysis

Reynolds (1983) argues that "readjustment facilitated [China's] search for macroeconomic balance, while reform greatly hindered it." Indeed, under China's economic reforms, foreign trade has expanded rapidly and, as we have shown, the rapid expansion of foreign trade has a tendency to worsen the shortage of consumer goods. The interesting question is, however, whether the same amount of increase in foreign trade would be less inflationary under the reforms than it would be under strict central planning. If the answer is positive, one would expect the level of foreign trade under economic reforms to be greater than that under strict central planning for the simple reason that the cost of foreign trade in terms of economic imbalance at the margin would be lower in the former case than in the latter. Put differently, if the government were to keep foreign trade at a relatively high level for the purpose of speeding up the process of technological transformation, it would be advisable for the government to continue with the policy of economic reform. This consideration provides an explanation as to why the recentralization of foreign trade and other economic powers in 1981 was relatively short-lived, only to be replaced by an even higher degree of decentralization in the following years.

In order to make a comparison of the effect of foreign trade on consumer goods imbalance under economic reforms with that under strict central planning, it is necessary first to determine the measurement of the level of consumer goods imbalance. This issue will be covered in great detail in Chapter 5. For simplicity and to provide a lead for discussion in Chapter 5, in this section I use the simplified version of the inflation rate approach as shown in Figure 4.2. In the figure, the price and quantity of consumer goods are represented by the vertical and horizontal axes, respectively. $\bar{Q}$ is the planned output and $\bar{P}$ is the planned price under strict central planning. The supply curve is $\bar{Q}S$, which is vertical to the horizontal axis and the demand curve is DD, which intersects $\bar{Q}S$ at E. $\bar{Q}S$ is vertical because under strict central planning the supply of con-

Price

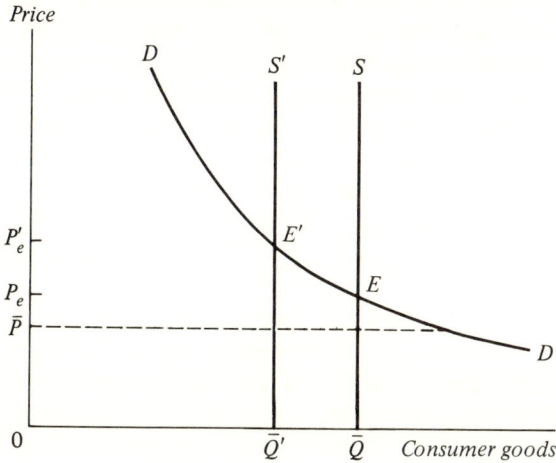

Figure 4.2.   Foreign trade and repressed inflation.

sumer goods is insensitive to price changes [equation (4.22)]. The market-clearing price P_e is greater than $\bar{P}$ because of the shortage of consumer goods that normally characterizes a strictly centrally planned economy. The difference between the market-clearing price and the planned price, $P_e - P$, reflects the degree of consumer goods shortage or the price increase which would have taken place had prices been allowed to adjust freely in the market. $(P_e - \bar{P})/\bar{P}$ is commonly referred to as the rate of repressed inflation. Nevertheless, if we define the rate of repressed inflation as the *change* in repressed inflationary pressure, $(P_e - \bar{P})/\bar{P}$ actually reflects the *accumulated* inflationary pressure which has been repressed. To explain, we assume both the planned price and the market-clearing price to be the same in the current period as they were in the previous period. Under this assumption, there is no change in inflationary pressure, open or repressed. Then, the rate of repressed inflation, by definition, is equal to zero, and $(P_e - \bar{P})/\bar{P}$, which is normally positive, remains as it is and still is greater than zero. In the discussion which follows, $\bar{P}$ is assumed to be fixed while P_e changes with the conditions in the consumer goods market. Under this assumption, the rate of repressed inflation, or the change in the degree of consumer goods shortage, is equal to the rate of change in P_e.

   To compare the effect of a foreign trade expansion on the degree of consumer goods imbalance under strict central planning with that under economic reforms, the rate of repressed inflation under strict central planning must be expressed so that it is comparable with the rate of inflation under economic reforms. For this purpose, we start with Figure 4.2, in which we assume that the expansion of foreign trade reduces the amount of consumer goods available for domestic consumption by $\overline{Q}\overline{Q}'$ (see Sections 4.3 and 4.4). The supply curve shifts from $\overline{Q}S$ to $\overline{Q}'S'$, intersecting the demand curve DD at E', at which the market-clearing price equals P_e'. Assuming that consumers are willing to spend all of their current wage incomes (W) on consumer goods, the DD curve is a rectangular hyperbola, and $P_e = W/\overline{Q}$ and $P_e' = W/\overline{Q}'$. Hence, the rate of repressed inflation is equal to $(\overline{Q} - \overline{Q}')/\overline{Q}'$, assuming unchanged planned prices.

Under economic reforms and given the assumption that consumers are willing to spend all of their wage incomes, the rate of inflation, which reflects the change in the degree of consumer goods imbalance, can be expressed in exactly the same way. To explain, let Q_g and Q_f be the outputs of consumer goods in the controlled (regulated) and free markets, respectively, and P_g and P_f be the corresponding prices. The price level of the economy, P, can be taken as the weighted average of P_g and P_f:

$$P = \frac{Q_g}{Q}P_g + \frac{Q_f}{Q}P_f, \tag{4.68}$$

where $Q = Q_g + Q_f$. Note that consumers are willing to spend all of their wage incomes:

$$P_g Q_g + P_f Q_f = W. \tag{4.69}$$

Substituting equation (4.69) into equation (4.68), we get

$$P = \frac{W}{Q}, \tag{4.70}$$

which is the price level at which the consumer goods market is cleared. Suppose that foreign trade expands, thus reducing the supply of consumer goods from Q to Q'. Then, the rate of inflation will be equal to $(Q - Q')/Q'$.

In general, one can expect $(\overline{Q} - \overline{Q}')/\overline{Q}'$ to be greater than $(Q - Q')/Q'$ because under strict central planning the supply of consumer goods is unresponsive to changes in inflationary pressure whereas under economic reforms the supply of consumer goods will tend to rise with the increase in their prices. The greater the responsiveness of the supply of consumer goods to changes in their prices, the smaller will be the reduction in the supply of consumer goods to the domestic market. In the extreme case where the price elasticity of the supply of consumer goods is infinity, there will be no reduction in the supply of consumer goods (i.e., $Q - Q' = 0$)

and the rate of repressed inflation under strict central planning, $(\bar{Q} - \bar{Q}')/\bar{Q}'$, must be greater than the rate of inflation under economic reforms, which is zero. Only in the case of the opposite extreme, where the price elasticity equals zero, will the two ratios be equal to each other. Therefore, the increase in the degree of consumer goods imbalance induced by foreign trade expansion will normally be smaller under economic reforms than under strict central planning, ceteris paribus.

4.6   Summary

Although Western economists have paid little attention to the likely effects of foreign trade on national output in centrally planned economies, Chinese economists have all along regarded foreign trade as having a decisive influence on China's economic growth. In this chapter, I started with a theoretical review of the imbalance concept advanced by Chinese economists and then analyzed how foreign trade may influence the level of consumer goods imbalance in the theoretical framework that embraces the concept. The analysis shows that foreign trade will affect the level of consumer goods imbalance primarily through its effect on (a) the total wage bill and (b) the growth rate of consumer goods relative to that of producer goods. More specifically, an expansion of foreign trade will raise the level of investment at the expense of current consumption; the growth of investment will require a greater labor input, thus raising the wage bill; and the tendency for the investment growth to be biased in favor of producer goods production will further aggravate the shortage of consumer goods.

All of the above effects are long-term in nature, and the short-term effects arising from the reallocation of domestic resources have not been considered. In the two-sector model, I consider the situation under which (a) an increase in foreign trade has no significant effect on the economy's capital stock, (b) the level of labor input as well as the total wage bill remains unchanged, and (c) work effort decreases (increases) with an increase (decrease) in the level of consumer goods shortage. It is shown that under these conditions an expansion in foreign trade will tend to cause a reallocation of the existing capital stock from the consumer goods sector to the producer goods sector, thus worsening the shortage of consumer goods. Such an effect will occur irrespective of whether imports of investment goods are financed by consumer goods or producer goods exports. In a strictly centrally planned economy, the effect will take the form of an increase in repressed inflation, but under economic reforms or in the presence of free markets, the effect will manifest itself, at least in part, as open inflation.

Finally, I showed that foreign trade expansion is less inflationary under economic reforms than under strict central planning. The reason is that consumer goods production would respond to price changes under economic reforms but it would not respond under strict central planning.

CHAPTER 5

Foreign trade and internal imbalance: empirical evidence

The theoretical model developed in Chapter 4 suggests that in a centrally planned economy such as China's an expansion of foreign trade will tend to worsen the degree of consumer goods imbalance. In this chapter, I discuss empirical evidence concerning the relation between foreign trade and the degree of consumer goods imbalance in China in the postreform period, leaving the empirical estimation of the contribution of foreign trade to the growth of the money supply (and open inflation) to Chapter 6. Two major tasks are involved: The first is to develop an indicator of the degree of consumer goods imbalance and the second is to use that indicator to determine the contribution of foreign trade fluctuations to the changes in the degree of consumer goods imbalance in China during the period of economic reforms. I first provide a detailed discussion of the concept of consumer goods imbalance in relation to central planning.

5.1   The concept of consumer goods imbalance

In this study, a consumer goods imbalance is considered to be present when there is an imbalance in the demand for and supply of consumer goods. In an economy characterized by price flexibility, and, therefore, full employment, prices will adjust to eliminate the excess demand for or supply of consumer goods. Hence, the rate of increase in consumer prices will be a proper indicator of the degree of consumer goods imbalance. Conversely, in an economy characterized by price stickiness and unemployment, the rate of unemployment will change with market imbalances. Therefore, the degree of market imbalance can be reflected by the rate of unemployment. However, when the economy is characterized by full employment and price stickiness, as is normally the case in a centrally planned economy, the question then arises of whether the rate of inflation can serve as an appropriate indicator of the degree of consumer goods imbalance. In the preceding chapter, I followed the traditional approach and took the inflation rate, which is the sum of open inflation and repressed inflation, as a measure of the degree of consumer goods imbalance. The problems involved in the use of this approach are discussed in detail in the following under the heading of "The inflation rate approach." I also showed in the preceding chapter that the degree of market imbalance can be measured in terms of the amount of unused purchasing power [equation (4.24)]. This approach is discussed later under the heading of the purchasing power imbalance approach. In addition to these two approaches, I also discuss the accumulation share approach, which has been widely used by Chinese economists for explaining the changes in the degree of macroeconomic imbalance in China.

The inflation rate approach

In a centrally planned economy, inflation may take the form of both open and repressed inflation. Most economists agree that the inflation rate can serve as an appropriate indicator of the change in the degree of consumer goods imbalance in such an economy, but they differ in their views of the importance of repressed inflation, and even open inflation, to such an economy. Economists who argue that centrally planned economies, using administrative controls over wages, money supply, and resource allocation among industries, would be, and always have been, able to maintain equilibrium in the consumer goods market, either dismiss the imbalance problem in such economies outright (Donnithorne 1974; Tsakok 1979; Portes and Winter 1980) or consider the problem to take place only in the form of open inflation (Reynolds 1983; Wanless 1985). Their use of the inflation rate approach to the problem of internal imbalance in centrally planned economies is based on an implicit assumption that open inflation itself must be sufficient to eliminate consumers' excess purchasing power, which will arise as a result of the lack of coordination between consumer demand and production. However, in view of the fact that in a centrally planned economy the rate of open inflation is administratively determined, it is rare that the inflation rate exactly eliminates consumers' excess purchasing power. In a more general case, consumers' excess purchasing power is only partly eliminated by open inflation and the rest is retained in the form of involuntary accumulation of monetary assets. In other words, open inflation in general cannot reflect fully the problem of internal imbalance in centrally planned economies, and repressed inflation must be taken into account. A diagrammatic illustration of the inflation rate approach is given in Figure 5.1.

Figure 5.1 depicts the consumer goods market in a centrally planned economy. The horizontal and vertical axes represent the quantity and price of consumer goods, respectively. The SS curve stands for the supply of consumer goods, which is insensitive to price changes, and $\bar{P}_0$ is the

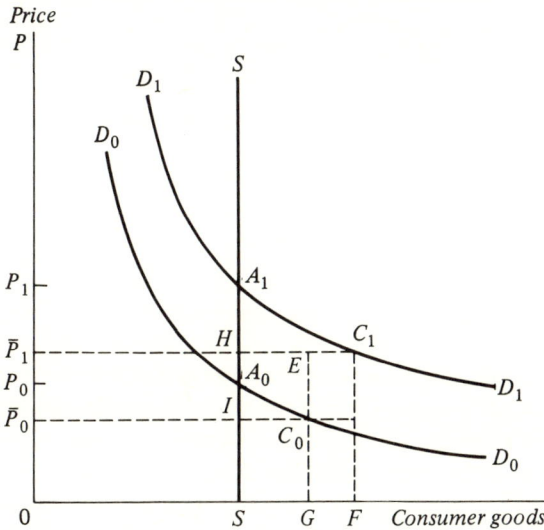

Figure 5.1. Consumer goods imbalance and open inflation.

initial price of consumer goods fixed by the planners. The demand curve $D_0 D_0$ intersects the SS curve at point A_0, at which the equilibrium price of consumer goods is P_0, which is greater than $\bar{P}_0$. Suppose that, for some reason, the price of consumer goods is adjusted upward to $\bar{P}_1$ and at the same time the demand curve is shifted rightward to $D_1 D_1$, crossing the SS curve at point A_1, at which the equilibrium price is equal to P_1.[1] The economy records a rate of open inflation measuring $(\bar{P}_1 - \bar{P}_0)/\bar{P}_0$, which is the rate of change in the planned price of consumer goods. The total inflationary pressure incurred in the current period can be measured in terms of the rate of movement of the equilibrium price from P_0 to P_1, that is, $(P_1 - P_0)/P_0$.

The total inflationary pressure is considered to be the sum of open inflation and repressed inflation. In accordance with this concept, we write

$$\frac{P_1 - P_0}{P_0} = \dot{P} + RI, \tag{5.1}$$

where

$$\dot{P} = \frac{\bar{P}_1 - \bar{P}_0}{\bar{P}_0},$$

which is the rate of open inflation, and RI is the rate of repressed inflation.

Based on Figure 5.1, the rate of total inflation can also be written as

$$\frac{P_1 - P_0}{P_0} = \dot{P} + \frac{\overline{P}_1}{P_0}\left(\frac{P_1 - \overline{P}_1}{\overline{P}_1} - \frac{P_0 - \overline{P}_0}{\overline{P}_0}\right). \tag{5.1'}$$

From equations (5.1) and (5.1'), we obtain the rate of repressed inflation as

$$RI = \frac{\overline{P}_1}{P_0}\left(\frac{P_1 - \overline{P}_1}{\overline{P}_1} - \frac{P_0 - \overline{P}_0}{\overline{P}_0}\right). \tag{5.2}$$

In equation (5.2), $(P_t - \overline{P}_t)/\overline{P}_t$ is the rate of increase in the price level above the current price level that is needed to eliminate the shortage of consumer goods or the amount of inflationary pressure that has been repressed. The change in the amount of accumulated repressed inflationary pressure, multiplied by the ratio of the price level in the current period to the equilibrium price level in the preceding period, is equal to the rate of repressed inflation in the current period. Since the amount of accumulated repressed inflationary pressure may rise, remain unchanged, or fall, the rate of repressed inflation can be positive, zero, or negative. This concept of repressed inflation must be distinguished from the concept behind the argument of some economists that repressed inflation is an ever-present phenomenon in centrally planned economies. The latter concept essentially implies the presence of consumer goods shortages, or a positive $(P_t - \overline{P}_t)/\overline{P}_t$ for all t, whereas the former concept attempts to capture the change in the degree of consumer goods shortage attributable to the change in the demand for the supply of consumer goods in the current period.[2]

The difficulty involved in the empirical estimation of total inflation based on equations (5.1) and (5.2) is that the market-clearing prices, P_0 and P_1, are unknown. To overcome this problem Chen and Hou (1986) use the simple quantity theory of money to estimate the rates of total inflation in their study of China for the period between 1979 and 1983. The "Quantity Equation of Exchange" identity they use can be written as

$$M^s V \equiv \Omega y, \tag{5.3}$$

where M^s is the money supply, V is the velocity of circulation of money, Ω is the "true" average price level, and y is the level of real output. From this identity, the rate of total inflation can be derived as

$$\dot{\Omega} = \dot{M}^s + \dot{V} - \dot{y}, \tag{5.4}$$

where the dot denotes the growth rate of a variable. The rate of total inflation $\dot{\Omega}$ is empirically estimated on the basis of a crucial assumption that the demand for real balances is a fixed proportion of real national output so that the desired V is a constant. Since by definition $\dot{\Omega}$ is the sum of the rates of open and repressed inflation, equation (5.4) can be rewritten as

$$RI = \dot{M}^s - (\dot{P} + \dot{y}). \tag{5.4'}$$

Equation (5.4′) states that the rate of repressed inflation is equal to the difference between the growth rate of the money supply and the growth rate of nominal national output at controlled prices. The rate of repressed inflation is positively related to the growth rate of the money supply and negatively related to the rates of open inflation and national output growth. In a market economy, RI will be equal to zero, given constant velocity of money, since the equality between the growth rate of real balances and the growth rate of real national output will always be maintained by price flexibility. In a centrally planned economy, in contrast, RI can be positive or negative, depending on the difference between the growth rates of the money supply and nominal national output.

Empirical estimation of the rate of total inflation or repressed inflation based on the above approach depends crucially on the availability of statistics on the growth rates of the money supply, the price level, and national output. In the case of China, because of its relatively underdeveloped statistical system as well as the inherent difficulty involved in output valuation in a centrally planned economy, these statistics are not readily available and have to be estimated. The resultant estimation of the inflation rate will clearly be sensitive to the method used in the estimation of these variables, thus rendering it relatively unreliable. Another problem is that although the desired velocity of money may be constant in the long run it could fluctuate significantly in the short run. Thus, the estimated rate of inflation could deviate significantly from the actual rate of change in consumer goods imbalance. The approach adopted by Huang Hsiao (1971) suffers from similar problems. Instead of directly estimating the rate of total inflation, she first estimates the rate of repressed inflation and then adds to it the rate of open inflation to arrive at the rate of total inflation. In her estimation, the rate of repressed inflation is derived as the additional rate of inflation that would have been incurred by the increased holdings of money balances by the public. The estimation is also based on the simple quantity theory of money which assumes the velocity of money to be constant.

The purchasing power imbalance approach

The difficulty involved in the empirical estimation of the actual inflationary pressure in the inflation rate approach can be avoided if it is possible to estimate directly the growth rate of excess demand for consumer goods, or the difference in the growth rates between the desired and actual aggregate spending on consumer goods. This is an approach adopted by Peebles (1983, 1986). He measures the rate of change in the excess demand for consumer goods in terms of purchasing power imbalance (PPI), which is defined as the excess of the growth rate of money incomes ($\dot{MI}$) over the growth rate of real national output ($\dot{y}$):

$$PPI = \dot{MI} - \dot{y}. \tag{5.5}$$

As can be seen from equation (5.4), PPI for a market economy is nothing more than the national income deflator so long as $\dot{MI}$ correctly reflects the growth rate of nominal national income.[3] However, if $\dot{MI}$ represents the growth rate of money incomes received by consumers and $\dot{y}$ represents the growth rate of consumer goods supplied to the market, PPI measures the growth rate of excess purchasing power (or unspent purchasing power) at the initial prices of consumer goods. For present purposes, the second concept is adopted. Official statistics on both money incomes and the consumer goods supply are readily available (see the more detailed discussion to be presented subsequently).

The difference between the inflation rate approach [equation (5.1)] and the purchasing power imbalance approach based on equation (5.5) can be explained with the aid of Figure 5.1. Assuming that, due to persistent shortages of consumer goods, consumers are willing to spend all their current income on consumption, the D_0D_0 and D_1D_1 curves are rectangular hyperbolas, and $\overline{P}_0C_0GO$ and $\overline{P}_1C_1FO$ are levels of money incomes in the previous and current periods, respectively. Note that in this figure real national output is unchanged at OS in the second period, that is, $\dot{y} = 0$. Then, PPI is equal to the rate of change in money incomes:

$$
\begin{aligned}
PPI &= \frac{\overline{P}_1C_1FO - \overline{P}_0C_0GO}{\overline{P}_0C_0GO} \\
&= \frac{\overline{P}_1EC_0\overline{P}_0 + EC_1FG}{\overline{P}_0C_0GO} \\
&= \frac{\overline{P}_1 - \overline{P}_0}{\overline{P}_0} + \frac{EC_1FG}{\overline{P}_0C_0GO}.
\end{aligned}
\tag{5.6}
$$

PPI is shown to be equal to the sum of the rate of open inflation and the ratio of excess money incomes (or the amount of income over the level which is needed to keep the real purchasing power unchanged) to the initial level of money incomes. The second term on the right-hand side of equation (5.6) may be positive or negative, depending on whether there is an increase or decrease in consumer goods shortage. This term reflects the growth of unused purchasing power which contributes to repressed infla-tion. Therefore, Peebles's purchasing power imbalance approach is essen-tially the same as the inflation rate approach; they differ only in how the degree of imbalance should be estimated. More specifically, whereas the inflation rate approach requires an explicit estimation of the rate of re-pressed inflation, Peebles's purchasing power imbalance approach re-quires no such estimation. The similarity between the two approaches can also be seen by comparing equation (5.4) with equation (5.5).

To explain the difference between the purchasing power imbalance approach based on equation (5.5) and the imbalance concept underlying the right-hand side of equation (4.24), define R as the accumulation of unused purchasing power in the current period:

$$R = MI - (C + U),$$
(5.7)

where C is the current supply of consumer goods or the aggregate con-sumption expenditure ($= C_s = C_d$). Equation (5.7) states that the accu-mulation of unused purchasing power is equal to the difference between the level of money incomes and the sum of consumption expenditure and increased demand for money. An increase (decrease) in R in the current year over the previous year will occur when there is a faster (slower) accumulation of unrealized purchasing power in the current year than in the previous year. Under the assumption that consumers are willing to spend all of their current money incomes on consumption, the ratio of unused purchasing power to the supply of consumer goods, R/C, can be used to denote the relative shortage of consumer goods in the current year, and an increase (decrease) in R/C implies an increase (decrease) in the degree of consumer goods imbalance. Dividing each term in equation (5.7) by C and totally differentiating the resultant equation, we get

$$r = d\left(\frac{MI}{C}\right) - d\left(\frac{U}{C}\right)$$
$$\approx \frac{MI}{C}(\dot{MI} - \dot{C}), \text{ since } d\left(\frac{U}{C}\right) \approx 0,$$
(5.8)

where $r = d(R/C)$. The degree of consumer goods imbalance worsens (improves) if r is positive (negative) or if the growth rate of money income is greater (smaller) than the growth rate of the nominal supply of con-sumer goods, ceteris paribus. Define Z as the excess of the growth rate of money incomes over the growth rate of nominal consumption, all in percentages:

$$Z = \dot{MI} - \dot{C}.$$
(5.9)

Since r is a monotonic (increasing) function Z, Z may replace r as an imbalances indicator.[4] The greater (smaller) the value of Z, the greater (smaller) the degree of consumer goods imbalance. This imbalance indicator is different from PPI in that the growth rate of the real supply of consumer goods in equation (5.5) has now been replaced by the growth rate of the nominal supply of consumer goods in equation (5.9).

The significance of this difference can be seen by rewriting equation (5.9) as

$$Z = \left(\frac{\dot{MI}}{P}\right) - \left(\frac{\dot{C}}{P}\right), \tag{5.10}$$

where P is the price level. This equation shows that the value of Z is independent of the rate of open inflation. In contrast, the rate of open inflation has an unambiguous effect on the value of PPI [equation (5.6)], which will be greater the higher the rate of open inflation. That Z is independent of the rate of open inflation is consistent with the fact that, in a centrally planned economy, an administrative increase or decrease in the price level itself will have no bearing on the relationship between the supply of and demand for consumer goods; it will increase or decrease the real purchasing power and the real supply of consumer goods by the same percentage, given the money incomes and the nominal supply of consumer goods. For instance, if the prices of all consumer goods have been adjusted upward by 10 percent and the level of money incomes has also been adjusted upward by 10 percent, the shortage of consumer goods in real terms will obviously be unaffected. Thus, the 10 percent increase in the price level is irrelevant to the degree of consumer goods imbalance. In view of this property, the use of Z (or r) as an imbalance indicator may be termed the real purchasing power imbalance approach.

It is of interest to note that Z as an indicator of the change in degree of consumer goods imbalance can be diagrammatically illustrated using Figure 5.1. Based on the assumption that consumers are willing to spend all of their money incomes, we can first obtain r as

$$
\begin{aligned}
r &= \frac{MI_1}{C_1} - \frac{MI_0}{C_0} \\
&= \frac{OFC_1\bar{P}_1}{OSH\bar{P}_1} - \frac{OGC_0\bar{P}_0}{OSI\bar{P}_0} \\
&= \frac{O\bar{P}_1 \cdot OF}{O\bar{P}_1 \cdot OS} - \frac{O\bar{P}_0 \cdot OG}{O\bar{P}_0 \cdot OS} \\
&= \frac{GF}{OS}.
\end{aligned}
\tag{5.11}
$$

Given r, we get, according to equation (5.8),

$$Z = \frac{C_0}{MI_0} \cdot \frac{GF}{OS} = \frac{GF}{OG}. \tag{5.12}$$

GF can be regarded as the increase in the level of consumer goods shortage in physical terms. Accordingly, Z is the ratio of the change in the level of consumer goods shortage to the consumers' purchasing power in the preceding period, where both are in physical terms. The ratio is clearly independent of the rate of open inflation.

The accumulation share approach

Chinese economists, including Xue (1985) and Liao (1985), have strongly stressed the importance of consumption – accumulation balance to the economy. Excessively high shares of accumulation (or low shares of consumption) in aggregate expenditure have been blamed for the failure of the Great Leap Forward in 1958 – 60 and the Four Modernizations movement in 1978, during which periods bottlenecks in the supplies of a large number of heavy industrial items developed, hampering the production of both producer goods and consumer goods. Among other things, the shortage of consumer goods had been aggravated. Xue (1985, p. 419) suggests that China, in view of past experience, should keep the accumulation share below 30 percent in order to achieve macroeconomic balance. He cites the extremely high accumulation share of between 33.9 and 43.8 percent during the years of the Great Leap Forward (1958 – 60) as a factor contributing to the decline in the standard of living during the period. He also deplores that the accumulation shares had been artificially kept above 30 percent in the later years of the Cultural Revolution (i.e., 1970 – 77), and he considers the dramatic rise of the share to 36.5 percent in 1978 to have caused an internal imbalance almost as severe as that of the years of the Great Leap Forward.

The use of the share of accumulation in aggregate expenditure by Xue and other Chinese economists to explain the severity of the problem of consumer goods imbalance may be termed the accumulation share approach. Although this approach apparently differs considerably from both the inflation rate approach and the purchasing power imbalance approach, it can actually be taken as a crude purchasing power imbalance approach. The basic argument of this approach is that an increase in the share of accumulation can only take place at the expense of consumption, given the amount of productive resources (Liao 1985, p. 65). Accordingly, the greater the share of accumulation, the greater will be the decline in the production of consumer goods, and the greater will be the level of unspent purchasing power (or the shortage of consumer goods).

The accumulation share approach is based on the crucial assumption that investment is the only factor that causes significant changes in the supply and demand conditions in the consumer goods market, whereas other factors, including technological changes, population growth, monetary growth, natural disasters, and so on, are relatively unimportant.[5] On the whole, this is not an unrealistic assumption in the short run as far as the prereform Chinese economy is concerned, given the relatively low rates of technological change in the prereform period. However, as the impacts of economic reforms on production and prices gain in importance, changes in the accumulation share may have, for instance, simply reflected the changes in relative prices instead of the changes in the degree of consumer goods shortages. An increase in the relative price of investment goods would raise the accumulation share, whereas a decrease would lower it. Furthermore, since investment activities have been increasingly diversified across all sectors of the economy, the degree of consumer goods imbalance caused by any given amount of investment is likely to have changed. Investments undertaken by individual enterprises and local governments are no longer focused on large-scale projects in the heavy industrial sector, and, unlike in the prereform economic plan, they do not involve massive, forced reallocation of resources from existing enterprises to new enterprises. Therefore, the accumulation share and its change have become increasingly inappropriate as an indicator of consumer goods imbalance for the Chinese economy. This point will be further elaborated on in Section 5.4.

5.2   Foreign trade and inflationary pressure: empirical evidence

The model in Chapter 4 suggests that the degree of consumer goods imbalance in a centrally planned economy such as China's will worsen (improve) with the expansion (contraction) of foreign trade. The purpose of this section is to provide an empirical test of this theoretical result. In the test, we use the real purchasing power imbalance approach [equation (5.7)], according to which a rise or fall in the money incomes – consumer goods supply ratio MI/C signifies a deterioration or an improvement in consumer goods imbalance. The question is therefore: Will the MI/C ratio increase (decrease) with an increase (decrease) in the relative importance of foreign trade in national output?

To carry out the test, we first derive the level of money incomes for each year from 1955 to 1985, using the official statistics published in the *Statistical Yearbook of China,* 1986. In the statistics, money incomes include (1) wages of staff and workers in state-owned units, (2) wages of staff and workers in collective-owned units, (3) wages of staff and workers in various jointly owned units, (4) incomes of other professions, (5) incomes of peasants from selling products, (6) service incomes of peasants, (7) government financial support to residents, (8) net increases in agricultural loans and downpayments for farm products from banks and credit unions, (9) other incomes of residents, (10) purchases of consumer goods by foreigners, and (11) purchases of consumer goods by urban social groups. The amount of disposable money incomes is, however, overstated by (a) peasants' expenditures on agricultural means of production and (b) the taxes paid to the government by residents. For this reason, *MI* is obtained by deducting these two terms from the official money income statistics. The results are presented in Table 5.1.

Turn now to the estimation of consumption expenditures, or the supply of consumer goods (*C*). We also use the official statistics published in the *Statistical Yearbook of China,* 1986, which takes monetary expenditures as the sum of the following items: (1) residents' purchases of commodities, (2) resident's expenses for cultural life, (3) taxes paid by residents to the government, (4) net changes in agriculture loans and downpayments for farm products from banks and cooperatives, and (5) residents' other expenditures. Note that item 1 includes agricultural means of production, which should be excluded from consumption expenditures. In addition, the tax payments in item 3 have no relation to the supply of consumer goods. Therefore, I deduct both peasants' purchases of agricultural means of production and the taxes paid by residents to the government from aggregate monetary expenditures to arrive at the level of aggregate consumption expenditures. The result of this calculation is given in Table 5.1.

Finally, I turn to the estimation of the relative importance of foreign trade in national output. The trade–GNP ratio is one of the most frequently used indicators of the relative importance of foreign trade in the economy. In general, the greater the ratio, the more dependent is the economy on foreign trade. Nevertheless, what is required here is an indicator which can reflect the relative size of trade-induced demand for domestic goods. For this purpose, the trade-induced demand for domestic goods, *T,* is set as

$$T = (X'' - M'') + \lambda M^* + X^* = X - M'' + \lambda M^*, \tag{5.13}$$

where X'' is consumer goods exports, M'' is consumer goods imports, M^* is producer goods imports, X^* is producer goods exports, $X = X'' + X^*$, and λ is a multiplier representing the amount of domestically produced producer goods needed to work with a unit of imported producer goods.

Table 5.1. Money incomes, consumption expenditure, and the foreign trade – national-output ratio, 1955 – 85

	MI^a (100 million yuan)	C^b (100 million yuan)	MI/C	$T/Y^{c,d}$ ($\lambda=2$)	T/Y ($\lambda=3$)
1955	393.0	378.6	1.0380	0.2025	0.2752
1956	474.0	455.1	1.0422	0.1680	0.2230
1957	492.0	478.6	1.0292	0.1569	0.2076
1958	548.9	518.1	1.0594	0.1589	0.2103
1959	652.9	615.7	1.0603	0.1729	0.2287
1960	668.6	648.8	1.0305	0.1512	0.2021
1961	626.0	600.8	1.0419	0.0850	0.1117
1962	555.2	602.5	0.9215	0.0750	0.0952
1963	587.2	596.1	0.9851	0.0743	0.0943
1964	635.7	625.3	1.0166	0.0715	0.0916
1965	669.7	648.4	1.0328	0.0732	0.0907
1966	722.3	684.8	1.0548	0.0865	0.1143
1967	745.7	726.2	1.0269	0.0855	0.1128
1968	722.6	697.1	1.0366	0.0880	0.1158
1969	743.0	746.2	0.9957	0.0799	0.1039
1970	777.4	783.3	0.9925	0.0726	0.0967
1971	863.1	835.9	1.0325	0.0713	0.0924
1972	939.1	917.5	1.0235	0.0802	0.1040
1973	1023.0	985.7	1.0378	0.1081	0.1423
1974	1073.0	1037.2	1.0345	0.1421	0.1914
1975	1146.3	1119.3	1.0241	0.1491	0.1994
1976	1207.2	1182.8	1.0206	0.1410	0.1872
1977	1283.5	1270.9	1.0099	0.1173	0.1555
1978	1423.4	1379.1	1.0321	0.1455	0.1961
1979	1720.2	1602.4	1.0735	0.1675	0.2265
1980	2141.4	1936.1	1.1060	0.1819	0.2442
1981	2350.3	2160.3	1.0880	0.2038	0.2717
1982	2582.6	2384.1	1.0833	0.2101	0.2510
1983	2958.2	2686.5	1.1011	0.2140	0.2842
1984	3893.5	3369.9	1.1554	0.2598	0.3500
1985	5035.8	4485.2	1.1226	—	—

[a] MI = money incomes.
[b] C = consumption expenditure.
[c] $T = X - M'' + \lambda M^*$, where X is total exports, M'' is consumer goods imports, λ is a constant, and M^* is producer goods imports.
[d] Y = national income.
Sources: MI and C: Estimated from State Statistical Bureau, *Statistical Yearbook of China* (Hong Kong: Economic Information and Agency, 1987, pp. 480 – 3). X, M,* and M'': State Statistical Bureau, *Statistical Yearbook of China* (Hong Kong: Economic Information and Agency, 1987, p. 519). Proportion of consumer goods in total imports: Table 1.5. Y: State Statistical Bureau, *Statistical Yearbook of China* (Hong Kong: Economic Information and Agency, 1987, pp. 38 – 9).

To estimate M'' and $M,*$ we use the renminbi value of imports, multiplied by the proportions of consumer goods and producer goods (or means of production) in total imports as published in the *Statistical Yearbook of China*. λ is assumed to equal two or three (Chao 1982, p. 125). Equation (5.13) states that the trade-induced demand for imports is equal to net consumer goods exports plus producer goods exports plus the amount of domestically produced producer goods working with imported producer goods.[6] Dividing T by national output, Y, yields the required indicator of the relative importance of foreign trade in national output. Here, we use the official national income statistics for Y, noting that services are excluded from both T and Y. The resultant T/Y ratios are shown in Table 5.1.[7] In the prereform period, the T/Y ratios (with $\lambda = 2$) were relatively high (above 14 percent for most of the years) in the periods between 1955 and 1960 and between 1974 and 1976, and relatively low (below 10 percent) in the period between 1961 and 1973. In the postreform period, the ratios were high and increasing, rising from 15 percent in 1978 to 26 percent in 1984.

To determine the extent to which the degree of consumer goods imbalance has been influenced by the growth of foreign trade, we regress MI/C on T/Y, using the ordinary least squares method, for the period from 1955 to 1984. The year of 1985 is excluded from the analysis because of the tendency for the MI/C ratio to understate the degree of consumer goods imbalance given the substantially increased price flexibility in that year (see Section 5.6). The regression results are given as follows:

i. $\lambda = 2.$

$$\frac{MI}{C} = 0.9832 + 0.6616 \frac{T}{Y},$$

$$(70.8746) \quad (6.8698)$$

$$R^2 = 0.6361, \quad D-W = 1.8181.$$

ii. $\lambda = 3.$

$$\frac{MI}{C} = 1.0078 + 0.4902 \frac{T}{Y},$$

$$(74.3243) \quad (7.70738)$$

$$R^2 = 0.6495, \quad D-W = 1.7979.$$

$D-W$ refers to Durbin-Watson Statistics, and figures in parentheses are t statistics.

These results show that the value of λ bears no significant effect on our regression analysis. In each regression, the coefficient of T/Y is of the correct sign, all coefficients are significant, the Durbin-Watson statistics show the absence of autocorrelation, and R^2 is above 60 percent. These results reveal that from 1955 to 1984 foreign trade growth had a significant influence on the degree of consumer goods imbalance in China. An increase in foreign trade would increase the trade-induced demand for domestic goods and cause an increase in the ratio of money income to consumption expenditure. A decrease in foreign trade would have the opposite effect.

5.3   The degree of consumer goods imbalance: empirical estimates

In Chapter 1, I discussed the growth of China's foreign trade in the prereform period. Foreign trade was shown to fluctuate closely with the country's investment policy. In the present chapter, I intend to show how the fluctuations in foreign trade (or investment in fixed capital) might have affected the country's consumer goods imbalance. For this purpose, I present the following indicators of consumer goods imbalance for comparison: the accumulation share (AS), the rate of open inflation $(\dot{P})$, the index of nominal purchasing power imbalance (PPI), and the index of real purchasing power imbalance (Z).

The first column of Table 5.2 provides the values of the accumulation share for the period from 1956 to 1985. These values represent the proportions of aggregate expenditure that take the form of net increases in fixed and working capital. The values fluctuate rather widely, ranging from the low of 10.4 percent in 1962 to the high of 43.8 percent in 1959. The changes in the accumulation share have been widely used by Chinese economists, including Xue (1985), as an indicator of the changes in the degree of macroeconomic imbalance.

Note that the statistics do not seem to lend support to Xue's argument that it can be deduced from past experience that 30 percent is the "proper" share at which macroeconomic balance can be maintained. For most of the years before 1970, the shares were far below 30 percent, whereas for most of the years after 1970, the shares were mostly above 30 percent. There was no apparent reason why the economy was more balanced in the years before 1970 than it was in the years after. Actually, it is the change in the value of the share, instead of the value of the share itself, that would serve as a more appropriate indicator of the extent to which consumer goods imbalance is worsened or improved. The reason is that if there is a significant increase (decrease) in AS, the economy is most likely to suffer a worsening (improvement) of consumer goods imbalance, since it implies a substantial increase (decrease) in the amount of resources reallocated from the consumer goods sector to the producer goods sector. It must be noted that, however, the usefulness of this indicator depends crucially on

Table 5.2. Consumer goods imbalance
indicators: empirical estimates, 1956–85 (in
percentages)

	AS	$\dot{P}$	PPI	Z
1956	24.4	0.0	6.58	0.48
1957	24.9	1.5	−0.65	−1.30
1958	33.9	0.2	−10.60	3.18
1959	43.8	0.9	10.68	0.09
1960	39.6	3.1	3.85	−2.96
1961	19.2	16.2	23.35	1.03
1962	10.4	3.8	−4.81	−11.59
1963	17.5	− 5.9	−4.94	6.83
1964	22.2	−3.7	−8.23	3.36
1965	27.1	−2.7	−11.65	1.66
1966	30.6	−0.3	−9.11	2.24
1967	21.3	−0.7	10.47	−2.81
1968	21.1	0.1	3.39	0.91
1969	23.2	−1.1	−16.49	−4.22
1970	32.9	−0.2	−18.62	−0.34
1971	34.1	−0.7	4.03	4.31
1972	31.6	−0.2	5.89	−0.95
1973	32.9	0.6	0.64	1.50
1974	32.3	0.5	3.81	−0.33
1975	33.9	0.2	−1.48	−1.08
1976	30.9	0.3	7.99	−0.36
1977	32.3	2.7	−1.48	−1.13
1978	36.5	0.7	−1.39	2.39
1979	34.6	2.0	13.86	4.66
1980	31.5	6.0	18.10	3.66
1981	28.3	2.4	4.86	−1.82
1982	28.8	1.9	1.58	−0.48
1983	29.7	1.5	4.75	1.85
1984	31.6	2.8	18.12	6.18
1985	35.3	8.8	16.63	−3.76

Notes: AS = the share of accumulation in aggregate expenditure, in percentages. $\dot{P}$ = the rate of open inflation, using the
annual growth rate of the prices of retail sales. *PPI* = the index
of nominal purchasing power imbalance, given as the excess
of the growth of money incomes over the growth rate of real
national output. *Z* = the index of real purchasing power imbalance, given as the excess of the growth rate of money incomes over the growth rate of the nominal supply of consumer goods.
Sources: AS: State Statistical Bureau, *Statistical Yearbook of
China* (Hong Kong: Economic Information and Agency,
1986, p. 49). $\dot{P}$: Ibid, p. 535. Growth rate of real national
output: Ibid, pp. 41–2. Money incomes: Table 5.1. *Z:* Estimated from Table 5.1.

the assumption of the absence of significant changes in such factors as technology, population, and price structure. For years of highly differentiated rates of price increases and technical changes in industry and agriculture, such as in the 1980s, changes in AS can no longer adequately reflect the direction in which the degree of consumer goods imbalance changes. For instance, a relatively fast increase in the (administered) prices of investment goods will raise the accumulation share and a relatively fast increase in the (administered) prices of consumer goods will lower it. Similarly, a relatively fast improvement in productivity in agriculture will lower the accumulation share, whereas a relatively fast productivity increase in heavy industry will raise it. These changes will tend to distort the picture of the effect of changes in the accumulation share on consumer goods imbalance.

Turn now to the rate of open inflation. Table 5.3 presents various price indexes, including the annual rates of increase in the price of retail sales, the cost of living for urban workers, and the retail prices of industrial goods in rural areas over the period 1956 to 1985. In the first column of the table, retail sales refer to all consumer items and agricultural means of production sold in state-owned shops and marketplaces. They exclude housing, medical care, transportation, and other personal services. This is also true for column 3, which covers only the retail sales of industrial products in rural areas. In column 2, the cost of living index is presumably more comprehensive than the other two indexes since it covers both goods and services consumed by urban workers. However, it suffers from the disadvantage of not covering the vast majority of rural areas. These three indexes are complementary to each other and none of them is by itself an ideal index of the rate of open inflation. However, since the patterns of their changes during the period do not differ significantly from one another, I incorporate only the general retail price index in Table 5.2 as an indicator of the rate of open inflation.

As for the estimates of *PPI*, I make use of the estimates of money incomes in Section 5.2 and, following Peebles (1983, 1986), approximate the growth rates of consumer goods supply with the growth rates of real national income given in the second column of Table A.1. The resultant estimates of *PPIs* are given in the third column of Table 5.1. These estimates are an improvement over those of Peebles (1986) in that, whereas Peebles has to make do with the limited data available to him by estimating the growth rates of money incomes using the growth rates of state wages, I make direct use of the recently published money incomes statistics which cover not only state wages but also a number of other important income items, such as collective wages and peasants' incomes. One major deficiency of the estimates so arrived at is that the growth rates

Table 5.3. Indexes of China's inflation,
1956–85 (in percentages)

	Prices of retail sales	Cost of living (urban)	Industrial retail prices (rural)
1956	0.0	−0.1	−1.0
1957	1.5	2.6	1.2
1958	0.2	−1.1	−0.6
1959	0.9	0.3	0.9
1960	3.1	2.5	2.8
1961	16.2	16.1	4.9
1962	3.8	3.8	4.5
1963	−5.9	−5.9	−1.0
1964	−3.7	−3.7	−1.9
1965	−2.7	−1.2	−3.7
1966	−0.3	−1.2	−2.9
1967	−0.7	−0.6	−0.8
1968	0.1	0.1	−0.3
1969	−1.1	1.0	−1.5
1970	−0.2	0.0	−0.2
1971	−0.7	−0.1	−1.5
1972	−0.2	0.2	−0.5
1973	0.6	0.1	0.0
1974	0.5	0.7	0.0
1975	0.2	0.4	0.0
1976	0.3	0.3	0.1
1977	2.0	2.7	0.1
1978	0.7	0.7	0.0
1979	2.0	1.9	0.1
1980	6.0	7.5	0.8
1981	2.4	2.5	1.0
1982	1.9	2.0	1.6
1983	2.5	2.0	1.0
1984	2.8	2.7	3.1
1985	8.8	11.9	3.2

Note: The urban cost of living index is also referred to as the index of the cost of living of staff and workers in the *Statistical Yearbook of China.*

Source: State Statistical Bureau, *Statistical Yearbook of China* (Hong Kong: Economic Information and Agency, 1986, p. 535).

of "real national income" as obtained from the *Statistical Yearbook of China* can differ greatly from the actual growth rates of real national output. In Chinese statistics, "national income" (*NI*) refers only to incomes generated in the "material sectors" and excludes those generated in the "nonmaterial sectors" (see Appendix A). Therefore, the estimate of *PPI*, which is the difference between the growth rates of money incomes and real national income, may overstate or understate the change in nominal purchasing power imbalance, depending on whether the actual growth rate of real national output is greater or smaller than the growth rate of real *NI*.

Finally, I estimate Z, the index of real purchasing power imbalance, on the basis of equation (5.9), which states that Z is the difference between the growth rate of money incomes $(\dot{MI})$ and the growth rate of monetary expenditure $(\dot{C})$. The estimates of both *MI* and *C* are as given in Table 5.1. The resultant estimates of Z are given in the last column of Table 5.2. Note that in using Z as a real purchasing power imbalance index I have ignored the increase in the demand for money [equation (5.8)], which will increase with national income and population and has a negative effect on consumer goods imbalance. Therefore, it must be borne in mind that the degree of consumer goods imbalance must to a certain extent be overstated by Z, especially in the years of rapid income growth where there is a rapid rise in the demand for money.

5.4   Foreign trade and consumer goods imbalance, 1956–77

In the years before the recent economic reforms, China's foreign trade grew relatively rapidly in the following periods: (a) 1958–9, or the years of the Great Leap Forward, (b) 1964–6, the years following the rapid recovery of the economy from the Great Leap Forward disaster, and (c) 1970–4, the years when China began to widen its contact with the Western world and when worldwide inflation occurred. In these periods, the economy's exports and imports rose by more than 10 percent per annum. Other than in these periods, the annual growth rates of both exports and imports were mostly negative or, if positive, below 10 percent. The question now is whether the degree of consumer goods imbalance in China had been worsened by the rapid foreign trade growth during the three high-trade-growth periods.

According to Liao (1985), any sudden and significant rise in the share of accumulation in aggregate expenditure would contribute to the worsening of consumer goods imbalance. Indeed, as shown in Table 5.2, *AS* rose significantly in all of the three high-trade-growth periods. The years of the Great Leap Forward registered the most significant increases in *AS*, which rose from 25 percent in 1957 to 34 percent in 1958 and rose further to 44 percent in 1959. In 1960, *AS* was slightly lowered but it remained as high as 40 percent. Owing to the corrective measures adopted by the government, *AS* dropped to 19 percent and below in the next three years. In the years between 1964 and 1966, the second period of relatively rapid trade growth, *AS* was lifted above 22 percent and reached a peak of 31 percent in 1966, signifying a moderate worsening of the consumer goods imbalance. However, foreign trade and investment were both dampened by the Cultural Revolution in the years from 1967 to 1969, resulting in a decline of *AS* to a level slightly above 20 percent in these three years. As foreign trade expanded rapidly in the early 1970s, *AS* was again raised above 30 percent, signifying another deterioration in the degree of consumer goods imbalance.

The rough picture of the changes in consumer goods imbalance presented above by the accumulation share approach shows that foreign trade growth had a close relation to the degree of consumer goods imbalance in the Chinese economy. However, the use of the rates of open inflation or Peebles's *PPIs* would draw different conclusions. Neither $\dot{P}$ nor *PPI* seems to rise or fall systematically with the country's foreign trade. Take the years of the Great Leap Forward, for instance. Based on $\dot{P}$, the years of both 1958 and 1959 experienced relatively stable prices, implying that there were no significant changes in the degree of consumer goods imbalance in the economy. But this is in contradiction with the widely recognized fact that the economy had experienced an unprecedented shortage of consumer goods during those years. Based on *PPI*, the degree of consumer goods imbalance appears to have improved in 1958 but deteriorated in 1959. For the two years as a whole, there was little change in the degree of consumer goods imbalance, again in contradiction with the fact that severe consumer goods shortages existed during those two years. The problem with the approach using the rates of open inflation lies with the fact that all prices were under government control and could not themselves respond to changes in market imbalances; and the problem with *PPI* lies with the fact that the growth of the so-called national income, which includes the value of producer goods, does not reflect the growth of the supply of consumer goods.

The only indicator which presents a similar picture of consumer goods imbalance to that presented by the accumulation share approach for the prereform period is the index of real purchasing power imbalance, *Z*. As shown in Table 5.2, the values of *Z* for all of the periods of high trade growth in the prereform period are positive except for 1972 (for which $Z = -0.95$). In contrast, the values of *Z* for all other years in the period are negative, with the exception of only 1961 and 1968, for which *Z* equals

1.03 and 0.91, respectively. Taking the simple arithmetic average of the values of Z in individual years, we get the following table.

Period	Average Z
1956-7	-0.41
1958-9	1.64*
1960-3	-1.67
1964-6	2.42*
1967-9	-2.04
1970-3	1.13*
1974-7	-0.73

* Denotes the period of high trade growth.

This result shows that the consumer goods imbalance was worsened in all of the periods with high trade growth and improved in all other periods when the growth of foreign trade slowed down.

Note that although the pictures of consumer goods imbalance painted by the accumulation share approach are similar to each other, the latter approach is superior to the former approach for the following reasons. First, the accumulation share approach depends crucially on the assumptions of unchanged technology, stable population growth, and unchanged price structure, whereas the real purchasing power imbalance approach, measuring the change in real unsatisfied consumer demand, is unaffected by these factors. Second, whereas neither the value of AS nor its change provides any unambiguous information about the change in the degree of consumer goods imbalance, the sign as well as the magnitude of Z, like the rate of inflation in the market economy, provide unambiguous information about the degree of improvement or deterioration in consumer goods imbalance. Nevertheless, for comparison purposes, I continue to use these two indicators in the following discussion.

5.5   Foreign trade, economic reforms, and consumer goods imbalance, 1978-80

Xue (1985) describes 1978 as the year of China's second "Great Leap Forward." This is a proper description in the sense that the country, as in the first Great Leap Forward, undertook a sudden and large-scale increase in investment that featured a dramatic rise in the imports of machinery and capital equipment for heavy industry. As shown in Table 5.4 imports increased by an unprecedented 57 percent and fixed capital formation

Table 5.4. Annual growth rates of foreign trade and fixed capital formation, 1978–85 (in percentages)

	1978	1979	1980	1981	1982	1983	1984	1985
Exports	24.32	34.49	38.37	15.51	6.16	2.22	19.17	13.32
Imports	57.12	39.24	33.04	−6.15	−7.07	9.65	36.95	54.96
Fixed capital formation	30.82	2.85	6.25	−21.10	25.61	6.89	23.26	37.21

Sources: Table A.2 and Table A.3.

rose by nearly 31 percent in that year. The rapid increase in investment raised the accumulation share to 37 percent from 32 percent in the previous year (Table 5.2). The significant increase in the share of accumulation in aggregate expenditure has been considered by Chinese economists as a clear indication of the worsening of the economy's consumer goods and producer goods shortages. The worsening of the economy's consumer goods shortage is also confirmed by our Z estimate, which gives a positive value of 2.39.

Due to the long gestation periods that characterize investment in heavy industrial projects and the lasting effects of the shortage of energy, raw materials, transportation facility, and so forth, the shortage of consumer goods continued to worsen in 1979 and 1980, for which Z increased to 4.66 and 3.66, respectively. The severity of this imbalance problem together with the inefficiency with which imported capital goods were absorbed by the economy prompted the government to revise downward its investment and import targets dramatically.[8] Both economists and policymakers in China started to advocate the adoption of readjustment policy as early as in late 1978. At the same time, the government carried out economic system reforms with a view to improving the efficiency with which enterprises and the agricultural sector operated. Several measures taken by the government had different degrees of impact on the consumer goods imbalance.

First, the imports of machinery and capital equipment were curtailed and the construction of new projects which were already under way was either canceled or delayed. As shown in Table 5.4, the growth rates of imports decreased from 57 percent in 1978 to about 39 percent in 1979 and further decreased to 33 percent in 1980. The decrease was substantial considering that a large proportion of these years' imports either had been ordered in 1978 or derived from many of the new investment projects which called for foreign parts and raw materials. As a matter of fact, the

Chinese government imposed a moratorium on the signing of new import contracts with foreign traders in 1979 (Chapter 3).

Second, as discussed in Chapter 1, economic reforms were implemented in order to increase the responsiveness of individual production units to changes in market demand. In agriculture, the government introduced the household responsibility system, freeing farmers from prereform bureaucratic management system that controlled nearly all aspects of farming before the reform, including the type of crops to grow, the amount of fertilizer to apply, and so on. In industry, enterprises were given some degree of autonomy with respect to production, management, sales, price setting, and input procurement. As a result of these changes as well as the readjustment policy which redirected resources from heavy industry to agriculture and light industry, agriculture and light industry grew more quickly than did heavy industry in both 1979 and 1980 (Chapter 3).

The impacts of these two policy changes on the supply of and demand for consumer goods were unlikely to be significant in the first few years. In the first place, it was a time-consuming process for individual enterprises to acquire additional resources to increase production and to find the outlets for their increased products within the rather primitive marketing and information networks. In addition, reduction in imports could only be achieved with a certain time lag. Hence, the economy was still very much under the influence of the 1978 Four Modernizations drive in 1979 and 1980, and it is not surprising that, according to the Z estimates, the economy witnessed a continued worsening of consumer goods imbalance in those two years.

In spite of the worsening consumer goods imbalance, not all policy measures adopted during 1979 and 1980 were in line with the objective of achieving economic balance. In light of the large trade deficit created by the import spree of 1978 and the government's continued interest in technology imports, exports were actively promoted. Among other export promotion measures, Special Economic Zones for export processing purposes in the Guangdong and Fujian provinces were set up, joint ventures with foreign firms in the areas where products could be exported were initiated, corporations were formed to export labor, and a foreign exchange retention scheme was introduced. As shown in Table 5.4, exports went up by as much as 34 percent and 38 percent in 1979 and 1980, respectively. As indicated in the previous chapter, such a rapid increase in exports had an unambiguous worsening effect on the economy's consumer goods imbalance.

Another policy measure which tended to aggravate the shortage of consumer goods was the substantial wage increase in agriculture and industry. Partly to solicit support from the people for the policy of economic modernization, the government substantially raised both agricultural procurement prices and industrial wage rates in 1979 and 1980. In 1979, industrial wage rates went up by nearly 9 percent, while agricultural procurement payments per worker increased by as much as 27 percent.[9] In the following year, industrial wage rates went up by an even higher 14 percent, while agricultural procurement payments per worker increased by about 15 percent. These increases were exceptionally high in China's recent history, and they tended to aggravate the shortage of consumer goods by raising their demand. Nevertheless, their effects on consumer goods imbalance should not be overstated since the wage increases had to some extent been accounted for by productivity improvements, as evidenced by the rapid growth of agricultural and light industrial outputs, which, in real terms, went up by 13 percent and 30 percent, respectively, in the period from 1979 to 1980 (State Statistical Bureau, *Statistical Yearbook of China,* 1987, p. 32).

On the whole, the years from 1978 to 1980 were characterized by deteriorating consumer goods imbalance. Although the programs of readjustment and reforms implemented in 1979 and 1980 helped alleviate the imbalance problems to a certain extent by raising productivity, the resultant increases in wages and investment spending by enterprises and local governments inevitably contributed to a worsening of the shortage of consumer goods. For a dramatic improvement in consumer goods imbalance, it was necessary for the economy to take a more drastic step to reduce the levels of investment and foreign trade.

5.6   Export expansion, free markets, and consumer goods imbalance, 1981–5

The year of 1981 was characterized by the recentralization of economic decision-making power as the economy, still struggling to correct the imbalances caused by the Four Modernizations drive, was faced with investment booms and seemingly uncontrollable wage hikes at the local government level. Stringent controls were imposed on imports, investments, and wage increases, to such an extent that it appeared that the government was moving toward abolishing the newly implemented economic reforms. Such a dramatic turnaround resulted in a sharp drop in the growth rates of foreign trade and fixed capital formation. As shown in Table 5.4, the level of imports recorded a decline of more than 6 percent, signifying the down-to-earth effort made by the government to contain the growth of investment. And, indeed, the level of capital formation dropped by 21 percent in that year, lowering the accumulation share to

28.3 percent from 31.5 percent in the previous year. As a result of these changes and the relatively slow export growth (16 percent), the economy finally witnessed an improvement in consumer goods imbalance in that year, as evidenced by the negative estimate of the real purchasing power imbalance index Z ($= -1.82$). The improvement continued into 1982, for which year Z equaled -0.48.

However, the government was far from ready to give up its ambition to modernize the economy through economic reforms for the sake of economic stability. The recentralization of economic decision-making power proved to be short-lived as China again pushed for economic reforms by late 1982. During the period between 1982 and 1985, exports continued to be promoted for the eventual import of foreign technology, which was still considered to be the single most important factor contributing to the economy's modernization. Nevertheless, partly as a result of the world economic recession, exports went up by an average of only 4 percent in the period 1982–3. As the world economy recovered in 1984, exports grew by a relatively high rate of 19 percent, followed by a slightly lower rate of 13 percent in 1985. As for imports, although they dropped by more than 7 percent in 1982, they were moving on the track of rapid growth in the years from 1983 to 1985, in which period they increased by an average of more than 32 percent per annum. At the same time, there was a rapid increase in fixed capital formation, which went up by 7 percent in 1983, 23 percent in 1984, and 37 percent in 1985. The government's loss of control of imports and investment quickly resulted in a worsening of the degree of consumer goods imbalance as the Z index turned positive and rose to 1.85 in 1983 and further to 6.18 in 1984.

The severity of the deterioration in consumer goods imbalance in 1983 and 1984, judging from the estimates of Z, seemed to surpass that in the years between 1978 and 1980. However, one must be careful in making such comparison. The reason is that as the economy has become increasingly less strictly centrally planned since late 1982, when economic reforms were again advocated by the government, the nature of consumer goods imbalance has also changed. Recall that the real purchasing power imbalance indicator Z is given as the difference between the growth rate of money incomes and the growth rate of the supply of consumer goods $(\dot{MI} - \dot{C})$. In the state where the economy is strictly centrally planned, a foreign trade or investment expansion would involve a relatively small increase in money incomes, since the government would be relatively reluctant to resort to deficit financing. For instance, the growth rate of money incomes in 1978 was only 10.9 percent, which was only slightly higher than the 6.32 percent of 1977. In contrast, in the state where economic decision-making power is decentralized, a substantial expansion in investment and foreign trade would usually involve a rapid credit expansion, with enterprises and local governments incurring debts with the central government and the central government incurring debts with foreign banks or governments (see Chapter 3 for the statistics on the annual foreign debts incurred by China during this period). A rapid expansion of credit will in turn lead to a rapid increase in money incomes (see Section 6.6 for a discussion of the effect of foreign trade expansion on money incomes). Take the year of 1984, for instance. In that year, investment and foreign trade grew rapidly: Exports went up by 19 percent, imports went up by 37 percent, and fixed capital formation went up by 23 percent (Table 5.4). As a result, money incomes went up by as much as 32 percent, compared with 10 percent and 15 percent in 1982 and 1983, respectively. The high growth rate of money incomes was also due in part to the competitive expansion in bank credits, which enterprises used to finance new investment projects and even wage increases. The fact that enterprises and local governments could raise their own investment funds through borrowings from the banking system implies that the level of investment was no longer limited by the size of "profits" accumulated in the traditional fiscal system. Thus, unusually high rates of increase in money incomes became possible under economic reforms.

The effect of foreign trade or investment expansion on the supply of consumer goods also changed with economic reforms. When the economy was under strict central planning, a significant increase in the level of investment would worsen the shortage of consumer goods, because an investment increase would lead to an increase in the demand for, but a decrease in the supply of, consumer goods. Wage payments would rise and boost the demand for consumer goods while resources would be reallocated from the consumer goods sector to the producer goods sector, lowering the supply of consumer goods. When reforms were undertaken and when the size of free markets began to increase, an increase in the level of investment would increase not only the demand for but also the supply of producer goods. Thus, given any investment increase, there would be a relatively small amount of resources which had to be reallocated from the consumer goods sector to the producer goods sector. In addition, as free markets gained in importance, any excess demand for consumer goods in controlled markets would spill over into free markets, raising the prices of consumer goods in these markets and stimulating their supply. Therefore, the effect of an investment increase on the supply of consumer goods under economic reform tended to be relatively small.

For the above reasons, the negative effect of an investment and foreign trade expansion on the supply of consumer goods was relatively important in explaining such consumer goods imbalance as that which occurred in 1978, whereas its positive effect on money incomes and, therefore, the demand for consumer goods (as a result of changes in money incomes) was relatively important in explaining such consumer goods imbalance as that which occurred in 1984.[10] In a low-income country like China, the government would obviously be more sensitive to the first type of consumer goods imbalance than to the second type, given the same degree of consumer goods imbalance. This explains at least partly why no drastic action was taken by the government to rectify the imbalance problem in or immediately after 1984.

Note that in the presence of free market transactions the imbalance indicator Z is likely to understate the degree of consumer goods imbalance when the amount of consumer goods transacted in the free and semifree markets becomes a relatively important part of the aggregate consumption expenditure. The reason is that the indicator fails to take into account the part of the consumer goods imbalance which takes the form of price increases in the free and semifree markets. In 1985, for instance, Z is negative and equal to -3.76, seemingly suggesting that there was an improvement in consumer goods imbalance during the year. Nevertheless, in that year, the economy was seen to suffer from the highest rate of open inflation in more than 20 years, measured at nearly 9 percent in terms of the prices of retail sales. In terms of the prices of consumer goods, which had greater flexibility than other prices did, the rate of open inflation was 8 percent in state-controlled markets and 17 percent in free markets, due mostly to sharp increases among food items. In state-controlled markets, the prices of food items rose by an unprecedented 13 percent, while in free markets, the prices of fresh vegetables rose by 22 percent, fishery products, 26 percent, and fresh fruits, 29 percent. If the inflation rate is taken into account, the degree of consumer goods imbalance is likely to be seen to have worsened in 1985.[11]

In the face of rising inflationary pressure, the government adopted several measures to control inflation. First, in addition to advising provincial officials to slow down capital construction and speed up investment in infrastructure, the central government from time to time postponed or canceled those investment projects which it considered to be cost-ineffective or to be putting an undue strain on electricity supply and other infrastructure. In 1983 alone, 5,350 projects were either canceled or postponed. The fact that they included about 3,000 projects which were outside the state plan suggests that the state had lost considerable control over investment at the local level. The effectiveness of such measure is subject to doubt, however, because the cancellation or delay of current projects could not in itself prevent new projects from starting up. Enterprises and local governments holding idle investment funds under the profit-sharing scheme would continue to seek outlet for these funds, by issuing bonuses to workers or starting up new projects. A fundamental rectification of the problem would require the use of incentives to induce enterprises and local governments to invest in the areas where the degree of consumer goods imbalance could be improved.

Second, the government temporarily relaxed its controls over consumer goods imports in late 1984 and early 1985 for the purpose of withdrawing currency from circulation. During this period, numerous organizations, including kindergartens and military establishments, sprang up to deal with imports, and consumers, armed with large amounts of unspent cash accumulated from past savings, took advantage of what they considered to be a once-in-a-lifetime opportunity by importing such "luxury" items as motor vehicles, cameras, electronic watches, television sets, and so forth. In less than a year, the import fever depleted about 30 percent of the country's foreign exchange reserves, or 5.41 billion U.S. dollars. This measure, though not sustainable, was clearly an effective means for controlling inflation, since it not only effected a large increase in the supply of consumer goods but also siphoned off a large amount of money in circulation.

Finally, to control the growth of consumer goods demand, the government imposed progressive taxes on bonus payments to workers. The scheme of the taxes has been discussed in Chapter 2. However, this measure was effective in controlling the wage rate but ineffective in controlling the total wage bill. Faced with the progressive taxes, enterprises were induced to spend their retained profits on new investment projects, thus increasing the number of workers hired and raising the total wage bill. In 1984, for instance, the average wage rate of the economy increased by about 13 percent, but the total wage bill went up by more than 21 percent. An effective control of the growth of consumer goods demand would call for a reduction in the level of profits retained by enterprises and local governments as well as a strict restriction on the amount of funds that could be extended to them by domestic and foreign banks.

In the absence of an effective inflation control policy, China continued to experience high inflationary pressures in 1986 and 1987. The rate of inflation, in terms of the rate of increase in the prices of retail sales, reached 6 percent in 1986 and 7.8 percent in the first half of 1987.[12] Since it feared that inflation might be further worsened, the government delayed the introduction of price reforms, which it regarded as a crucial step toward a successful economic reform (see Chapter 6 for a detailed discussion on the problem of price reform). In early 1988, the government started to link the wage rate with the rate of inflation by providing workers with cost-of-living subsidies so as to alleviate the resentment of workers toward economic reforms. This measure was most likely to fuel further inflation unless the subsidies were accompanied by a commensurate reduction in other government expenditures.

5.7   Summary and conclusion

In the present chapter, I developed the index of real purchasing power imbalance as an indicator of the change in the degree of consumer goods imbalance. The empirical analysis shows that there were significant fluctuations in the degree of consumer goods imbalance in China in the past three decades. Notably, the fluctuations in the degree of consumer goods imbalance were closely related to the fluctuations in the growth of the country's foreign trade. In general, consumer goods imbalance deteriorated when there was rapid foreign trade growth and improved when there was a contraction in the volume of foreign trade. Moreover, I also showed that the picture of the fluctuations in the degree of consumer goods imbalance as presented by the real purchasing power imbalance index is similar to that which is perceived by some leading Chinese economists who regard the degree of consumer goods imbalance as being influenced mostly by changes in the share of accumulation in aggregate expenditure. The similarity between the two pictures is particularly striking for the period between 1956 and 1977.

In the post-1978 years, the degree of consumer goods imbalance was influenced by two major factors: the ambitious modernization program launched in 1978 and the program of readjustment and reform implemented starting in 1979. Because of the large-scale increase in imports and investment in heavy industry in 1978, the economy was faced with severe supply bottlenecks in the production of both producer goods and consumer goods. As a result, the government had to abolish the modernization program in 1979 and start to remedy the situation by pushing for economic readjustment. According to my analysis, the readjustment policy in the years of 1979 and 1980 resulted only in a slowdown in the rate at which the degree of consumer goods imbalance deteriorated, and it was not until 1981, the year when the government drastically reduced the growth rates of imports and investment, that there was an improvement in consumer goods imbalance. Nevertheless, the improvement continued for only two years, and by 1983, because of the rapid increase in the scope of economic reforms which loosened the central government's control over investment and bank credits, the economy was again faced with deteriorating consumer goods imbalance. However, the imbalance in and after 1983 was due partly to the lack of coordination in central planning and partly to the loss of government control over the money supply, which went up quickly with the investment spendings at the enterprise and local government levels. As a result of the lack of government control over the money supply, prices in free and semifree markets rose quickly. Beginning in 1985, the index of real purchasing power imbalance, which is based on the assumption that the supply of consumer goods is insensitive to changes in their prices, can no longer adequately account for the problem of consumer goods imbalance in the Chinese economy. The problem of consumer goods imbalance must now be assessed by placing an increasing emphasis on the phenomenon of inflation.

CHAPTER 6

Conclusion: The prospect of foreign trade reforms

Under China's prereform foreign trade system, exports were determined by the level of planned surpluses and imports by the level of planned shortages. It was important that foreign trade was fully integrated into the national economic plan. A deficiency in raw material imports, for instance, would hamper domestic production and create a ripple of coordination problems. In contrast, under the postreform system, exports and imports are no longer determined by an elaborate coordination process. Specialized ministries, local governments, and enterprises, now sharing with the central government the power to engage in foreign trade, are to a certain extent allowed to make their own foreign trade decisions. Foreign trade is not, and does not have to be, rigidly planned, because enterprises and local governments are now faced with relatively flexible supplies of material inputs from domestic and foreign sources. The central government only has to draw up a rough foreign trade plan and deal with major exports and imports. Under this new economic system, foreign trade is much less destabilizing than it was under the prereform system, given that foreign trade is no longer strictly associated with massive and forced reallocation of resources from one sector to the other. The 1981–2 foreign trade slump and the 1984–6 foreign trade boom had relatively little impact on China in terms of national output.

Although foreign trade is less destabilizing under the postreform economic system, the economic efficiency of foreign trade has not necessarily improved with economic reforms. Under the present foreign trade system, the decisions on what and how much to export and import, though having been decentralized to a certain extent, are made within the institutional framework inherited from the prereform economic system. Except for the case where foreign-owned enterprises were involved, changes in market conditions would have little influence on foreign trade since exports are indirectly determined by the government's procurement policy whereas imports are determined by the government's discretionary control measures. Unless a further reform is implemented to improve the responsiveness of exports and imports to changes in market conditions at home and abroad, the economic efficiency of foreign trade is unlikely to improve significantly in the future.

The crucial question is this: Can economic reforms in China be further advanced? In his recent study of the Hungarian reform process, Kornai (1986) raises a similar question: "Does contemporary Hungary exhibit more or less the ultimate limits of reforms?" Given that Hungary has been implementing reforms since 1968, it is conceivable that it has already reached a more "mature" stage of reforms such that a further advancement of reforms is considerably more difficult than it would be in China. However, the process of reforms in China has slowed down considerably since 1985 as various measures with far-reaching economic consequences have been proposed but failed to be put into practice. The proposed measures include the bankruptcy law and a realignment of domestic prices, both being regarded as a precondition for a significant improvement in the efficiency of resource allocation. In these proposed measures, China has essentially followed its past practice of forcing changes upon enterprises rather than creating an environment to induce enterprises to respond. As in the past, the proposed reforms lack a comprehensive study of their possible effects on such important problems as price stability, employment, regional balance, fiscal revenues at local and central levels, and income distribution. Thus, strong resistance from enterprises and even the planning authorities themselves arose, hindering a further reform of enterprises and foreign trade.

The present chapter is divided into two parts. The first part, including Section 6.1 through Section 6.5, discusses the problems which have to be tackled by future foreign trade reforms with a view to improving the economic efficiency of foreign trade. Section 6.1 points to the need for establishing a foreign exchange market. Section 6.2 shows the need for a fundamental change in China's foreign trade objectives. Section 6.3 suggests that China's foreign trade reform will have to be preceded by a general reform. Section 6.4 examines the problems involved in the price reform proposed by the government. Section 6.5 points to the need for a basic reform of the incentive system as a prerequisite of a thorough price reform. In the second part of this chapter, that is, Section 6.6, I look at the increasingly important problem of inflation in the Chinese economy in light of the rapid expansion of foreign trade. This is a supplement to Chapters 4 and 5, which looked at the problem of real purchasing power imbalance caused primarily by changes in the supply of consumer goods. Section 6.7 provided some concluding remarks.

6.1   The role of the exchange rate in foreign trade

Since 1979, markets for commodities and services have expanded rapidly in China as a result of the economic reforms which allow enterprises to sell their above-plan output at free-market or negotiated prices. However, nearly a decade after the implementation of economic reforms, the country still has not established a foreign exchange market as a basis for the control of foreign trade. In the absence of this market, the exchange rate does not serve to convey to exporting enterprises the economic benefit of foreign exchange earnings or to importing enterprises the economic costs of foreign exchange expenditures. A devaluation of the renminbi, for instance, will have no effect on export procurement prices and therefore will not affect the decisions of enterprises and local governments concerning exports. Imports will be affected only to the extent that a devaluation raises the renminbi costs of foreign exchange entitlement quotas, thus effectively reducing the amount of foreign exchange allocated to enterprises and local governments under the foreign exchange retention scheme. Other imports, which are financed by centrally allocated foreign exchange, will not be affected, as they involve no renminbi payments.

One pertinent question is: Have certain economic changes, including the decentralization of foreign trade power and the development of the black market for foreign exchange, increased the role of the exchange rate in China's foreign trade? Under economic reforms, municipal and provincial governments are empowered to establish their own foreign trade corporations and conduct their own trade with foreign traders. This decentralization of foreign trade power, however, has not increased the role of the exchange rate in the decision making of those foreign trade corporations, because under the present system local governments are as likely to benefit from as to be hurt by exchange rate changes. For instance, when the exchange rate depreciates, local governments will be paid more for the portion of foreign exchange earnings that they turn over to the central government and thus benefit from higher retained profits, but, at the same time, they will also have to pay more for the use of foreign exchange within the foreign exchange quotas. The net benefit for them is indeterminate, and the exchange rate change does not have an unambiguous effect on the decisions of local governments on exports and imports.

The growth of the black market for foreign exchange also has not enhanced the role of the exchange rate in foreign trade. In the prereform period, private holdings of foreign exchange were strictly prohibited, and, because there was limited contact with the outside world, people did not normally receive or use foreign exchange. Therefore, there were few transactions of foreign exchange outside government control. However, during the postreform period, domestic residents have had an increasingly wider range of contacts with the outside world and they can in various ways benefit from the holding and use of foreign exchange. First, residents possessing foreign exchange may surrender it to the banks in exchange for foreign exchange certificates, which provide them with access to those consumer goods which are normally in short supply in the market, such as brand name bicycles and electric appliances. Second, residents may deposit foreign exchange in their foreign exchange savings accounts in their banks to hedge against the devaluation of renminbi or to provide their children with the foreign exchange funds needed for foreign education.[1] Third, foreign exchange may be sold at a premium to foreign traders and investors who have to convert their renminbi earnings into foreign exchange but are unable to do so through the official channel.[2] Fourth, foreign exchange may also be sold at a premium to people engaged in the smuggling of high-quality consumer goods from Hong Kong and Taiwan. Motivated by these benefits, black market transactions in foreign exchange have increased substantially in recent years. The exchange rate in the black market has consistently been more than 50 percent higher than the official rate. In August 1988, when it was rumored that the renminbi was about to be devalued, the black market rate for the Hong Kong dollar, a widely used foreign currency in Guangdong, was reported by tourists coming out of China as having shot up from the usual 0.78 Hong Kong dollars to about 0.9 Hong Kong dollars per renminbi yuan, compared to the official rate of 0.47 Hong Kong dollars per renminbi yuan. Nevertheless, the transactions in the black market, depending chiefly on tourists and some foreign enterprises for the supply of foreign exchange, are relatively small and unlikely to have played any significant role in China's international trade.

Since the role of the exchange rate in foreign trade has not increased with the increased responsiveness of exports and imports to prices, the establishment of local foreign trade corporations, and the development of the black market for foreign exchange, China still has to rely on administrative methods to control exports and imports. Under these circumstances, there is no guarantee that foreign trade would not become over- or underexpanded.

6.2 The need for a change in foreign trade objectives

In the absence of an official foreign exchange market for regulating foreign trade, China's foreign trade policy hinges crucially on the perception of the political leadership of the importance of foreign trade to the economy. The recent economic reforms have not been accompanied by any change in the view of Chinese political leaders on the role of foreign trade in China's economic modernization. As in the prereform period, exports are still considered to be a necessary evil and imports are still considered to be a necessary means for the achievement of economic modernization. Both exports and imports are still arranged by the government rather than determined by the market, and foreign trade is still aimed at increasing the imports of foreign technology and equipment. In his address to the 13th Chinese Communist Party Congress (October 26, 1987), Premier Zhao Ziyang stated that[3]

The [economy's] export earning capability determines to a great extent the degree and scope of the openness of the country and it will affect the scale and speed of domestic economic construction. We should, on the basis of the demand of the world market and the country's comparative advantage, actively promote those industries and products which are competitive, characterized by short gestation periods, and cost-effective, greatly raise the quality and quantity of exports, rationally arrange the commodity structure of exports, and widely open up international markets, so as to achieve rapid and sustained growth of exports. At the same time, we should actively promote tourism and develop service and technology exports, raising nonmerchandise export earnings. Imports should be centered on technology and key equipment.

China's emphasis on technology imports stems from the widely held belief among Chinese economists and political leaders that China's low level of economic development is attributable primarily to its backward production technology and that the use of foreign technology is a short cut to technological modernization. Indeed, China's technology level has been low and its industrial machinery and equipment have mostly been imported from industrialized countries, such as Japan and the Soviet Union, and such imports have saved China much time and effort which it would otherwise have had to invest in the development of its own machinery and equipment. However, the basic question is how much and what technology should be imported? Zhao Ziyang's speech essentially suggests that China should import as much foreign technology as permitted by the economy's import capacity, and that enterprises can be counted on to decide the technology to be imported. Accordingly, the major task to be performed by the foreign trade authorities is to promote exports and raise the economy's import capacity.

In this regard, the MFERT has drawn up some guidelines for exports.[4] First, goods which are essential to the livelihood of people, such as food grains and edible oil, can be exported only in limited quantities; second, goods produced by those enterprises which have been set up with foreign capital or foreign trade loans extended by the government must be exported; third, "luxury" industrial items produced by coastal cities should normally be exported; and fourth, goods for which demand exists in both domestic and foreign markets should be partly exported. These guidelines are based on an implicit assumption that the economic costs of most domestically produced goods are lower than the economic benefits of imports. This was probably a realistic assumption for most of the prereform years when foreign trade was relatively small. In recent years, however, the marginal rate of return on technology imports must have decreased dramatically because of the rapid expansion in these imports, given the relatively slow improvement in the environment for investment. By the investment environment is meant the general perception of the role of the market, the availability of technical personnel, the quality and quantity of the services of infrastructure, and the legal and political framework governing investment activities. Since all of these elements tend to take a long time to improve, it is not surprising that numerous imported projects have in past years been reported as having been significantly underutilized, for such reasons as inadequate feasibility studies, shortages of technical personnel, poor infrastructure, bureaucratic foot-dragging, and so on.

To improve the economic efficiency of foreign trade, the government should first recognize that technology imports are neither necessary nor sufficient to bring about economic modernization. Technology imports will contribute to economic modernization only if the benefits from their use can generate sufficiently large economic benefits to cover their costs. The major benefit associated with foreign trade is that it enables the economy to specialize in and export those goods in which it has a comparative cost advantage in exchange for those goods in which it has a comparative cost disadvantage. The latter category of goods is by no means restricted to advanced technology; they may consist of raw materials, intermediate products, machine parts, and even consumer goods. To determine the goods in which the economy has a comparative cost advantage or disadvantage, the government should rely more on the market than on discretionary measures in foreign trade decision making. And, to increase the role of the market in foreign trade, it should implement a further reform of the present foreign trade system.

6.3   The need for further reform of the economic system

Although the eventual improvement in the economic efficiency of foreign trade will have to come from a further reform of the foreign trade system, any foreign trade reforms must be preceded by a general economic reform, since foreign trade activities cannot be strictly separated from the rest of the economy. The role of the market in foreign trade cannot be increased without an increase in the role of the market in the economy as a whole. For instance, the responsiveness of exports to changes in international prices cannot be raised without raising the responsiveness of the enterprises as a whole to changes in domestic market conditions. Also, for imports to respond to changes in market conditions at home, the decisions of the importing enterprises on investment will first have to be guided by the profitability determined by the market, which is possible only if the production and investment of domestic enterprises are also guided mainly by their market profitability. In the past, China's foreign trade reforms, characterized by the import agent system and relatively flexible export procurement prices, have all occurred in parallel with general reforms.

By reform, we have adopted Kornai's definition that it occurs when the economic system of a centrally planned economy is so changed that "it diminishes the role of bureaucratic coordination and increases the role of the market" (Kornai 1986, p. 1691). Efforts made by China (a) to pool together trading and nontrading enterprises to augment exports and (b) to step up the use of imported technology in exporting enterprises are not reforms in this sense because they do not involve any increase in the role of the market.

How the foreign trade system will be changed in the future will depend on the course that will be taken in general economic reforms. Zhao Ziyang has provided the following guidelines for China's future economic reforms in his speech to the 13th Communist Party Congress.[5]

Separation of management from ownership: Public ownership of all productive means will be maintained while the right to manage will be relinquished to individual enterprises. Enterprises will in turn be responsible for their own profits and losses, irrespective of whether they are engaged in domestic or foreign trade. Leasing and contracting as a form of management responsibility system will be encouraged and adopted in appropriate industries.

Horizontal linkages: To improve the mobility of labor, capital, knowhow, and productive materials, China will encourage enterprises and regional governments to open up and trade with each other, so as to exploit the benefits of specialization and scale economies. Joint corporations crossing different regions and ministries will also be encouraged.

Price reform: In order to make better use of the market mechanism, price reforms will be carried out in both the factor and goods markets. The state will be responsible for setting the prices of only a few key services and commodities, while allowing other prices to fluctuate and regulate supply and demand.

Macroeconomic management: China will reform the banking, financial, and fiscal systems to facilitate the government's indirect control over the level of prices, the distribution of income, the level of investment, and the structure of industrial growth. For this purpose, a comprehensive system of commercial laws will be created for regulating exchange and production, supervising and disciplining enterprises and markets, and protecting consumer and national interest.

Private economy: Recognized as being useful in supplementing the public sector, in creating employment, and in increasing the quantity and variety of products, private economy will not only be tolerated but will also be encouraged. To promote and regulate private economic activities, the government will publish its policy on the matter and promulgate related law. At the same time, foreign investment will continue to be encouraged.

Income distribution: Labor will be paid according to its contribution to production, and incomes in the form of interest and profit will be permitted.

According to the above guidelines, the reform is to transform China into a market-oriented economy. Such a reform would greatly facilitate the government's introduction of the export agent system which it considers to be crucial to the improvement of the economic efficiency of foreign trade. In the export agent system, enterprises can themselves decide on what and how much to export, and foreign trade corporations will act only as exporting agents. Since they will no longer be faced with fixed procurement prices, exports will now become sensitive to changes in the exchange rate as well as foreign demand, thus improving in economic efficiency. At the same time, the reform would also improve the economic efficiency of imports by increasing their sensitivity to import costs. Of course, the government is likely to maintain a relatively high degree of control over foreign trade when compared with internal trade. Consumer goods imports may still be curtailed, technology imports may continue to receive priority, the exports and imports of some key commodities are likely to be put under the direct control of the foreign trade authorities, and tariffs, quotas, and administrative measures will still be used to regulate inessential imports and exports.

The importance of the above guidelines should not be overemphasized, however. In fact, they have already been set out in the recent reform.[6] The repetition is mainly to reassure the country and the rest of the world that

China is still firmly on the road of reform following the political uncertainty that led to the resignation of Hu Yaobang, a reformist, from the post of the General Secretary of the Communist Party in early 1987. The country still has to draw up a comprehensive reform program in order to achieve the targets embodied in the above guidelines. Before this is done, China's foreign trade system is likely to remain as it is.

6.4   Price reforms and problems

One of the concrete steps that has been taken by China to push for a further reform of the economic system is the introduction of the manager responsibility system in 1984. During the economic reforms, each enterprise is accorded certain decision-making power and made eligible to share its profits with the state. However, being an economic decision-making unit, the enterprise does not have to take the responsibility for the decisions it makes. In the case where losses are incurred as a result of, say, wrong investment decisions, the enterprise will not be disciplined and all losses will be paid for by the government. China intends to rectify this problem by consolidating the management power in the hands of enterprise managers and making them responsible for the performance of the enterprises. This system is known as the manager responsibility system. Under this system, managers, in place of party officials, would be empowered to make production, investment, and sales decisions and be responsible for the decisions they make. The government is attempting to create a system similar to the agricultural household responsibility system (Li 1987, pp. 10–12).

One of the most important benefits associated with such a system is that it would be possible for the government to control the performance of the enterprise through the incentives and disincentives provided to the manager. What is needed is only a "proper" incentive system to determine how the manager would be rewarded or disciplined in association with the performance of the enterprise. The government has long believed that enterprises should be made responsible for their profits and losses, so that they would become cost-conscious and break the habit of pursuing self-sufficiency. Under the present system, enterprises' insensitivity to costs has created tens of thousands of "small and comprehensive" and "large and comprehensive" production units in the industrial sector. They produce as much machine parts and intermediate goods for themselves as possible so as to minimize their dependence on other production units for the supply of inputs. It would be beneficial to the economy if the cost-minimizing behavior of enterprises would lead to increased specialization and interenterprise trade. Another important benefit of the system is that it would help streamline the enterprise decision-making process and enable the enterprise to respond quickly to changes in market conditions.

In its implementation of the manager responsibility system, China, however, has encountered serious problems. One of the greatest problems is that, in the presence of irrational prices, managers cannot be asked to take full responsibility for the enterprises' profits and losses even if they were given full management power. Enterprises may incur losses for the simple reason that their inputs have been overpriced or that their products have been underpriced, or both, rather than due to management inefficiency. Similarly, the presence of profits may be attributable to artificially low input prices or artificially high output prices, or both, instead of efficient management. The profitability of enterprises can be used to evaluate management efficiency only if all prices are rational or determined by the enterprises themselves, a condition that cannot be satisfied without a fundamental price reform.

In preparing for a price reform, the Price Study Center of the State Council has undertaken the task of mapping out a reform strategy and studying how rational prices may be determined. Nevertheless, the government had yet to come up with a workable program as recently as early 1989, more than four years after the launch of the manager responsibility system. To understand the problems involved, I first discuss below the view of Chinese economists on price irrationality and then show how they have proposed to tackle the problems.

Price irrationality: the Chinese view

Chinese economists generally agree that prices in China are irrational, in the sense that they do not reflect the "values" of the products. In Marxian theory, the value of a product is the sum of labor costs, material costs, and surplus, and the price of the product should be set equal to its value. If the product is overpriced, it will incur inordinately high profits; and if the product is underpriced, it will incur inordinately high losses. As pointed out earlier, however, since there is no objective rule as to how labor costs, material costs, and surplus may be determined empirically, all planned prices have to be to a certain extent arbitrarily determined. In most centrally planned economies, the problem is "solved" by pricing all goods on a cost-plus basis. Thus, planned prices would generally be higher the greater the number of processing stages involved in production, ceteris paribus. In some cases, planned prices are set at so low a level that inordinately large losses are incurred in production, whereas in some other cases, planned prices are set at so high a level as to generate inordinately high profits. Under economic reforms, operation losses would be paid for by the government, and operation profits would be shared between enterprises and the government. These losses and profits form a major part of the government's expenditures and revenues.

Chinese economists, focusing on the fiscal function of prices, consider price irrationality to have manifested itself in the following phenomena (Wang 1985, pp. 10–18). First, energy (oil, coal, and natural gas), raw materials, housing, and transportation services are underpriced, whereas a majority of manufactured goods, which normally undergo a number of processing stages, are overpriced. The following criteria are used to determine whether a goods is under- or overpriced: (a) the profits or losses incurred by the industry, (b) the degree of shortage of the goods in the market, and (c) the difference between domestic and foreign prices. Although inconsistency exists in these criteria, the first two are cited most frequently by the government and Chinese economists, presumably because enterprise losses and material imbalance are still important problems of the economy under the economic reforms. According to these criteria, the industries that are shortage-ridden and operating at a loss, including coal, oil, cotton, iron ore, natural gas, city water, and public transportation, are seriously underpriced. One problem with these goods and services being underpriced is that the subsidies on these industries represent a heavy fiscal burden on the government, particularly at the time when a large budget deficit is being incurred.[7] Another problem is that under the profit-sharing scheme, enterprises and local governments have little incentive to expand the production of these loss-incurring goods regardless of the fact that they are mostly in short supply in the market; they would expand the production of those goods which are "profitable" even if these goods were in excess supply in the market. As a result, according to Chinese economists, wastages have been incurred in the form of uneconomic use of underpriced goods and excessive production of overpriced goods.

Second, the procurement prices of agricultural goods, following a significant increase in 1979, had been set well above their retail prices until the summer of 1985, when the retail prices were adjusted upward. The policy was to stimulate agricultural production while keeping the cost of living in the nonagricultural sector unchanged. However, it had given rise to two major problems. On the one hand, the amount of subsidies tended to rise with the improvement of agricultural productivity. From 1979 to 1982, for instance, the subsidies on food grains and edible oil increased from 2.4 billion yuan to 4.7 billion yuan primarily as a result of the rapid increase in agricultural productivity following the implementation of the agricultural household responsibility system (Wang 1985, p. 13). On the other hand, the subsidies represented the operation losses of the commerce department undertaking the sales of agricultural goods. Faced with the losses, the commerce department was discouraged from promoting the procurement and sales of agricultural goods, thus hindering the inter-regional flow of foods and raw materials.

Third, in each commodity group, the price differentials are often so small that they do not reflect the differences in the quality of the goods. Under these circumstances, enterprises would not be rewarded for turning out high-quality products or penalized for turning out low-quality products, and, in a sense, consumers would not be compensated for shifting their purchases from high- to low-quality products. As a result, high-quality products tend to be in persistent shortage, whereas low-quality products tend to be in persistent surplus.

Of these three problems, the first one is generally considered to be the most serious and its rectification is regarded by some Chinese economists as what the future price reforms are all about. Such an assessment of the irrationality problem is understandable because the market prices of energy and raw materials have generally been substantially higher than the planned prices.[8] Most Chinese economists, of course, also recognize that the problem of price irrationality is attributable primarily to the economy's heavy reliance on directive planning. They believe that the problem should be dealt with by widening the scope of the guidance plan, under which prices are determined by the market. The question is to what extent should the scope of the guidance plan be expanded at the expense of the directive plan? The government's line is that the market should be used only as a supplement to central planning, presumably because it fears that a dramatic change to guidance planning could prove politically unpopular. With most productive activities still under central planning, the problem of price irrationality can only be dealt with by adjustment of the planned prices. The central problem of the price reform, from the government's point of view, is therefore how the planned prices should be adjusted, not so much as how much market forces should be allowed to operate and determine individual commodity prices. The two-tier pricing system will continue to operate.

Price reforms and difficulties

Under China's present two-tier pricing system, planned prices are fixed by the state and nonplanned prices are determined by the (distorted) market. By normally fixing the planned prices below the market-determined prices for the portion of the goods under central planning, the system opens the door for widespread favoritism and corruption in planned allocation and sends inconsistent signals to enterprises with respect to how much and what to produce and which inputs to use. This problem is particularly severe for heavy industrial products, since most of them are still subject to the rigid central economic plan and their market prices have been driven up significantly by the shortages of centrally allocated supplies. Since planned prices are normally lower than nonplanned prices, enterprises and local governments, motivated by the profit-sharing scheme, compete with one another for planned supplies but are discouraged from producing for planned allocation. As a result, shortages tend to prevail in the controlled market, or among the goods which are subject to the directive plan. In addition, many enterprises whose output prices are prohibited from being adjusted upward by the directive plan have reported making large losses because the costs of their production have been raised by the upward adjustment of the prices of some of their inputs. These enterprises, instead of turning over surpluses to the government, now have to depend on the government for subsidizing their losses. Such subsidies have worsened the budget deficit since the amount involved tended to be greater than the increase in the revenues from the enterprises whose prices had been adjusted upward. Since prices and outputs of most enterprises are no longer under central control, it has not been uncommon for enterprises to underreport their profits or overreport their production costs. Such practices enable them to accumulate funds for payments for workers' bonus and investment expenditures, on the one hand, and cause a decrease in government revenues from each unit of output produced by enterprises, on the other. In the course of rising government expenditures on infrastructure and price subsidies, the government budget deficit has been rising in recent years. One of the consequences of the enlarged budget deficit is that it has created an upward pressure on the general price level. The two-tier pricing system has added complications to the irrational pricing system.

Chinese economists generally view the present two-tier pricing system as an improvement over the previous rigid pricing system mainly because, under the former system, production would respond to changes in market conditions whereas it would not under the latter system. They believe that the system should continue to be adopted in order to ensure the stability of the supply of some "key" industrial products, including energy and raw materials. The rationalization of the planned prices of these products will therefore be a major task of the government in the future price reforms.

Wang (1985) suggests that to ensure a successful price reform, the government should first determine the so-called theoretical prices as substitutes for the current irrational planned prices. The theoretical prices are the prices which would have prevailed had they been determined freely by the market, subject to certain policy constraints. The determination of the theoretical prices clearly has to involve a general equilibrium model which is sophisticated enough to take into account the effects of various frequently changing economic and noneconomic factors. Building such a model for such a large and distortion-ridden economy such as China's is obviously difficult, if not impossible. Recently, a simpler approach has been considered by the planning authorities. In this approach, the theoretical prices are approximated by Little and Mirrlees's "shadow" prices, which are calculated as foreign exchange prices multiplied by the shadow exchange rate (Baldwin 1972, pp. 16–21; Little and Mirrlees 1974, pp. 29–37). One difficulty with this approach lies in the estimation of the shadow exchange rate, which is defined as the additional domestic resource costs that would be incurred when exports are increased by one foreign exchange unit or the domestic resource costs that would be saved as a result of an increase in the production of one foreign exchange unit of import substitutes. As pointed out in Chapter 2, the estimation of the domestic resource costs is particularly difficult in the presence of China's highly distorted factor markets, making it nearly impossible to calculate the shadow exchange rate. Nevertheless, since the major concern of the price reform is the determination of a rational price structure, the estimation of the shadow exchange rate, which determines the absolute shadow prices, is of secondary importance. According to the present approach, a rational price structure would be consistent with the structure of international prices.

The structure of the theoretical prices thus obtained would most likely be different dramatically from the prevailing price structure. The same old question then arises as to whether all or part of the planned prices should be replaced by the theoretical prices. Most Chinese economists suggest that the price reform should proceed cautiously, starting out with only a few industries, in order to avoid creating a dramatic shock to the economy (Wang 1985, pp. 32–43). The attention has been focused on energy and raw materials, which are widely recognized as being seriously underpriced. However, even with this relatively unambitious plan, its fiscal implications and possible inflationary effects turn out to be a major obstacle to its being put into practice.

Consider, first, the fiscal implications of an increase in the price of heavy industrial goods. Under China's fiscal system, the profits and losses of enterprises account for the most important part of the government's fiscal revenues and expenditures. In a suppliers' market, an enterprise's profits (losses) will normally increase (decrease) with an increase in its output price, and vice versa. Therefore, a price rise will increase the government's revenue from or decrease the government's subsidy of the product. However, this positive effect on the government budget will be at least partially offset by the negative effect of the ensuing increase in the production costs of the industries using the goods as an intermediate input. Whether there will be a net increase or decrease in fiscal expenditures will depend on the quality of the prevailing accounting practice as well as on the price elasticities of the demand for the goods in other industries. The government, having little control over the accounting procedure adopted by enterprises, fears that the net result will be an increase rather than a decrease in fiscal expenditures. This fear is not unfounded in view of its previous experience with the coal industry's report of an increase in losses following an upward adjustment of coal prices. If the price reform were almost certain to aggravate the budget deficit, there would be little incentive on the part of the government to implement the reform.

Price reforms would also change the distribution of fiscal revenues between central and local governments. This is due to the fact that the production of energy and raw materials is mostly under the control of the central government whereas the production of goods using energy and raw materials as inputs is under the dual control of central and local governments. As a result, an increase in the prices of energy and raw materials may increase or decrease the expenditures of the central government, whereas it can only lead to an increase in the expenditures of local governments. Under these circumstances, local governments are likely to seek compensation from the central government for losses in revenues, or else they would oppose the reform for the simple reason that their budget position would be adversely affected.

Now, turn to the likely effects of price reforms on general prices. An increase in the prices of energy and raw materials will inevitably raise the relative prices of those goods which use them intensively. It will also raise the absolute price level if it results in an increase in the budget deficit. The implication is that the real wages of those workers who receive fixed money wages and who work in the enterprises where profits decrease will necessarily be adversely affected. If they were to be compensated for the decrease in real wages, as has been implemented in the form of cost-of-living subsidies since April 1988, fiscal expenditures would have to be further raised. An increase in the budget deficit will result and it will raise the inflationary pressure.

In view of these difficulties, the government had made little progress in price reform since 1984. Without a price reform, the feasibility of the manager responsibility system, which is regarded as a crucial step in the reform process by the government, is in question. In October 1987, the Economic Commission announced that two-thirds of the state-owned enterprises had already adopted the manager responsibility system while the rest were expected to join the ranks before the end of 1988.[9] The present manager responsibility system, however, is a far cry from what was initially proposed. Under the present system, managers are not required to bear full responsibility for the profits and losses of the enterprises, and it aims only to reduce the management power of party officials, who traditionally have had a greater say in the management of the enterprises. The change is therefore a pure restructuring of enterprise management. Important as it may be for future price reforms, it does not have an unequivocal impact on the efficiency with which individual enterprises operate. No analogy can therefore be made between the present manager responsibility system and the agricultural household responsibility system, which has resulted in a significant increase in agricultural productivity in the past years.

6.5   The need for a basic reform of the incentive system

The price reform proposed by the government is only a piecemeal approach to the problem of price irrationality. It fails to recognize the need for the market to be given a greater role in price determination. It does not undertake a fundamental reform of the incentive system which determines how labor, land, capital, and entrepreneurship will be rewarded in relation to their contribution to production. In the absence of a fundamental reform of the incentive system, enterprise managers, whose salaries are unrelated to the "true" profitability of the enterprises, cannot be expected to make a rational pricing decision. The government therefore has to take the responsibility of determining what might be considered as rational prices. Unfortunately, administered prices are no substitutes for market-determined prices. The former, however determined, will not be as sensitive to changes in market conditions as are the latter. Moreover, any attempt to change the administered prices would encounter resistance from those parties whose interests are likely to be adversely affected. To avoid causing undesirable political consequences, the government would tend to keep the administered prices unchanged or adjust them as infrequently as possible. For instance, the government would be reluctant to raise grain prices in the time of a bad harvest for fear of causing resentment among the politically influential urban workers, though an upward adjustment in prices is necessary to bring about required changes in the quantity of grain supplied and demanded. Under these circumstances, prices would still be irrational, and enterprises would still be unable to take full responsibility for their own profits and losses. The main obstacle to the implementation of the manager responsibility system remains.

Li (1987) goes a step further and casts doubt on the desirability of pushing price reforms ahead of other reforms. He argues that even if the prices set by the government were all rational, state-owned enterprises would still lack the incentives to improve economic efficiency. He believes that enterprises will be pressured to improve economic efficiency only if they are incorporated and under the indirect control of shareholders, which may include the state, ministries, enterprises, and individuals. As for price reforms, he suggests that they should be undertaken in parallel with enterprise reforms so that enterprises would be allowed to compete with each other on the basis of rational prices (Li 1987, p. 83).

As a matter of fact, what Li proposes can be taken as part of the task of a price reform which should ideally involve the creation of an environment conducive to a smooth operation of market forces in both the factor and the goods markets. Such an environment includes private ownership of the means of production, the separation of management from state ownership, a high degree of factor mobility, freedom of entry and exit for enterprises, a comprehensive system of legal framework for regulating economic activities, supporting tax, monetary, and banking systems to facilitate the provision of public services and the exercise of macroeconomic control, and so forth. Obviously, no country can create such an environment overnight, but the reform should initiate a change which would create a pressure on the government and private individuals to respond and undertake changes in the direction of establishing a rational pricing system. Li essentially suggests that the change should start with the diversification of enterprise ownership. However, since he fails to tackle the problem of how prices should be determined, there is no mechanism in his proposal that will create any pressure on the government to establish a rational pricing system. Furthermore, under his proposed scheme, enterprises will remain under the control of central and local governments and no incentives will be provided to them for an improvement in the efficiency with which they operate.

China may follow the Hungarian practice, in which the determination of output and prices has mostly been devolved to enterprises (Hussain 1983, p. 107). In doing so, the state can relieve itself from the difficult task of determining the level of rational prices; it only has to be concerned about the environment within which prices and outputs are determined. Improvement in the efficiency with which enterprises operate can take place gradually with the implementation of a sequence of reforms that aim at improving the environment within which prices and outputs are determined. The pressure for such reforms would come from enterprises which seek to maximize profits.

The important point is that future price reforms should take place from the "bottom-up" instead of from the "top-down," using the terms in the World Bank's country report (World Bank 1985, p. 117). The former approach emphasizes the allocation function of prices, whereas the latter approach emphasizes their fiscal function. Since price flexibility is a necessary condition for prices to fulfill their allocation function (or to reflect the values of the products), a price reform that pursues price rationality must aim at reducing the importance of the fiscal function. The government may levy consumption taxes, income taxes, and profit taxes and use subsidies and transfers to perform the fiscal function currently performed by the pricing system. For instance, relatively high taxes may be imposed on monopolistic profits, luxury consumption, and conspicuously high personal incomes; investment financing, in a departure from the current profit-sharing scheme, may be undertaken by a profit-oriented banking system. Given these changes, fiscal considerations would no longer be a major obstacle to price reforms, and the government could focus on the allocation function of the pricing system by providing individuals and enterprises with price determination power.

6.6   Foreign trade policy and changes in nominal purchasing power

In a predominantly centrally planned economy like that of prereform China, foreign trade expansion would worsen consumer goods shortage primarily through its effect on the allocation of resources between the consumer goods and the producer goods sectors. Foreign trade would expand mainly to increase the imports of investments goods, and resources would be mobilized to the expanding sector. As a result, the production of consumer goods would be adversely affected. In the years starting from 1985, free markets in China have developed significantly as the prices of many nonstaple foods have been decontrolled. Consumer goods imbalance has occurred mainly in the form of open inflation.[10] The contribution of foreign trade to open inflation can now be better understood by looking at its effect on the level of unused money incomes (or nominal purchasing power). For this purpose, I focus on the right-hand side of equation (4.24), which shows the imbalance in the assets market. That is, I will now take a brief look at the other side of the same coin by examining how foreign trade affects aggregate nominal purchasing power and therefore the price level.

According to Peebles (1983), De Wulf and Goldsbrough (1986), and Feltenstein and Farhadian (1987), in a centrally planned economy money is injected into the economy through the government's payments for agricultural procurements, the total wage bill of the public sector, net government transfers to residents, and net increases in bank credits to households, on the one hand, and withdrawn from the economy through residents' purchases of consumer goods, on the other. The money supply will increase (decrease) if money injections exceed (fall short of) money withdrawals:

$$\Delta M2 = AP + W + TR + \Delta BC - C, \tag{6.1}$$

where $\Delta M2$ is the change in money supply, which is broadly defined to include currency balances and personal deposits, AP is agricultural procurement, W is the total wage bill (net of taxes paid by residents) in the public sector, ΔBC is the change in the amount of credits extended by banks to residents, and C is residents' purchases of consumer goods. Note that this equation is an expanded version of the term $W - C$ in equation (4.24) and that $\Delta M2$ is also the change in unspent purchasing power.

Equation (6.1) is a useful description of how money incomes or nominal purchasing power are created and used in a centrally planned economy. To show the role of foreign trade and fiscal policy in the money creation process, we set

$$AP = DAP + XAP, \tag{6.2}$$
$$W = (DIP + XIP - DE - ME) + (G' - T), \tag{6.3}$$
$$C = DC + MC, \tag{6.4}$$

where DAP is procurements of agricultural products for domestic consumption, XAP is procurements of agricultural products for export, DIP is procurements of industrial products for domestic uses, XIP is procurements of industrial products for export, DE is enterprise purchases of domestic goods and services, ME is enterprise purchases of imported goods and services, G' is government expenditures, including the change in net bank credits to enterprises but excluding government budgeted imports (MGB), government transfers to residents, and changes in bank credits to residents, T is taxes paid by enterprises and residents to the government, DC is residents' purchases of domestically produced consumer goods and services, and MC is residents' purchases of imported consumer goods and services.

Agricultural procurement is given in equation (6.2) as the sum of the components for domestic use and export. The total wage bill in the public sector is given in equation (6.3) as the sum of the following two terms: industrial procurements net of enterprise purchases, and government expenditures net of taxes paid by enterprises and residents. In this equation, the change in net bank credits to the public sector is considered as part of government expenditures because the credits would be used by enterprises and other production and nonproduction units for buying supplies and paying wages. Government budgeted imports are not included in G' because they involve no renminbi payments to the central bank on the part of the government or end-users. In equation (6.4), consumer goods purchased by residents are given as the sum of domestically produced and imported components.

Since peasants' purchases of agricultural means of production constitute a decrease in nominal purchasing power, they must be subtracted from $\Delta M2$ in equation (6.1). For this purpose, we set

$$AM = DAM + MAM, \tag{6.5}$$

where DAM and MAM are the domestically produced and imported components of agricultural means of production.

Substituting equations (6.2), (6.3), and (6.4) into equation (6.1), and subtracting equation (6.5), we get

$$\begin{aligned} \Delta M2 = (DAP + DIP) - (DAM + DE) + (G' - T) \\ + TR + BC + (X - M') - DC, \end{aligned} \tag{6.6}$$

where

$$X = XAP + XIP, \tag{6.7}$$
$$M' = ME + MC + MAM. \tag{6.8}$$

Equation (6.6) shows that money incomes are created through government procurement payments for agricultural and industrial goods for domestic uses $(DAP + DIP)$ and for export (X), and other government renminbi expenditures $(G' + TR + BC)$; and money incomes are spent through peasants' purchases of domestically produced agricultural means of production (DAM), enterprises' purchases of domestically produced goods and services (DE), government taxes on enterprises and residents (T), enterprises' and residents' renminbi payments for imported goods and services (M'), and residents' purchases of domestically produced goods and services (DC).

Equation (6.6) can be simplified by making the same assumption as we did in Chapter 4 that the actual demand for domestically produced goods is constrained by domestic supply. That is, we assume the following equality to hold true:

$$DAP + DIP = DAM + DE + DC. \tag{6.9}$$

Substituting equation (6.9) into equation (6.6), we get

$$\Delta M2 = (G' - T) + (X - M') + TR + \Delta BC. \tag{6.10}$$

The contribution of foreign trade to the change in money supply or unused nominal purchasing power is equal to $(X - M')$. Given the renminbi payments for imports M', which consist mainly of consumer goods and raw materials, the government's decision on exports and government budgeted imports will have an unambiguous effect on both the money supply and the level of money incomes. A large increase in exports for the purpose of financing imports and investments, for instance, will significantly raise the money supply and the level of money incomes.

Note that G' in equation (6.10) differs from government expenditures on goods and services G by government transfers TR and government budgeted imports MGB, and that M' differs from total imports M by MGB. The differences arise as a result of the fact that in the Chinese government the monetary authorities are not strictly separated from the fiscal authorities and the creation of money is linked strictly to the budgetary process. Were the two branches strictly separated from each other, the fiscal authorities would be required to purchase from the monetary authorities the foreign exchange needed for importing goods and services for central allocation. Under the current system, foreign exchange for import purposes is allocated to the MFERT directly, resulting in no withdrawal of money from the economy in the process. This is one of the most important institutional characteristics that must be taken into account in studying the effect of foreign trade on the money supply in a centrally planned economy.

In the present study, the change of unused money incomes, $\Delta M2$, can be readily obtained by subtracting C from MI in Table 5.1. However, to estimate the contribution of foreign trade to the increase in the money supply, it is necessary to determine the amount of imports which involve renminbi payments on the part of end-users. In general, government budgeted imports *(MGB)*, which involve no renminbi payments, are confined to capital goods for infrastructure and new investment projects initiated by the central government. Other imports, which include consumer goods, raw materials, and capital equipment for investment projects initiated by enterprises and local governments, normally require renminbi payments by end-users. Official statistics show that in the period between 1983 and 1985 major consumer goods and raw materials accounted for more than 60 percent of the economy's total imports in each year. Thus, it can be argued that the portion of imports which required renminbi payments might well have exceeded 70 percent in those years.

Table 6.1 provides the estimates of the percentage contribution of foreign trade to the growth of the money supply based on two hypothetical ratios for M'/M: 0.7 and 0.8. The estimates of annual changes in the money supply are obtained by subtracting C from MI in Table 5.1. The table shows that the money supply increased by about 20 billion yuan in each of the years between 1980 and 1983. Assuming that the M'/M ratio

Table 6.1. Foreign trade and unused money incomes, 1980–5

	$\Delta M2$ (billion yuan)	X^b	M^c	$(X - M')/\Delta M2$ (%)	
				$e = 0.7^d$	$e = 0.8$
1980	20.53	27.24	29.14	33.32	19.14
1981	19.00	36.76	36.67	58.05	38.95
1982	19.85	41.43	35.77	82.57	64.53
1983	27.17	43.83	42.18	52.63	37.14
1984	52.36	58.06	62.05	27.94	16.08
1985	55.00	80.93	125.78	−13.01	−35.81

[a] $\Delta M2$ = changes in the money supply.
[b] X = exports, in renminbi.
[c] M = imports, in renminbi.
[d] $e = M'/M$, where M' is residents' and enterprises' renminbi payments for imports.
Source: State Statistical Bureau, *Statistical Yearbook of China* (Hong Kong: Economic Information and Agency, 1987, pp. 480–1 and 519).

was equal to 0.7, foreign trade would account for between 33 percent and 83 percent of the increase in the money supply $(\Delta M2)$. The rising and relatively significant contribution of foreign trade to $\Delta M2$ was attributable to the foreign trade policy adopted in those years that both promoted exports and curtailed imports.

In the period between 1983 and 1985, $\Delta M2$ increased from 27 billion yuan in 1983 to 55 billion yuan in 1985. However, foreign trade accounted for only 53 percent of the increase in the money supply in 1983, much lower than the 83 percent of 1982. The decrease in the percentage contribution of foreign trade to $\Delta M2$ was due primarily to the government's easing of restrictions on capital goods imports in that year. The percentage contribution of foreign trade continued to decrease in the following two years when the government temporarily relaxed its control over consumer goods imports. In view of the fact that most of the increased imports in these two years were initiated and undertaken by enterprises and local governments, the M'/M ratio might have increased substantially. Assuming that the ratio was increased to 0.8, foreign trade would be responsible for only 16 percent of $\Delta M2$ in 1984. In 1985, the percentage contribution of foreign trade to the level of unused money incomes even turned negative. This result shows that the high $\Delta M2$, which was above 50 billion yuan, was due not to the expansion of foreign trade but to the rapid growth of bank credits and the government budget deficit.[11]

This empirical analysis presents a striking result: In China, foreign trade would normally have a significant effect on the change of the money supply or the level of unused nominal purchasing power during the period dominated by central planning. It follows from the result that even as free markets expanded in recent years, unused nominal purchasing power must have accumulated in the controlled sector and generated an upward pressure on free market prices, partly as a result of the expansion of foreign trade. The inflationary pressure arising from foreign trade would depend on the relative strength of the positive effect of the expanding exports and the negative effect of the increased decentralization of foreign trade power. The former effect was likely to be greater than the latter in the period of rapid foreign trade growth such as that which China experienced in 1986 and 1987, since the pace of foreign trade decentralization was slowed down by the loss of reform momentum in those two years.

Implications for future reforms

The above analysis points to the need for China, before successfully separating the government budget from the the issue of money, to reform its foreign trade system in order to alleviate the inflationary pressure brought about by foreign trade. In this regard, several reform measures discussed in the preceding sections are relevant. First, the government may stop promoting exports and technology imports, so that the efficiency with which foreign exchange is used can be improved on the one hand and the growth of unused money incomes can be reduced on the other. Such a change would require a fundamental change in the government's perception of the role of foreign trade in China's economic development as discussed in Section 6.2. Second, the government may further decentralize foreign trade and provide enterprises and local governments with greater foreign exchange quotas. In so doing, imports would increase in parallel with exports and, since all imports by enterprises and local governments would involve renminbi payments, a proportionally greater amount of the money incomes created by exports would be siphoned off by imports. The temporary relaxation of import controls between mid-1984 and mid-1985 provided a similar effect.

However, before prices are rationalized, China is unlikely to abolish its administrative control over foreign trade. So long as foreign trade is under administrative control, it would be difficult to convince the foreign trade authorities that technology imports are not necessary for the modernization of the economy. In addition, the central government would be reluctant to devolve import power to enterprises and local governments, who would similarly have the problem of having to determine what and how much to import without the assistance of the market mechanism. In general, enterprises and local governments, motivated by private benefits, would tend to import as much as permitted while paying relatively little attention to the efficiency with which foreign exchange is utilized. In the absence of import controls, they would be tempted to import consumer goods, which have been in persistent shortage. In this case, foreign trade would involve an exchange of much needed consumer goods and producer goods at home for "luxury" consumer items from abroad. The desirability of such an exchange is not only questionable but also in contradiction to the government's long-established policy of fostering economic growth with foreign trade. Suppose that foreign trade decentralization takes place in the form of providing enterprises and local governments with greater decision-making power in the import of capital goods. The change would be more in line with the government's present foreign trade policy. However, high imports would mean high investments, and high investments would call for a reallocation of domestic resources from existing uses to new investment projects, thus putting strain on the supply of consumer goods and producer goods at home in the short run. More importantly, the efficiency with which the new investment projects would be utilized would be subject to question given that any losses incurred by them would still be paid for by the government.

A fundamental reform of the pricing system would facilitate a further decentralization of foreign trade power and increase the role of the exchange rate in foreign trade. With foreign trade decentralization, the amount of government budgeted imports can be greatly reduced, and foreign trade would affect the rate of inflation primarily through the balance in the current account. A surplus in the current account would be inflationary since it would lead to an expansion in the money supply. Conversely, a deficit would contribute to a decrease in the rate of inflation since it would lead to a contraction in the money supply. To control the inflationary effect of foreign trade the government would only have to use exchange rate policy to control exports and imports and, therefore, the current account balance.

6.7 Conclusion

Since its implementation of economic reforms in 1979, China has to a certain extent devolved foreign trade power to enterprises and local governments, thus breaking the state monopoly of foreign trade and reducing the importance of central foreign trade plan to the economy. Nevertheless, these changes have done little to increase the role of the exchange rate in foreign trade, a key to improving the responsiveness of foreign trade to economic costs and benefits. Government intermediation in foreign trade continues to be practiced, and a majority of imports and, in particular, exports remain unresponsive to changes in the exchange rate and the market conditions in foreign trade. In addition, with direct government involvement, foreign trade, through government budgeted imports, can have a significant inflationary effect.

To summarize, China's foreign trade reforms have incurred two major problems. The first problem is the low economic efficiency of foreign trade. In order to improve the economic efficiency of foreign trade it is necessary for China to increase the sensitivity of exports and imports to economic costs and benefits. For this purpose, a further reform of the economic system will be required, but such reform has been stalled since 1985 by the problems involved in the proposed price reform. The basic reason for the government's failure to implement the proposed price reform lies in the government's inability to design a comprehensive reform program. Most of the changes that have been made or proposed are reactionary in nature without the benefit of an in-depth study of their economic, political, and social impacts. Therefore, a substantial reform of enterprises is increasingly hard to come by. But until any such reform is implemented, it is unlikely that there will be any substantial change in the foreign trade system, nor any significant improvement in the economic efficiency of foreign trade. The second problem is trade-induced inflation. The problem arises mainly as a result of China's continued practice of centralized allocation of foreign exchange, under which a significant part of export earnings are allocated to enterprises directly, without requiring renminbi payments. Therefore, foreign trade would tend to contribute to monetary expansion so long as a significant portion of the economy's foreign exchange earnings remained under central allocation. In addition, foreign trade expansion, through the export of domestically produced producer goods and consumer goods and by raising the level of investment, will tend to create a strain on the supply of consumer goods, thus raising the inflationary pressure. If China is to improve its gain from foreign trade, these two problems will first have to be tackled.

Notes

Chapter 1

1 The relation between investment and imports will be explored at length in Sections 1.2 and 1.4.

2 China's distrust of foreign powers, which colonized some parts of the country at the beginning of the 20th century, also contributed to the country's reluctance to open up and trade with the rest of the world. See Holzman (1976, pp. 24–6) for a further discussion on factors contributing to trade aversion in centrally planned economies.

3 Our discussion of China's prereform era falls in the period between 1956 and 1977. The former year is the year by which nearly all private economic activities had been nationalized, whereas the latter year is the year preceding a dramatic Four Modernizations movement in 1978. This period is referred to here as either the prereform period or the pre-1978 period, with a view to distinguishing it from the post-1978 years when economic reforms were under way.

4 In evaluating China's foreign trade and national output, one would inevitably encounter the problem that prices in the country, like in other communist countries, are irrational and do not reflect their market values. Therefore, the ratio of foreign trade to national output does not necessarily reflect the importance of foreign trade to the economy. For more discussions on the estimation of China's foreign trade and national output, see Appendix A. In this study, I use the CIA's estimates of GNP and foreign trade for the entire pre-1978 period for the simple reason that they are the most complete of all available estimates. For 1978 and the post-1978 period, I continue to use the CIA's estimates of GNP.

5 The foreign trade–national output ratios of Brazil and India are obtained from IMF, *International Financial Statistics,* August 1975.

6 For the growth rates of foreign trade of China and Hungary in domestic currency between 1979 and 1985, see IMF, *International Financial Statistics,* September 1986.

7 See China Handbook Editorial Committee (1984, pp. 1–12).

8 By leaning to one side, China established economic and diplomatic relations with only the Soviet bloc countries. This "lean to one side" policy was adopted primarily because Western countries sided mostly with the defeated Nationalist government during the civil war. Western powers were considered as a threat to the new communist regime.

9 In 1956, 99.8 percent of national output was produced by state enterprises, compared to 49.8 percent in 1955. See China Handbook Editorial Committee (1984, pp. 29–30).

10 In China's official statistics, light industry is so defined as to include mostly labor-intensive products.

11 See Xue (1985, pp. 89, 209, 377–9, and 419).

12 See Hare (1983, p. 196). Xue (1985) also points out that "At present, there are only a few hundred products (but more than a half of national product) which are under the direct

201

control of the State Planning Commission. Among these products, less than a hundred are carefully calculated, and the rest are only roughly estimated and can differ considerably from actual conditions. Even for those carefully calculated products, the specifications and design cannot possibly be determined entirely by the State Planning Commission; they must be analyzed by the industrial ministries or by the suppliers and end-users" (p. 243).

13 The growth rates are based on the real outputs of light and heavy industries. See Table 1.4.

14 The growth rates of investment are based on the nominal values of investment deflated by the industrial output deflator.

15 For a more detailed discussion on how national output is estimated, see Eckstein (1980, pp. 7-39). A more specific discussion can be seen in Liu and Yeh (1965).

16 This example was given by Qian Jiaqu in his speech to the Chinese People's Political Consultative Conference on March 26, 1987. See *South China Morning Post*, April 11, 1987.

17 See Li Choh-Ming (1960) for a discussion of China's statistical system in the 1950s. In his discussion, he gives a detailed account of what he calls "the statistical fiasco of 1958."

18 See Sah and Stiglitz (1984) for a theoretical discussion of the conditions under which surplus resources can be generated from the agricultural sector and transferred to the industrial sector in the presence of price scissors.

19 As indicated in Appendix A, Chinese output statistics are arrived at as the sum of the values of output at all stages of production. Therefore, the net contribution of each sector to national income cannot be seen from the commodity composition of the total product of the society. In spite of this statistical deficiency, the growth rate of the output of a certain sector can be used as a good approximation of the actual growth rate of the value-added in that sector so long as the output structure in that sector is unchanged or changes very slightly over time.

20 The data on the per capita consumption of food grains and cloth are from State Statistical Bureau, *Statistical Yearbook of China*, 1984, p. 477.

21 As shown in Table A.2, in Appendix A, the CIA's estimates of foreign trade growth differ only slightly from the official trade statistics.

22 See Table A.3 in Appendix A for the estimation of the growth rate of real investment.

23 As before, fixed capital formation is obtained as "investment in capital construction" deflated by the industrial output deflator.

24 Fixed capital formation went up by 30 percent in 1959 and 12 percent in 1960.

25 State Statistical Bureau, *Statistical Yearbook of China*, 1984, p. 395.

26 A more detailed discussion of the new incentive scheme will be given in Chapter 2.

Chapter 2

1 China's focus on the short-run, static benefits of foreign trade has to do with the fact that most of its economic plans have been short-term in nature owing to the lack of sophisticated planning techniques.

2 Boltho (1971), Holzman (1974), and Holzman (1976) have all given a detailed discussion of the role of foreign trade under central planning. Empirical studies related to China prior to its recent economic reforms can be found in Eckstein (1966), Mah (1971), Chen (1975), Hsiao (1977), Bastsavage and Davie (1978), and Kravalis (1978).

3 By controlling imports for investment purposes, the planners aimed at achieving a certain rate of accumulation and technical change. In view of the absence of a market mechanism by which the rate of accumulation may be determined, designing an opti-

mum rate of accumulation has become one of the most important policy problems in China's recent economic history. In this connection, what to import has also become an important concern of the government during the economic reforms. This problem will be further elaborated on in Chapter 4.

4 The years of the Great Leap Forward (1958–60) and the Four Modernizations campaign (1978) can be considered as the years of high investment growth, and the years from 1961 to 1977 can be considered as the years of low investment growth.

5 According to MFERT, ten of MFERT's fifteen FTCs conducted about 70 percent of China's foreign trade in 1986 (*Ming Pao,* January 26, 1987, p. 30). Based on this finding, it can be reasoned that the fifteen FTCs as a whole were likely to have conducted more than 80 percent of China's foreign trade.

6 The number of export items under the central procurement plan was reduced from more than 900 to about 100 in 1982 (He and Wang 1983, p. 472).

7 The number of import items under the directive plan was about 50 in 1982 (He and Wang 1983, p. 471). Nevertheless, it is unclear how broadly these items were classified.

8 For a detailed discussion of the institutional changes taking place in industry and agriculture under the general economic reforms, see Zhang and Meng (1985).

9 A number of studies point out that the responsibility system adopted by the village varies in form and substance due to a number of factors, such as leadership, crop types, and transportation.

10 Floating prices are applicable mostly to those goods which are characterized by volatile demand and supply and which have a variety of designs and specifications, such as electronic products, honey, and walnuts.

11 Negotiated prices are applicable to agricultural sideline products, some industrial household items, and some productive raw materials.

12 Free market prices are applicable to all items which are traded in marketplaces.

13 It must be noted that in China an enterprise is a branch of the local government or a certain ministry. Therefore, the foreign trade incentives provided to the enterprises can to a certain extent be regarded as part of the incentives provided to the local governments and ministries (Riskin 1987, p. 345).

14 Note that the structure of the export procurement prices does not necessarily have any relation to the structure of the foreign exchange prices determined in the world market. The use of export procurement prices is to insulate the profitabilities of exporting enterprises from being directly affected by foreign prices.

15 According to He and Wang (1983, p. 470), about 10 percent of the total imports were financed by the foreign exchange retained by enterprises, ministries, and local governments. This implies that the central government was still controlling a major proportion of the country's foreign exchange earnings. Nevertheless, in recent years the proportion retained by enterprises and local governments appears to have increased in view of the fact that the central government has met with increasing difficulty in controlling the imports initiated at the local level.

16 In general, enterprises and local governments are allowed to make use of most of their retention quotas, since the government fears that restrictions on their uses would dampen the enthusiasm of enterprises and local governments to export.

17 For a discussion by Chinese economists of how the social cost saved can be estimated, see Huang (1985, p. 262).

18 Note that in a multicommodity economy, resource allocation is influenced by the relative profit rates, instead of their absolute values.

19 See Zhang and Meng (1985, pp. 545–6). The progressive taxes on wage increases certainly have a dampening effect on work effort, but they serve to stem the depletion of

investment funds by profitable enterprises, which the government considers to be ones that should be encouraged to expand.

20 The following discussion of the import procedure is based on Hong Kong Trade Development Council, "A Guide for Selling to China," monograph, September 1986.

21 Enterprises are allowed to keep 60 percent of their depreciation funds (Riskin 1987, p. 344).

22 Enterprises have been accorded with the right to set the prices of their new products in the initial promotion period. The purpose is to encourage enterprises to produce the goods which are needed but not yet available at home. See Zhang and Meng (1985, pp. 583–4).

23 The serious abuse of foreign exchange and investment funds is highlighted in a recent finding of an official investigation. The following is a newspaper's account of the finding:

Foreign and Chinese equipment worth millions of dollars is rusting, unused or still unpacked, the official press reported on Thursday in its latest exposé of industrial mismanagement and stupidity. The newspaper Economic Information said textile concerns in the central province of Anhui had imported 3,500 machines from Japan and West Germany but many of them had not been used or were not used enough. In one factory, 531 machines had not even been unwrapped while the enterprise still had to meet heavy interest payments. In another, the imported machines had produced 37,500 garments in two years, one-seventh of their capacity. [See *South China Morning Post*, September 11, 1987.]

Chapter 3

1 According to official statistics, the per capita agricultural output of China increased by only 24 percent and the per capita consumption of food and clothing remained virtually unchanged in the period from 1956 to 1977. See State Statistical Bureau, *Statistical Yearbook of China*, 1985, pp. 25, 185, and 576.

2 China's real light industrial and heavy industrial output increased by 4 times and 8 times, respectively, in the period from 1956 to 1977. Ibid., p. 25.

3 The table below shows the amounts of foreign debt incurred by China during the period between 1978 and 1985 (in billion yuan):

1978	1979	1980	1981	1982	1983	1984	1985
0.0	3.5	4.3	7.4	4.0	3.8	3.5	2.9

Source: State Statistical Bureau, *Statistical Yearbook of China.* Hong Kong: Economic Information and Agency, 1986, pp. 509–10.

Figures in the table are arrived at by subtracting the total financial revenues exclusive of foreign borrowings from the total financial revenues inclusive of foreign borrowings in the official statistics.

4 The following table shows the annual growth rates of the prices of Saudi Arabian crude oil between 1978 and 1985 (in percentages):

1978	1979	1980	1981	1982	1983	1984	1985
2.56	33.33	70.07	13.10	2.65	13.61	−1.80	−1.52

Source: IMF, *International Financial Statistics,* 1984–7.

5 Lin (1985) points out that "a number of people take export merely as a means to earn foreign exchange. This created a one-sided tendency of pursuing foreign exchange earnings. They would sell any exportable commodities without regard to their costs of production. Some of the commodities exported by us cost 5 yuan, 10 yuan, or even more than 10 yuan per U.S. dollar of foreign exchange earnings. For instance, it costs as much as 15 yuan to earn one U.S. dollar of foreign exchange when we export binoculars." The export of some heavy manufacturers could well be a result of the government's indiscriminate promotion of exports. In the foreign trade plan, enterprises, local governments, and foreign trade corporations were given an annual export target to fulfill and did not have to be concerned about the cost of production (see Lin 1985, p. 55). See also *South China Morning Post,* May 30, 1987.

6 In a CIA report, prepared at the request of a congressional committee, it was pointed out that "traditionalists in the Chinese government believe Western-style reforms, [which] began in 1983 to loosen the tightly controlled Soviet style economy, have gone too far and are seeking an end to the movement." The "traditionalists" were likely to have gained influence in view of the problems of trade imbalance, budget deficits, and inflation faced by the economy. See *South China Morning Post,* August 24, 1987.

7 See Appendix C for an analysis of the commodity composition of China's trade with communist countries.

8 According to Guo (1987), China's trade with Latin America rose from 736 million U.S. dollars in 1978 to 1.7 billion U.S. dollars in 1985, accounting for not more than 3 percent of China's total trade. In 1985, China's major exports to the region were oil, natural gas, coal, and lubricants, which were valued at 420 million U.S. dollars. They accounted for nearly 70 percent of China's total exports to the region. Manufactured products amounted to only 113 million U.S. dollars. Guo points out that "China does not know well the technological level [of] equipment required by industries in [Latin American] countries, nor does it know which commodities these countries need to import and which commodities they can offer to export." This was an obstacle to the growth of China's direct exports to the region. He also points out that local traders in Latin America found it to their advantage to buy from Hong Kong and other countries rather than from China directly. See Guo (1987, pp. 19–21).

9 Sri Lanka intended to follow the development strategy adopted by Singapore, Taiwan, and South Korea by setting up export-processing zones to attract foreign investors in the early 1980s. However, the strategy has not been successful. One of the reasons is likely to be the lack of competitiveness in its exports in comparison with the fast-growing Chinese exports.

10 In 1981, according to Jao (1983), Hong Kong investors accounted for no less than 91 percent of the 841 contracts signed with the Shenzhen authorities. The investments were mostly engaged in export-processing operations. See Jao (1983, p. 50).

11 For a brief discussion of the role of Hong Kong in China's exports and imports in connection with Hong Kong's investment in China, see Hsu (1983, pp. 173–8).

12 One report indicated that over 900 joint ventures had been set up in China by 1984. The value of these joint ventures amounted to 1.4 billion U.S. dollars. Investment from Hong Kong and Macao accounted for about 80 percent of these joint ventures. See Arthur Andersen, *China Flash,* April 1985, p. 14.

13 All of China's national foreign trade corporations have set up their agents in Hong Kong. These include China Resources Corporations (the buying and selling agent of all foreign trade corporations trading with Hong Kong), Ng Fung Hong (the agent of the China National Cereals, Oils, and Foodstuffs Import and Export Corporation), Teck Soong Hong Ltd. (the agent of the China National Native Produce and Animal By-products Imports and Export Corporation), Hua Yuan Company (the agent of the China Na-

tional Light Industrial Products Import and Export Corporations), Cheerglory Traders Ltd. (the agent of the China National Instruments Import and Export Corporation), and China Everbest Enterprise Co., Ltd. (the agent of China National Machinery and Equipment Import and Export Corporation). For more details, see Policy Research Department, Ministry of Foreign Economic Relations and Trade (1984).

14 See Census and Statistics Department, Hong Kong Government, *Hong Kong Review of Overseas Trade,* 1986, p. 62.

15 Hong Kong export statistics are classified into domestic exports and reexports. The classification depends on the extent to which the products have been processed in Hong Kong. If the goods have been processed to such an extent that their shape, nature, form, or utility have been changed, their exports will be considered as Hong Kong's domestic exports. Otherwise, they will be considered as reexports.

16 For a similar point, see Jao (1983, p. 22).

17 China's Foreign Minister Wu Xueqian called on the United States to import more from China in his recent address to the U.S. Congressional Foreign Affair Committee. He remarked that the United States should cease its "unreasonable" treatment of Chinese exports in view of the fact that in 1986, whereas the United States was China's third largest trading partner, the share of China's exports to the United States was only 0.6 percent of the United States' total imports. See *Ming Pao,* October 1, 1987.

18 China's indirect trade with Taiwan and South Korea has increased dramatically in recent years, as can be seen in the following table (in millions of U.S. dollars):

	1981	1982	1983	1984	1985	1986
Exports to						
Taiwan	76	90	96	128	116	144
South Korea	74	94	115	185	249	377
Imports from						
Taiwan	390	208	169	426	988	811
South Korea	145	56	45	160	355	276

Source: South China Morning Post, October 13, 1987.

In its direct trade with Taiwan, China exports mainly crude materials and imports mainly textile products, textile machinery, and telecommunication equipment. It should be noted, however, that direct trade relations between China and South Korea have been established since early 1988.

19 Chow (1985) gives a positive assessment of the impact of the reform on agriculture. He suggests that, under the responsibility system, farmers would behave in a fashion no different from those in a market economy. Partly as a result of the reform, agricultural output increased by 8.6 percent and 3.9 percent in 1979 and 1980, respectively.

Chapter 4

1 Yueh (1959) and Liu (1959) are two of the Chinese economists who pioneered the study of the issue of the sectoral imbalance in China. They were followed by Shih (1961), Wu (1961), Dong (1962), Sung (1962), and Dong (1963). See C. Lin (1981, pp. 27–34), for a brief summary of the theoretical arguments advanced by Chinese economists.

2 The symbols in this section must not be mixed up with those used in the rest of this book.

3 The formula can be rewritten as

$$I(C + V + M) > IC + IIC,$$

which implies that the output of producer goods must be greater than the amount of producer goods used up in the producer goods and consumer goods sectors.

4 See Liu (1980) for a review of the discussions by Chinese economists on the issue in the late 1970s. It can be clearly seen from the review that many Chinese economists rarely talk to each other in discussing the issue. They put forward their arguments without much regard to what has been discussed by other economists before.

5 It is assumed here that the rate of depreciation is zero.

6 For a discussion of the phenomenon of consumer goods shortages, see Kornai (1980, 1982, 1986).

7 Such a feedback effect has also been noted by Liao (1985), who suggests that the shortage of consumer goods will tend to damage people's attitudes toward production, thus hindering economic growth. See Liao (1985, p. 60).

8 The demand for monetary assets, including savings deposits and money in circulation, will increase when the volume of transactions increases in the consumer goods market mainly because of the role of money as a medium of transactions.

9 Note that both a and b are normally less than unity.

10 Again, domestically produced producer goods and imported producer goods are assumed to be imperfect substitutes. Whereas the former can be used immediately to turn out producer goods or consumer goods, the latter are often characterized by long gestation periods except for raw material imports.

11 As will be shown in Chapter 5, the problem was particularly serious in 1978 when the imports of producer goods suddenly rose by a significant amount.

12 By semifree markets, I refer to the markets in which prices are allowed to adjust in response to changes in market conditions, subject to the approval of the government.

13 A theoretical analysis would be required to determine such a threshold.

Chapter 5

1 Note that in a centrally planned economy, prices do not necessarily adjust in response to imbalances in the market. Prices may be adjusted for administrative reasons. In 1979, for instance, the Chinese government significantly raised the procurement prices of agricultural products but kept the prices of industrial consumer goods relatively stable, since the government at the time saw the need to reduce the degree of price discrimination against agriculture to stimulate agricultural production. The policy by no means implied that there was a greater shortage in the market for agricultural products than in the market for industrial products in that year.

2 That is, even if there is a persistent shortage of consumer goods, such that the inflationary pressure must be suppressed, the degree of shortage may or may not have worsened in the current period. Therefore, the rate of repressed inflation, which is the change in repressed inflationary pressure, may be positive or negative, depending on the market conditions in the current period.

3 In equation (5.3), M^sV can be taken as the level of nominal national income.

4 The use of Z in place of r is particularly useful when MI and/or C are unknown but when their growth rates can be estimated from available data.

5 If there is a technological change in production, a decrease in the share of accumulation will be required in order to keep the degree of consumer goods imbalance unchanged. That is, for each given accumulation share, the degree of consumer goods imbalance will

have improved as a result of technical changes. Similarly, when there is a large increase in population, keeping the same accumulation share will give rise to a lowered supply of consumer goods to each individual and, therefore, a worsening of the degree of consumer goods imbalance. Thus, any changes which affect the supply of and demand for consumer goods unequally will affect the degree of consumer goods imbalance even if the share of accumulation is held constant.

6 Implicitly, we assume imported producer goods and domestically produced producer goods to be nonsubstitutes, so that an increase in M^* itself will not reduce the demand for domestic resources whereas an increase X^* will result in an immediate withdrawal of domestic resources from domestic production.

7 Strictly speaking, the T/Y ratio does not adequately reflect the relative importance of foreign trade in the economy, since T is based on the renminbi value of foreign trade, for which various artificial exchange rates have been used, and since Y differs from both GNP and GDP. However, the change in T/Y does serve as a good indicator of the change in the relative size of the investment fund mobilized in conjunction with foreign trade.

8 See Chapter 2 for the discussion of the change in China's import policy in 1979.

9 Peasants obviously had benefited from the rise in agricultural procurement prices in view of the relatively small increase in industrial prices. The differential price increases were part of the government's effort at rectifying the price scissors against agriculture.

10 More specifically, the consumer goods imbalances that occurred before or immediately following the economic reforms were attributable mostly to the negative effect of investment on the growth rate of consumer goods supply, whereas the consumer goods imbalances that took place during the economic reforms were attributable mostly to the expansionary effect of investment on money incomes.

11 When the economy is not strictly centrally planned, prices in free and semifree markets will rise in response to an increase in the demand for consumer goods, thereby stimulating the supply of consumer goods. That is, given any increase in MI, the growth rate of C will tend to be greater than under rigid central planning. As a result, Z will be relatively small. In the case where the supply of consumer goods is extremely sensitive to price increases, Z can even turn negative.

12 See *Ming Pao,* October 19, 1987.

Chapter 6

1 The yuan–U.S. dollar exchange rate depreciated from 1.5303 yuan per U.S. dollar in 1980 to 3.7221 yuan per U.S. dollar in 1986 partly as a result of the government's effort to promote exports.

	1980	1981	1982	1983	1984	1985	1986
Yuan/US$	1.5303	1.7455	1.9227	1.9809	2.7957	3.2015	3.7221

Source: International Monetary Fund, *International Financial Statistics,* October 1987.

2 Many joint ventures in China have been faced with the problem of foreign exchange shortage because they fail to export as much of their products as required to pay for their expenses on imported materials, labor, and machinery. See *South China Morning Post,* June 25, 1986.

3 See *Ming Pao,* October 26, 1987.

4 See MFERT, *On China's Foreign Trade,* Foreign Trade Education Press, 1985.

5 See *Ming Pao,* October 26, 1987.

6 See, for instance, Yang Xian et al. (1985, pp. 125–239).

7 Official statistics show that the government incurred a total budget deficit of nearly 42 billion yuan in the period between 1979 and 1985. Even so, the budget deficit has been grossly understated since there has been a substantial increase in bank credits to enterprises in recent years.

8 For instance, the market price–planned price ratio for steel rods was 2.33, for coal, 1.65, and for aluminum ingots, 2.08, according to a report on the prices in Guangzhou in January 1986. See Chan (1986, p. 28).

9 See *Ming Pao,* November 16, 1987.

10 The prices of retail sales rose by 8.8 percent in 1985, 6 percent in 1986, and 7.8 percent in the first half of 1987. See *Ming Pao,* October 19, 1987.

11 See footnote 8.

References

Alexander, Sidney S. 1952. "Effects of a Devaluation on a Trade Balance," *IMF Staff Papers,* 2: 263–78. Reprinted in *Readings in International Economics,* Richard E. Caves and Harry G. Johnson, eds. Homewood, IL: Irwin, pp. 359–73.

Ashbrook, Arthur G., Jr. 1982. "China: Economic Modernizations and Long-term Performance," in *China under the Four Modernizations,* Joint Economic Committee, U.S. Congress, ed. Washington, DC: U.S. Government Printing Office.

Baldwin, G. B. 1972. "A Layman's Guide to Little-Mirrlees," *Finance and Development,* 9(1): 16–21.

Barro, Robert J. and Herschel J. Grossman. 1971. "A General Disequilibrium Model of Income and Employment," *American Economic Review,* 61: 82–93.

Bastsavage, Richard E. and John L. Davie. 1978. "China's International Trade and Finance," in *Chinese Economy Post Mao,* Joint Economic Committee, U.S. Congress, ed. Washington, DC: U.S. Government Printing Office, pp. 707–41.

Bayard, Thomas, James Orr, Joseph Pelzman, and Jorge Perez-Lopez. 1982. "U.S.-PRC Trade Normalization: Effects on U.S. Imports and Employment," in *China under the Four Modernizations,* Part 2, Joint Economic Committee, U.S. Congress, ed. Washington, DC: U.S. Government Printing Office, pp. 172–209.

Boltho, Andrea. 1971. *Foreign Trade Criteria in Socialist Economies.* Cambridge: Cambridge University Press.

Brada, Joseph C. 1982. "Real and Monetary Approach to Foreign Trade Adjustment Mechanisms in Centrally Planned Economies," *European Economic Review,* 19: 229–44.

Bruno, Michael. 1965. "The Optimal Selection of Export Promotion and Import-Substituting Projects," in *Planning the External Sector: Techniques, Problems and Policies.* New York: United Nations.

Chan, Thomas M. H. 1986. "China's Price Reforms in the 1980's." Discussion Paper No. 78, Department of Economics, University of Hong Kong.

Chao, Arnold. 1982. "Economic Adjustment and the Open-Door Policy," in *China's Economic Reforms,* Lin Wei and Arnold Chao, eds. Philadelphia: University of Pennsylvania Press, pp. 205–19.

Chao, Kang. 1964. "Pitfalls in the Use of China's Foreign Trade Statistics," *China Quarterly,* 19 (July–September): 47–65.

Chen, Edward K. Y. 1983. "The Impact of China's Four Modernizations on Hong Kong's Economic Development," in *China and Hong Kong: the Economic Nexus,* Alexander J. Youngson, ed. Hong Kong: Oxford University Press, pp. 77–103.

Chen, Jiaqin and Wei Jiang. 1985. "The Macroeconomic Effects of Foreign Trade: An Analysis" (in Chinese), in *Studies on Financial, Trade and Economic Problems,* vol. 2, Fong Qi, Jiwei Gao, and Weixin Liu, eds. Beijing: Chinese Academy of Social Sciences, pp. 268–75.

Chen, Nai-Ruenn. 1975. "China's Foreign Trade 1950–1974," in *China: A Reassessment of the Economy,* Joint Economic Committee, U.S. Congress, ed. Washington, DC: U.S. Government Printing Office, pp. 617–52.

and Chi-Ming Hou. 1986. "China's Inflation, 1979–1983: Measurement and Analysis," *Economic Development and Cultural Change,* 34(4): 811–35.

China Handbook Editorial Committee. 1984. *Economy.* Beijing: Foreign Language Press.

Chow, Gregory C. 1985. *The Chinese Economy.* New York: Harper and Row.

De Wulf, Luc and David Goldsbrough. 1986. "The Evolving Role of Monetary Policy in China," *IMF Staff Papers,* 33(2): 209–42.

Deng, Liquen, Hung Ma, and Heng Wu. 1985. *Contemporary Chinese Economic Management* (in Chinese). Beijing: Chinese Academy of Social Sciences.

Dong, Fureng. 1963. "Questions on Studying the Practical Applications of Marx's Reproduction Formulae from the Angle of Unifying the Production and Use of Social Products" (in Chinese), *Jingji Yanjiu,* March: 39–51.

Dong, Yuanshi. 1962. "An Investigation into the Sources of Simple and Expanded Reproduction" (in Chinese), *Jingji Yanjiu,* December: 36–43.

Donnithorne, Audrey G. 1967. *China's Economic System.* London: Allen and Unwin.

1974. "China's Anti-Inflationary Policy," *The Three Banks Review,* September: 3–25.

Eckstein, Alexander. 1966. *Communist China's Economic Growth and Foreign Trade.* New York: McGraw-Hill.

1977. *China's Economic Revolution.* Cambridge: Cambridge University Press.

(ed.). 1980. *Quantitative Measures of China's Economic Output.* Ann Arbor: University of Michigan Press.

Feltenstein, Andrew and Ziba Farhadian. 1987. "Fiscal Policy, Monetary Targets, and the Price Level in a Centrally Planned Economy: An Application to the Case of China," *Journal of Money, Credit, and Banking,* 19(2): 137–56.

Fung, Lawerence. 1984. *China Trade Handbook.* Hong Kong: The Adsale People.

Gullo, Damian T. 1982. "China's Hard Currency Export Potential and Import Capacity through 1985," in *China Under the Four Modernizations,* Part 2, Joint Economic Committee, U.S. Congress, ed. Washington, DC: U.S. Government Printing Office, pp. 83–108.

Guo, Chongdao. 1987. "Economic and Trade Relations between China and Latin

America – Current Development and Further Consideration." Paper presented in the Third International Congress of Professors World Peace Academy, August, in Manila.

Hare, Paul. 1983. "China's System of Industrial Economic Planning," in *The Chinese Economic Reforms,* Stephan Feuchtwang and Athar Hussain, eds. London: Croom Helm, pp. 185–223.

He, Jianpin and Jiye Wang. 1983. *Problems of Plan Management in China* (in Chinese). Beijing: Chinese Academy of Social Sciences.

Ho, Henry C. Y. 1986. "Distribution of Profits and the Change from Profit Remission to Tax Payments for State Enterprises in China." Paper presented in Conference on China's System Reform, University of Hong Kong.

Holzman, Franklyn D. 1960. "Soviet Inflationary Pressures, 1928–1957," *Quarterly Journal of Economics,* 74: 167–88.

1974. *Foreign Trade under Communism–Politics and Economics.* London: Macmillan Press.

1976. *Foreign Trade under Central Planning.* Cambridge, MA: Harvard University Press.

Howard, David H. 1976. "The Disequilibrium Model in a Controlled Economy: An Empirical Test of the Barro-Grossman Model," *American Economic Review,* 66: 871–9.

Hsiao, Gene T. 1977. *The Foreign Trade of China: Policy, Law and Practices.* Berkeley: University of California Press.

Hsu, John C. 1982. "Economic Reforms in China: An Assessment," *Asian Affairs,* 4(3): 253–62. Reprinted in *China in the Modern World,* Center for Development Research, ed. Dhaka: Powel Printing Press, 1983, pp. 50–9.

1983. "Hong Kong in China's Foreign Trade: A Changing Role," in *China and Hong Kong: The Economic Nexus,* Alexander J. Youngson, ed. Hong Kong: Oxford University Press, pp. 156–83.

Huang, Jing. 1985. "The Use of Statistics to Reflect the Economic Effects of Foreign Trade – with a Discussion on the Meaning of the Economic Effects of Foreign Trade" (in Chinese), in *Studies on Financial, Trade and Economic Problems,* vol. 2, Fong Qi, Jiwei Gao, and Weixin Liu, eds. Beijing: Chinese Academy of Social Sciences, pp. 255–67.

Huang Hsiao, Katherine H. Y. 1971. *Money and Monetary Policy in Communist China.* New York: Columbia University Press.

1982. "Money and Banking in the People's Republic of China: Recent Developments," *China Quarterly* (September): 462–75.

Hussain, Athar. 1983. "Economic Reforms in Eastern Europe and Their Relevance to China," in *The Chinese Economic Reforms,* Stephan Feuchtwang and Athar Hussain, eds. London: Croom Helm, pp. 91–120.

International Monetary Fund. 1988. *International Financial Statistics Yearbook.* Washington, DC: International Monetary Fund.

Jao, Y. C. 1983. "Hong Kong's Role in Financing China's Modernization," in *China and Hong Kong: The Economic Nexus,* Alexander J. Youngson, ed. Hong Kong: Oxford University Press, pp. 12–76.

Joint Economic Committee, U.S. Congress. 1972. *People's Republic of China: An Economic Assessment.* Washington, DC: U.S. Government Printing Office.

Kornai, János. 1980. *Economics of Shortage.* Amsterdam: North Holland.

1982. *Growth, Shortage and Efficiency.* Oxford: Blackwell Publisher.

1986. "The Hungarian Reform Process," *Journal of Economic Literature,* 24(4): 1687–737.

Kravalis, Hedija H. 1978. "An Analysis of China's Hard Currency Exports: Recent Trends, Present Problems, and Future Potential," in *Chinese Economy Post Mao,* Joint Economic Committee, U.S. Congress, ed. Washington, DC: U.S. Government Printing Office, pp. 789–811.

Lardy, Nicholas. 1983. *Agricultural Prices in China.* Washington, DC: World Bank.

Li, Choh-Ming. 1960. *The Statistical System of Communist China.* Berkeley: University of California Press.

Li, Qianheng, Long Liu, Xuchang Zhou, and Tianxiang Peng (eds). 1988. *International Economics and Foreign Trade Handbook* (in Chinese). Beijing: Jiangsu People's Press.

Li, Yining. 1987. *Searching for the Way to Economic System Reforms* (in Chinese). Beijing: People's Daily Press.

Liao, Jili. 1985. *Chinese Economic System Reform: An Analysis* (in Chinese). Beijing: China Finance and Economics Press.

Lin, Cyril C. 1981. "The Reinstatement of Economics in China Today," *China Quarterly,* 85: 1–48.

Lin, Jingzhou. 1985. *On International Economics under Socialism* (in Chinese). Fuzhou: Fujian People's Press.

Lin, Paul T. K. 1981. "The People's Republic of China and the New International Economic Order: The Strategy of Domestic Development," in *Asian and the New International Economic Order,* Jorge A. Lozoya, ed. Elmsford, NY: Pergamon, pp. 39–52.

Little, I. M. D. and J. A. Mirrlees. 1974. *Project Appraisal and Planning for Developing Countries.* London: Heinemann.

Liu, Guoguang. 1959. "Lenin's Contribution to the Theory of Relation of Proportion between the Two Categories of Social Production and Its Significance to the Socialist Construction" (in Chinese), *Jingji Yanjiu,* 11: 11–20.

1962. "A Preliminary Discussion on the Quantitative Relationship between the Rate and Proportions of Socialist Reproduction" (in Chinese), *Jingji Yanjiu,* 66: 16–31.

Liu, Ta-Chung. 1968. "Quantitative Trends in the Economy," in *Economic Trends in Communist China,* Alexander Eckstein, Walter Galenson, and Ta-Chung Liu, eds. Hawthorne, NY: Aldine.

and Kung-Chia Yeh. 1965. *The Economy of the Chinese Mainland: National Income and Economic Development, 1933–1959.* Princeton, NJ: Princeton University Press.

Liu, Xun. 1980. "A Review of the Discussions in the Past Year on the Question of Priority Increase of the Means of Production" (in Chinese), *Jingji Yanjiu,* 12: 32–6.

Mah, Feng-hwa. 1971. *The Foreign Trade of Mainland China.* Hawthorne, NY: Aldine.

Moore, Michael J. 1985. "Demand Management with Rationing," *Economic Journal,* 95: 73–86.

Muellbauer, J. and Richard Portes. 1978. "Macroeconomic Model with Quantity Rationing," *Economic Journal,* 88: 788–821.

Nanto, Richard K. 1982. "Sino-Japanese Economic Relations," in *China under the Four Modernizations,* Part 2, Joint Economic Committee, U.S. Congress, ed. Washington, DC: U.S. Government Printing Office, pp. 83–108.

Peebles, Gavin. 1983. "Inflation, Money and Banking in China: In Support of the Purchasing Power Approach," *ACEs Bulletin,* Summer: 81–103.

    1986. "Chinese Monetary Management, 1953–1982." Paper presented in Conference on China's System Reform, University of Hong Kong.

Perez-Lopez, Jorge. 1982. "U.S.-PRC Trade Normalization: Effects on U.S. Imports and Employment," in *China under the Four Modernizations,* Part 2, Joint Economic Committee, U.S. Congress, ed. Washington, DC: U.S. Government Printing Office, pp. 172–209.

Perkins, Dwight H. 1966. *Market Control and Planning in Communist China.* Cambridge, MA: Harvard University Press.

Policy Research Department, Ministry of Foreign Economic Relation and Trade. 1984. *Guide to China's Foreign Economic Relations and Trade: Import-Export Special* (in Chinese). Hong Kong: Economic Information and Agency.

Portes, Richard. 1979. "Internal and External Balance in a Centrally Planned Economy," *Journal of Comparative Economics,* 3: 325–45.

    and David Winter. 1980. "Disequilibrium Estimates for Consumption Goods Markets in Centrally Planned Economies," *Review of Economic Studies,* 47: 137–59.

Reynolds, Bruce L. 1983. "Economic Reforms and External Imbalance in China, 1978–81," *American Economic Review,* 73 (May): 325–8.

Riskin, Carl. 1987. *China's Political Economy: The Quest for Development since 1949.* Oxford: Oxford University Press.

Sah, Raaj K. and Joseph E. Stiglitz. 1984. "The Economics of Price Scissors," *American Economic Review,* 74(1): 125–38.

Scherer, John L. 1980, 1984, 1985, and 1987. *China: Facts & Figures Annual.* Gulf Breeze: Academic International Press.

Shih, Xue. 1961. "Preliminary Studies of Formulae for Expanded Reproduction" (in Chinese), *Guangming Ribao,* December 4: 4.

Srinivasan, T. N. and Jagdish N. Bhagwati. 1978. "Shadow Prices for Project Selection in the Presence of Distortions: Effective Rates of Protection and Domestic Resource Costs," *Journal of Political Economy,* 86(1): 97–116.

Sung, Zexing. 1962. "On the Issues of the Quantitative Relationship between the Two Categories of Social Production" (in Chinese), *Jingji Yangjiu,* 8: 1–14.

Trade Development Council. 1986. "A Guide for Selling to China." Monograph, Hong Kong Government.

Tsakok, I. 1979. "Inflation Control in the People's Republic of China 1949–1974," *World Development*, 7: 865–75.

Wanless, P. T. 1985. "Inflation in the Consumer Goods Market in Poland, 1971–1982," *Soviet Studies*, 37: 305–29.

Wang, Qing. 1985. *On Price Reform* (in Chinese). Chengdu: Sichuan Academy of Social Sciences.

Wei, Lin and Arnold Chao. 1982. *China's Economic Reforms*. Philadelphia: University of Pennsylvania Press.

World Bank. 1985. *China: Long-Term Development Issues and Options*. Baltimore, MD: The John Hopkins University Press.

Wu, Shuqing. 1962. "The Marxist Theory of the Two Major Categories of Social Production and Its Application in Socialist Reproduction" (in Chinese), *Guangming Ribao*, January 8: 4.

Xue, Muqiao. 1985. *Selective Essays by Xue Muqiao* (in Chinese). Taiyuan: Shansi People's Press.

Yang, Xian, Jiafang Du, Xiyan Wang, Shunrong Li, Jiwu Tu, Guizhen Xi, Mingfang Zhang, and Zuoyu Jiao. 1985. *Socialist Economy in China*. Beijing: Current Affair Press.

Yueh, Wei. 1959. "Leaping Speed and Social Proportions" (in Chinese), *Jingji Yanjiu*, 10: 26–33.

Zhang, Qi and Jiquen Meng. 1985. *Economic System Reform Handbook* (in Chinese). Shenyang: Liaoning People's Press.

Zheng, Li. 1985. "The Reform of China's Economic Planning Management System" (in Chinese), *Almanac of China's Economy*, 2: 3–5.

Index